DOMINIC COPY
PERSONAL COPY

AF378582

Solaris Volume Manager
Administration Guide

Sun Microsystems, Inc.
4150 Network Circle
Santa Clara, CA 95054
U.S.A.

Part No: 806–6111–10
May 2002
ISBN 0-595-73087-6

Copyright 2002 Sun Microsystems, Inc.   4150 Network Circle, Santa Clara, CA 95054 U.S.A.   All rights reserved.

This product or document is protected by copyright and distributed under licenses restricting its use, copying, distribution, and decompilation. No part of this product or document may be reproduced in any form by any means without prior written authorization of Sun and its licensors, if any. Third-party software, including font technology, is copyrighted and licensed from Sun suppliers.

Parts of the product may be derived from Berkeley BSD systems, licensed from the University of California. UNIX is a registered trademark in the U.S. and other countries, exclusively licensed through X/Open Company, Ltd.

Sun, Sun Microsystems, the Sun logo, docs.sun.com, AnswerBook, AnswerBook2, and Solaris are trademarks, registered trademarks, or service marks of Sun Microsystems, Inc. in the U.S. and other countries. All SPARC trademarks are used under license and are trademarks or registered trademarks of SPARC International, Inc. in the U.S. and other countries. Products bearing SPARC trademarks are based upon an architecture developed by Sun Microsystems, Inc.

The OPEN LOOK and Sun™ Graphical User Interface was developed by Sun Microsystems, Inc. for its users and licensees. Sun acknowledges the pioneering efforts of Xerox in researching and developing the concept of visual or graphical user interfaces for the computer industry. Sun holds a non-exclusive license from Xerox to the Xerox Graphical User Interface, which license also covers Sun's licensees who implement OPEN LOOK GUIs and otherwise comply with Sun's written license agreements.

Federal Acquisitions: Commercial Software–Government Users Subject to Standard License Terms and Conditions.

DOCUMENTATION IS PROVIDED "AS IS" AND ALL EXPRESS OR IMPLIED CONDITIONS, REPRESENTATIONS AND WARRANTIES, INCLUDING ANY IMPLIED WARRANTY OF MERCHANTABILITY, FITNESS FOR A PARTICULAR PURPOSE OR NON-INFRINGEMENT, ARE DISCLAIMED, EXCEPT TO THE EXTENT THAT SUCH DISCLAIMERS ARE HELD TO BE LEGALLY INVALID.

Copyright 2002 Sun Microsystems, Inc.   4150 Network Circle, Santa Clara, CA 95054 U.S.A.   Tous droits réservés

Ce produit ou document est protégé par un copyright et distribué avec des licences qui en restreignent l'utilisation, la copie, la distribution, et la décompilation. Aucune partie de ce produit ou document ne peut être reproduite sous aucune forme, par quelque moyen que ce soit, sans l'autorisation préalable et écrite de Sun et de ses bailleurs de licence, s'il y en a. Le logiciel détenu par des tiers, et qui comprend la technologie relative aux polices de caractères, est protégé par un copyright et licencié par des fournisseurs de Sun.

Des parties de ce produit pourront être dérivées du système Berkeley BSD licenciés par l'Université de Californie. UNIX est une marque déposée aux Etats-Unis et dans d'autres pays et licenciée exclusivement par X/Open Company, Ltd.

Sun, Sun Microsystems, le logo Sun, docs.sun.com, AnswerBook, AnswerBook2, et Solaris sont des marques de fabrique ou des marques déposées, ou marques de service, de Sun Microsystems, Inc. aux Etats-Unis et dans d'autres pays. Toutes les marques SPARC sont utilisées sous licence et sont des marques de fabrique ou des marques déposées de SPARC International, Inc. aux Etats-Unis et dans d'autres pays. Les produits portant les marques SPARC sont basés sur une architecture développée par Sun Microsystems, Inc.

L'interface d'utilisation graphique OPEN LOOK et Sun™ a été développée par Sun Microsystems, Inc. pour ses utilisateurs et licenciés. Sun reconnaît les efforts de pionniers de Xerox pour la recherche et le développement du concept des interfaces d'utilisation visuelle ou graphique pour l'industrie de l'informatique. Sun détient une licence non exclusive de Xerox sur l'interface d'utilisation graphique Xerox, cette licence couvrant également les licenciés de Sun qui mettent en place l'interface d'utilisation graphique OPEN LOOK et qui en outre se conforment aux licences écrites de Sun.

CETTE PUBLICATION EST FOURNIE "EN L'ETAT" ET AUCUNE GARANTIE, EXPRESSE OU IMPLICITE, N'EST ACCORDEE, Y COMPRIS DES GARANTIES CONCERNANT LA VALEUR MARCHANDE, L'APTITUDE DE LA PUBLICATION A REPONDRE A UNE UTILISATION PARTICULIERE, OU LE FAIT QU'ELLE NE SOIT PAS CONTREFAISANTE DE PRODUIT DE TIERS. CE DENI DE GARANTIE NE S'APPLIQUERAIT PAS, DANS LA MESURE OU IL SERAIT TENU JURIDIQUEMENT NUL ET NON AVENU.

020115@3062

Contents

Tables

Figures

Preface

The *Solaris Volume Manager Administration Guide* explains how to use Solaris Volume
Manager to manage your system's storage needs, including creating, modifying, and
using RAID 0 (concatenation and stripe) volumes, RAID 1 (mirror) volumes, and
RAID 5 volumes, in addition to soft partitions and transactional log devices.

Who Should Use This Book

System and storage administrators will use this book to identify the tasks that Solaris
Volume Manager supports and how to use Solaris Volume Manager to provide more
reliable and accessible data.

How This Book Is Organized

The *Solaris Volume Manager Administration Guide* includes the following information:

Chapter 1 provides a detailed "roadmap" to the concepts and tasks described in this
book and should be used solely as a navigational aid to the book's content.

Chapter 2 provides an introduction to general storage management concepts for those
readers who are new to this technology.

Chapter 3 describes Solaris Volume Manager and introduces essential product-related
concepts.

Chapter 4 provides an overall scenario for understanding the Solaris Volume Manager
product.

Chapter 5 describes concepts related to state databases and state database replicas.

Chapter 6 explains how to perform tasks related to state databases and state database replicas.

Chapter 7 describes concepts related to RAID 0 (stripe and concatenation) volumes.

Chapter 8 explains how to perform tasks related to RAID 0 (stripe and concatenation) volumes.

Chapter 9 describes concepts related to RAID 1 (mirror) volumes.

Chapter 10 explains how to perform tasks related to RAID 1 (mirror) volumes.

Chapter 11 describes concepts related to the Solaris Volume Manager soft partitioning feature.

Chapter 12 explains how to perform soft partitioning tasks.

Chapter 13 describes concepts related to RAID 5 volumes.

Chapter 14 explains how to perform tasks related to RAID 5 volumes.

Chapter 15 describes concepts related to hot spares and hot spare pools.

Chapter 16 explains how to perform tasks related to hot spares and hot spare pools.

Chapter 17 describes concepts related to transactional volumes.

Chapter 18 explains how to perform tasks related to transactional volumes.

Chapter 19 describes concepts related to disk sets.

Chapter 20 explains how to perform tasks related to disk sets.

Chapter 21 explains some general maintenance tasks that are not related to a specific Solaris Volume Manager component.

Chapter 22 provides some "best practices" information about configuring and using Solaris Volume Manager.

Chapter 23 provides concepts and instructions for using the Solaris Volume Manager SNMP agent and for other error checking approaches.

Chapter 24 provides information about troubleshooting and solving common problems in the Solaris Volume Manager environment.

Appendix A lists important Solaris Volume Manager files.

Appendix B provides tables that summarize commands and other helpful information.

Appendix C provides a brief introduction to the CIM/WBEM API that allows open Solaris Volume Manager management from WBEM-compliant management tools.

Related Books

Solaris Volume Manager is one of several system administration tools available for the Solaris operating environment. Information about overall system administration features and functions, as well as related tools are provided in the following:

- *System Administration Guide: Basic Administration*
- *System Administration Guide: Advanced Administration*

Accessing Sun Documentation Online

The docs.sun.com^{SM} Web site enables you to access Sun technical documentation online. You can browse the docs.sun.com archive or search for a specific book title or subject. The URL is `http://docs.sun.com`.

Typographic Conventions

The following table describes the typographic conventions used in this book.

TABLE P–1 Typographic Conventions

Typeface or Symbol	Meaning	Example
`AaBbCc123`	The names of commands, files, and directories; on-screen computer output	Edit your `.login` file. Use `ls -a` to list all files. `machine_name% you have mail.`
`AaBbCc123`	What you type, contrasted with on-screen computer output	`machine_name%` **`su`** `Password:`

TABLE P–1 Typographic Conventions   *(Continued)*

Typeface or Symbol	Meaning	Example
AaBbCc123	Command-line placeholder: replace with a real name or value	To delete a file, type **rm** *filename*.
AaBbCc123	Book titles, new words, or terms, or words to be emphasized	Read Chapter 6 in *User's Guide*. These are called *class* options. You must be *root* to do this.

Shell Prompts in Command Examples

The following table shows the default system prompt and superuser prompt for the C shell, Bourne shell, and Korn shell.

TABLE P–2 Shell Prompts

Shell	Prompt
C shell prompt	`machine_name%`
C shell superuser prompt	`machine_name#`
Bourne shell and Korn shell prompt	`$`
Bourne shell and Korn shell superuser prompt	`#`

## CHAPTER 1

Getting Started with Solaris Volume Manager

The *Solaris Volume Manager Administration Guide* describes how to set up and maintain systems using Solaris Volume Manager to manage storage for high availability, flexibility, and reliability.

This chapter serves as a high-level guide to find information for certain Solaris Volume Manager tasks, such as setting up storage capacity. This chapter does not address all the tasks that you will need to use Solaris Volume Manager. Instead, it provides an easy way to find procedures describing how to perform common tasks associated with the following Solaris Volume Manager concepts:

- Storage Capacity
- Availability
- I/O Performance
- Administration
- Troubleshooting

Caution – If you do not use Solaris Volume Manager correctly, you can destroy data. Solaris Volume Manager provides a powerful way to reliably manage your disks and data on them. However, you should always maintain backups of your data, particularly before you modify an active Solaris Volume Manager configuration.

Getting Started With Solaris Volume Manager

Solaris Volume Manager Roadmap—Storage Capacity

TABLE 1–1 Solaris Volume Manager Roadmap—Storage Capacity

Task	Description	For Instructions
Set up storage	Create storage that spans slices by creating a RAID 0 or a RAID 5 volume. The RAID 0 or RAID 5 volume can then be used for a file system or any application, such as a database that accesses the raw device	"How to Create a RAID 0 (Stripe) Volume" on page 74 "How to Create a RAID 0 (Concatenation) Volume" on page 75 "How to Create a RAID 1 Volume From Unused Slices" on page 95 "How to Create a RAID 1 Volume From a File System" on page 97 "How to Create a RAID 5 Volume" on page 138
Expand an existing file system	Increase the capacity of an existing file system by creating a RAID 0 (concatenation) volume, then adding additional slices.	"How to Expand Space for Existing Data" on page 76
Expand an existing RAID 0 (concatenation or stripe) volume	Expand an existing RAID 0 volume by concatenating additional slices to it.	"How to Expand an Existing RAID 0 Volume" on page 78
Expand a RAID 5 volume	Expand the capacity of a RAID 5 volume by concatenating additional slices to it.	"How to Expand a RAID 5 Volume" on page 142
Increase the size of a UFS file system on a expanded volume	Grow a file system by using the `growfs` command to expand the size of a UFS while it is mounted and without disrupting access to the data.	"How to Grow a File System" on page 229

TABLE 1–1 Solaris Volume Manager Roadmap—Storage Capacity   *(Continued)*

Task	Description	For Instructions
Subdivide slices or logical volumes into smaller partitions, breaking the 8 slice hard partition limit	Subdivide logical volumes or slices by using soft partitions.	"How to Create a Soft Partition" on page 126
Create a file system	Create a file system on a RAID 0 (stripe or concatenation), RAID 1 (mirror), RAID 5, or transactional volume, or on a soft partition.	"Creating File Systems (Tasks)" in *System Administration Guide: Basic Administration*

Solaris Volume Manager Roadmap—Availability

TABLE 1–2 Solaris Volume Manager Roadmap—Availablity

Task	Description	For Instructions
Maximize data availability	Use Solaris Volume Manager's mirroring feature to maintain multiple copies of your data. You can create a RAID 1 volume from unused slices in preparation for data, or you can mirror an existing file system, including root (/) and /usr.	"How to Create a RAID 1 Volume From Unused Slices" on page 95 "How to Create a RAID 1 Volume From a File System" on page 97
Add data availability with minimum hardware cost	Increase data availability with minimum of hardware by using Solaris Volume Manager's RAID 5 volumes.	"How to Create a RAID 5 Volume" on page 138
Increase data availability for an existing RAID 1 or RAID 5 volume	Increase data availability for a RAID 1 or a RAID 5 volume, by creating a hot spare pool then associate it with a mirror's submirrors, or a RAID 5 volume.	"Creating a Hot Spare Pool" on page 154 "Associating a Hot Spare Pool With Volumes" on page 156
Increase file system availability after reboot	Increase overall file system availability after reboot, by adding UFS logging (transactional volume) to the system. Logging a file system reduces the amount of time that the `fsck` command has to run when the system reboots.	"About File System Logging" on page 165

Solaris Volume Manager Roadmap—I/O Performance

TABLE 1–3 Solaris Volume Manager Roadmap—I/O Performance

Task	Description	For Instructions
Tune RAID 1 volume read and write policies	Specify the read and write policies for a RAID 1 volume to improve performance for a given configuration.	"RAID 1 Volume Read and Write Policies" on page 86 "How to Change RAID 1 Volume Options" on page 110
Optimize device performance	Creating RAID 0 (stripe) volumes optimizes performance of devices that make up the stripe. The interlace value can be optimized for random or sequential access.	"Creating RAID 0 (Stripe) Volumes" on page 74
Maintain device performance within a RAID 0 (stripe)	Expands stripe or concatenation that has run out of space by concatenating a new component to it. A concatenation of stripes is better for performance than a concatenation of slices.	"Expanding Storage Space" on page 76

Solaris Volume Manager Roadmap—Administration

TABLE 1–4 Solaris Volume Manager Roadmap—Administration

Task	Description	For Instructions
Graphically administer your volume management configuration	Use the Solaris Management Console to administer your volume management configuration.	Online help from within Solaris Volume Manager (Enhanced Storage) node of the Solaris Management Console application
Graphically administer slices and file systems	Use the Solaris Management Console graphical user interface to administer your disks and file systems, performing such tasks as partitioning disks and constructing UFS file systems.	Online help from within the Solaris Management Console application
Optimize Solaris Volume Manager	Solaris Volume Manager performance is dependent on a well-designed configuration. Once created, the configuration needs monitoring and tuning.	"Solaris Volume Manager Configuration Guidelines" on page 45 "Working with Configuration Files" on page 224

Task	Description	For Instructions
Plan for future expansion	Because file systems tend to run out of space, you can plan for future growth by putting a file system into a concatenation.	"Creating RAID 0 (Concatenation) Volumes" on page 75 "Expanding Storage Space" on page 76

Solaris Volume Manager Roadmap—Troubleshooting

TABLE 1–5 Solaris Volume Manager Roadmap—Troubleshooting

Task	Description	For Instructions
Replace a failed slice	If a disk fails, you must replace the slices used in your Solaris Volume Manager configuration. In the case of RAID 0 volume, you have to use a new slice, delete and recreate the volume, then restore data from a backup. Slices in RAID 1 and RAID 5 volumes can be replaced and resynchronized without loss of data.	"Responding to RAID 1 Volume Component Failures" on page 112 "How to Replace a Component in a RAID 5 Volume" on page 143
Recover from boot problems	Special problems can arise when booting the system, due to a hardware problem or operator error.	"How to Recover From Improper /etc/vfstab Entries" on page 258 "How to Recover From Insufficient State Database Replicas" on page 265 "How to Recover From a Boot Device Failure" on page 261
Work with transactional volume problems	Problems with transactional volumes can occur on either the master or logging device, and they can either be caused by data or device problems. All transactional volumes sharing the same logging device must be fixed before they return to a usable state.	"How to Recover a Transactional Volume With a Panic" on page 192 "How to Recover a Transactional Volume With Hard Errors" on page 193

## CHAPTER 2

Storage Management Concepts

This chapter provides a brief introduction to some common storage management concepts. If you are already familiar with storage management concepts, you can proceed directly to Chapter 3.

This chapter contains the following information:

- "Introduction to Storage Management" on page 27
- "Configuration Planning Guidelines" on page 29
- "Performance Issues" on page 30
- "Optimizing for Random I/O and Sequential I/O" on page 31

Introduction to Storage Management

Storage management is the means by which you control the devices on which the active data on your system is kept. To be useful, active data must be available and remain unchanged (persistent) even after unexpected events (hardware failure, software failure, or other similar event).

Storage Hardware

There are many different devices on which data can be stored. The selection of devices to best meet your storage needs depends primarily on three factors:

- Performance
- Availability
- Cost

You can use Solaris Volume Manager to help manage the tradeoffs in performance, availability and cost. You can often mitigate many of the tradeoffs completely with Solaris Volume Manager.

Solaris Volume Manager works well with any supported storage on any system that runs the Solaris™ Operating Environment.

RAID Levels

RAID is an acronym for Redundant Array of Inexpensive (or Independent) Disks. Basically, this term refers to a set of disks (called an array, or, more commonly, a *volume*) that appears to the user as a single large disk drive. This array provides, depending on the configuration, improved reliability, response time, and/or storage capacity.

Technically, there are six RAID levels, 0-5,. Each level refers to a method of distributing data while ensuring data redundancy. (RAID level 0 does not provide data redundancy, but is usually included as a RAID classification because it is the basis for the majority of RAID configurations in use.) Very few storage environments support RAID levels 2, 3, and 4, so they are not described here.

Solaris Volume Manager supports the following RAID levels:

- RAID Level 0–Although they do not provide redundancy, stripes and concatenations are often referred to as RAID 0. Basically, data are spread across relatively small, equally-sized fragments that are allocated alternately and evenly across multiple physical disks. Any single drive failure can cause data loss. RAID 0 offers a high data transfer rate and high I/O throughput, but suffers lower reliability and availability than a single disk

- RAID Level 1–Mirroring uses equal amounts of disk capacity to store data and a copy (mirror) of it. Data is duplicated, or mirrored, over two or more physical disks. Data can be read from both drives simultaneously (either drive can service any request), providing improved performance. If one physical disk fails, you can continue to use the mirror with no loss in performance or loss of data.

  Solaris Volume Manager supports both RAID 0+1 and (transparently) RAID 1+0 mirroring, depending on the underlying devices. See "Providing RAID 1+0 and RAID 0+1" on page 83 for details.

- RAID Level 5–RAID 5 uses striping to spread the data over the disks in an array. RAID 5 also records parity information to provide some data redundancy. A RAID level 5 volume can withstand the failure of an underlying device without failing, and, if used in conjunction with hot spares, can withstand multiple failures, albeit with a substantial performance degradation when operating with a failed device.

  In the RAID 5 model, every device has one area that contains a parity stripe and others that contain data. The parity is spread over all of the disks in the array, reducing the write time for large independent writes because the writes do not have to wait until a single parity disk can accept the data.

Configuration Planning Guidelines

When you are planning your storage management configuration, keep in mind that for any given application there are trade-offs in *performance*, *availability*, and *hardware costs*. You might need to experiment with the different variables to determine what works best for your configuration.

This section provides guidelines for working with Solaris Volume Manager RAID 0 (concatenation and stripe) volumes, RAID 1 (mirror) volumes, RAID 5 volumes, soft partitions, transactional (logging) volumes, and file systems that are constructed on volumes.

Choosing Storage Mechanisms

Before you implement your storage management approach, you need to decide what kinds of storage devices to use. This set of guidelines compares the various storage mechanisms to help you choose among them. Additional sets of guidelines apply to specific storage mechanisms as implemented in Solaris Volume Manager. See specific chapters about each volume type for details.

Note – The storage mechanisms listed are not mutually exclusive. You can use them in combination to meet multiple goals. For example, you could create a RAID 1 volume for redundancy, then create soft partitions on it to increase the number of discrete file systems that are possible.

TABLE 2–1 Choosing Storage Mechanisms

Requirements	RAID 0 (Concatenation)	RAID 0 (Stripe)	RAID 1 (Mirror)	RAID 5	Soft Partitions
Redundant data	No	No	Yes	Yes	No
Improved read performance	No	Yes	Depends on underlying device	Yes	No
Improved write performance	No	Yes	No	No	No
More than 8 slices/device	No	No	No	No	Yes

TABLE 2–1 Choosing Storage Mechanisms   *(Continued)*

Requirements	RAID 0 (Concatenation)	RAID 0 (Stripe)	RAID 1 (Mirror)	RAID 5	Soft Partitions
Larger available storage space	Yes	Yes	No	Yes	No

TABLE 2–2 Optimizing Redundant Storage

	RAID 1 (Mirror)	RAID 5
Write operations	Faster	Slower
Random read	Faster	Slower
Hardware cost	Higher	Lower

- RAID 0 devices (stripes and concatenations), and soft partitions do not provide any redundancy of data.

- Concatenation works well for small random I/O.

- Striping performs well for large sequential I/O and for random I/O distributions.

- Mirroring might improve read performance; write performance is always degraded.

- Because of the read-modify-write nature of RAID 5 volumes, volumes with greater than about 20 percent writes should probably not be RAID 5. If redundancy is required, consider mirroring.

- RAID 5 writes will never be as fast as mirrored writes, which in turn will never be as fast as unprotected writes.

- Soft partitions are useful for managing very large storage devices.

Note – In addition to these generic storage options, see "Hot Spare Pools" on page 44 for more information about using Solaris Volume Manager to support redundant devices.

Performance Issues

General Performance Guidelines

When you design your storage configuration, consider the following performance guidelines:

- Striping generally has the best performance, but it offers no data redundancy. For write-intensive applications, RAID 1 volumes generally have better performance than RAID 5 volumes.

- RAID 1 and RAID 5 volumes both increase data availability, but they both generally have lower performance, especially for write operations. Mirroring does improve random read performance.

- RAID 5 volumes have a lower hardware cost than RAID 1 volumes, while RAID 0 volumes have no additional hardware cost.

- Identify the most frequently accessed data, and increase access bandwidth to that data with mirroring or striping.

- Both stripes and RAID 5 volumes distribute data across multiple disk drives and help balance the I/O load.

- Use available performance monitoring capabilities and generic tools such as the `iostat` command to identify the most frequently accessed data. Once identified, the access bandwidth to this data can be increased using striping, RAID 1 volumes or RAID 5 volumes.

- The performance of soft partitions can degrade when the soft partition size is changed multiple times.

- RAID 5 volume performance is lower than stripe performance for write operations, because the RAID 5 volume requires multiple I/O operations to calculate and store the parity.

- For raw random I/O reads, the stripe and the RAID 5 volume are comparable. Both the stripe and RAID 5 volume split the data across multiple disks, and the RAID 5 volume parity calculations aren't a factor in reads except after a slice failure.

- For raw random I/O writes, the stripe is superior to RAID 5 volumes.

Optimizing for Random I/O and Sequential I/O

This section explains Solaris Volume Manager strategies for optimizing your particular configuration.

In general, if you do not know if sequential I/O or random I/O predominates on file systems you will be implementing on Solaris Volume Manager volumes, do not implement these performance tuning tips. These tips can degrade performance if they are improperly implemented.

The following optimization suggestions assume that you are optimizing a RAID 0 volume. In general, you would want to optimize a RAID 0 volume, then mirror that volume to provide both optimal performance and data redundancy.

Random I/O

If you have a random I/O environment, such as an environment used for databases and general-purpose file servers, you want all disk spindles to be approximately equal amounts of time servicing I/O requests.

For example, assume that you have 40 Gbytes of storage for a database application. If you stripe across four 10 Gbyte disk spindles, and if the I/O load is truly random and evenly dispersed across the entire range of the table space, then each of the four spindles will tend to be equally busy, which will generally improve performance.

The target for maximum random I/O performance on a disk is 35 percent or lower usage, as reported by the `iostat` command. Disk use in excess of 65 percent on a typical basis is a problem. Disk use in excess of 90 percent is a significant problem. The solution to having disk use values that are too high is to create a new RAID 0 volume with more disks (spindles).

Note – Simply attaching additional disks to an existing volume will not improve performance. You must create a new volume with the ideal parameters to optimize performance.

The interlace size of the stripe doesn't matter because you just want to spread the data across all the disks. Any interlace value greater than the typical I/O request will do.

Sequential Access I/O

You can optimize the performance of your configuration to take advantage of a sequential I/O environment, such as DBMS servers that are dominated by full table scans and NFS servers in very data-intensive environments, by setting the interlace value low relative to the size of the typical I/O request.

For example, assume a typical I/O request size of 256 Kbyte and striping across 4 spindles. A good choice for stripe unit size in this example would be: 256 Kbyte / 4 = 64 Kbyte, or smaller.

This strategy ensures that the typical I/O request is spread across multiple disk spindles, thus increasing the sequential bandwidth.

Note – Seek time and rotation time are practically zero in the sequential case. When you optimize sequential I/O, the internal transfer rate of a disk is most important.

In sequential applications, the typical I/O size is usually large (greater than 128 Kbytes, often greater than 1 Mbytes). Assume an application with a typical I/O request size of 256 Kbytes and assume striping across 4 disk spindles. 256 Kbytes / 4 = 64 Kbytes. So, a good choice for the interlace size would be 32 to 64 Kbyte.

## CHAPTER 3

Solaris Volume Manager Overview

This chapter explains the overall structure of Solaris Volume Manager and provides the following information:

- "What Does Solaris Volume Manager Do?" on page 35
- "Solaris Volume Manager Requirements" on page 38
- "Overview of Solaris Volume Manager Components" on page 38
- "Solaris Volume Manager Configuration Guidelines" on page 45
- "Overview of Creating Solaris Volume Manager Elements" on page 46

What Does Solaris Volume Manager Do?

Solaris Volume Manager is a software product that lets you manage large numbers of disks and the data on those disks. Although there are many ways to use Solaris Volume Manager, most tasks include the following:

- Increasing storage capacity
- Increasing data availability
- Easing administration of large storage devices

In some instances, Solaris Volume Manager can also improve I/O performance.

How Does Solaris Volume Manager Manage Storage?

Solaris Volume Manager uses virtual disks to manage physical disks and their associated data. In Solaris Volume Manager, a virtual disk is called a *volume*. For historical reasons, some command-line utilities also refer to a volume as a "metadevice."

A volume is functionally identical to a physical disk in the view of an application or a file system (such as UFS). Solaris Volume Manager converts I/O requests directed at a volume into I/O requests to the underlying member disks.

Solaris Volume Manager volumes are built from slices (disk partitions) or from other Solaris Volume Manager volumes. An easy way to build volumes is to use the graphical user interface built into the Solaris Management Console. The Enhanced Storage tool within the Solaris Management Console presents you with a view of all the existing volumes. By following the steps in wizards, you can easily build any kind of Solaris Volume Manager volume or component. You can also build and modify volumes by using Solaris Volume Manager command-line utilities.

If, for example, you want to create more storage capacity as a single volume, you could use Solaris Volume Manager to make the system treat a collection of many small slices as one larger slice or device. After you have created a large volume from these slices, you can immediately begin using it just as any "real" slice or device.

For a more detailed discussion of volumes, see "Volumes" on page 39.

Solaris Volume Manager can increase the reliability and availability of data by using RAID 1 (mirror) volumes and RAID 5 volumes. Solaris Volume Manager hot spares can provide another level of data availability for mirrors and RAID 5 volumes.

Once you have set up your configuration, you can use the Enhanced Storage tool within the Solaris Management Console to report on its operation.

How to Interact With Solaris Volume Manager

Use either of these methods to interact with Solaris Volume Manager:

- Solaris Management Console–This tool provides a graphical user interface to volume management functions. Use the Enhanced Storage tool within the Solaris Management Console as illustrated in Figure 3–1. This interface provides a graphical view of Solaris Volume Manager components, including volumes, hot spare pools, and state database replicas. This interface offers wizard-based manipulation of Solaris Volume Manager components, enabling you to quickly configure your disks or change an existing configuration.

- The command line–You can use several commands to perform volume management functions. The Solaris Volume Manager core commands begin with `meta` for example the `metainit` and `metastat` commands. For a list of Solaris Volume Manager commands, see Appendix B.

Note – Do not attempt to administer Solaris Volume Manager with the command line and the graphical user interface at the same time. Conflicting changes could be made to the configuration, and the behavior would be unpredictable. You can use both tools to administer Solaris Volume Manager, but not concurrently.

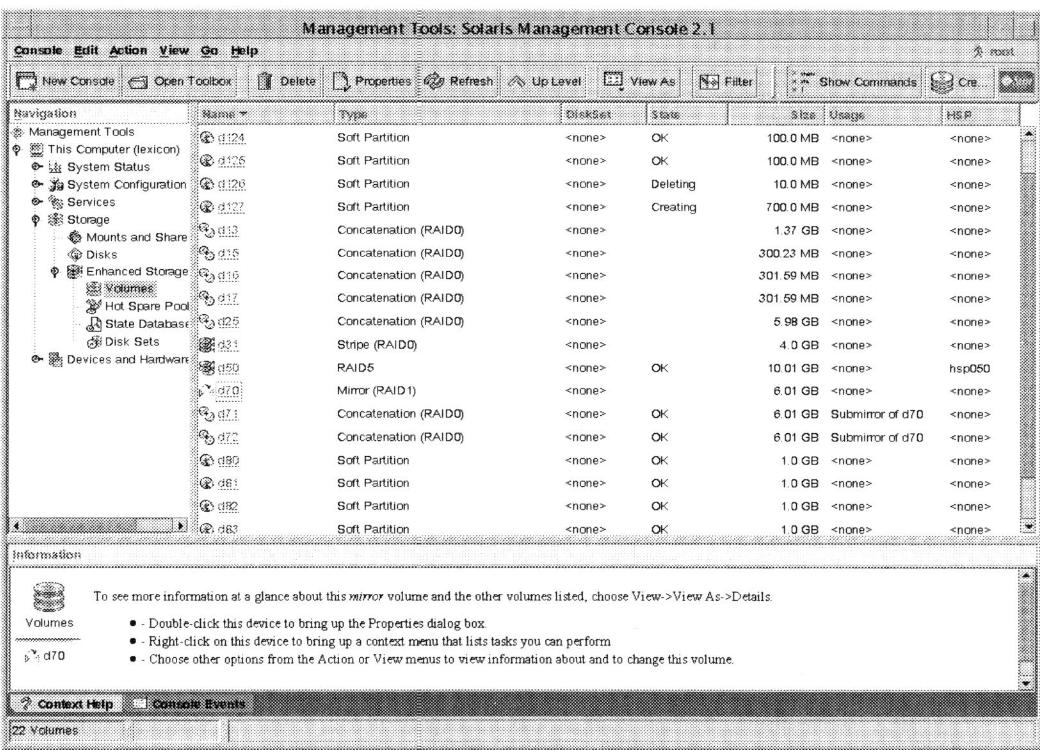

FIGURE 3–1 View of the Enhanced Storage tool (Solaris Volume Manager) in the Solaris Management Console

▼ How to Access the Solaris Volume Manager Graphical User Interface

The Solaris Volume Manager graphical user interface (Enhanced Storage) is part of the Solaris Management Console. To access it, use the following instructions:

1. **Start Solaris Management Console on the host system by using the following command:**

```
% /usr/sbin/smc
```

2. **Double-click This Computer.**

3. **Double-click Storage.**

4. **Double-click Enhanced Storage to load the Solaris Volume Manager tools.**

5. **If prompted to log in, log in as root or as a user who has equivalent access.**

6. **Double-click the appropriate icon to manage volumes, hot spare pools, state database replicas, and disk sets.**

Tip – To help with your tasks, all tools in the Solaris Management Console display information in the bottom section of the page or at the left side of a wizard panel. Choose Help at any time to find additional information about performing tasks in this interface.

Solaris Volume Manager Requirements

Solaris Volume Manager requirements include the following:

- You must have root privilege to administer Solaris Volume Manager. Equivalent privileges granted through the User Profile feature in the Solaris Management Console allow administration through the Solaris Management Console, but only the root user can use the Solaris Volume Manager command-line interface.

- Before you can create volumes with Solaris Volume Manager, state database replicas must exist on the Solaris Volume Manager system. At least three replicas should exist, and they should be placed on different controllers and disks for maximum reliability. See "About the Solaris Volume Manager State Database and Replicas" on page 51 for more information about state database replicas, and "Creating State Database Replicas" on page 58 for instructions on how to create state database replicas.

Overview of Solaris Volume Manager Components

The four basic types of components that you create with Solaris Volume Manager are volumes, disk sets, state database replicas, and hot spare pools. The following table gives an overview of these Solaris Volume Manager components.

TABLE 3–1 Summary of Solaris Volume Manager Components

Solaris Volume Manager Component	Definition	Purpose	For More Information
RAID 0 volumes (stripe, concatenation, concatenated stripe), RAID 1 (mirror) volumes, RAID 5 volumes	A group of physical slices that appear to the system as a single, logical device	To increase storage capacity, performance, or data availability.	"Volumes" on page 39
Soft partitions	Subdivisions of physical slices or logical volumes to provide smaller, more manageable storage units	To improve manageability of large storage volumes.	
State database (state database replicas)	A database that stores information on disk about the state of your Solaris Volume Manager configuration	Solaris Volume Manager cannot operate until you have created the state database replicas.	"State Database and State Database Replicas" on page 43
Hot spare pool	A collection of slices (hot spares) reserved to be automatically substituted in case of component failure in either a submirror or RAID 5 volume	To increase data availability for RAID 1 and RAID 5 volumes.	"Hot Spare Pools" on page 44
Disk set	A set of shared disk drives in a separate namespace that contain volumes and hot spares and that can be non-concurrently shared by multiple hosts	To provide data redundancy and availability and to provide a separate namespace for easier administration.	"Disk Sets" on page 44

Volumes

A *volume* is a name for a group of physical slices that appear to the system as a single, logical device. Volumes are actually pseudo, or virtual, devices in standard UNIX® terms.

Note – Historically, the Solstice DiskSuite™ product referred to these as "metadevices." However, for simplicity and standardization, this book refers to them as "volumes."

Classes of Volumes

You create a volume as a RAID 0 (concatenation or stripe) volume, a RAID 1 (mirror) volume, a RAID 5 volume, a soft partition, or a UFS logging volume.

You can use either the Enhanced Storage tool within the Solaris Management Console or the command-line utilities to create and administer volumes.

The following table summarizes the classes of volumes:

TABLE 3–2 Classes of Volumes

Volume	Description
RAID 0 (stripe or concatenation)	Can be used directly, or as the basic building blocks for mirrors and transactional devices. By themselves, RAID 0 volumes do not provide data redundancy.
RAID 1 (mirror)	Replicates data by maintaining multiple copies. A RAID 1 volume is composed of one or more RAID 0 volumes called submirrors.
RAID 5	Replicates data by using parity information. In the case of disk failure, the missing data can be regenerated by using available data and the parity information. A RAID 5 volume is generally composed of slices. One slice's worth of space is allocated to parity information, but it is distributed across all slices in the RAID 5 volume.
Transactional	Used to log a UFS file system. (UFS logging is a preferable solution to this need, however.) A transactional volume is composed of a master device and a logging device. Both of these devices can be a slice, RAID 0 volume, RAID 1 volume, or RAID5 volume. The master device contains the UFS file system.
Soft partition	Divides a slice or logical volume into one or more smaller, extensible volumes.

How Are Volumes Used?

You use volumes to increase storage capacity, performance, and data availability. In some instances, volumes can also increase I/O performance. Functionally, volumes behave the same way as slices. Because volumes look like slices, they are transparent to end users, applications, and file systems. Like physical devices, volumes are accessed through block or raw device names. The volume name changes, depending on whether the block or raw device is used. See "Volume Names" on page 42 for details about volume names.

You can use most file system commands (`mkfs`, `mount`, `umount`, `ufsdump`, `ufsrestore`, and so forth) on volumes. You cannot use the `format` command, however. You can read, write, and copy files to and from a volume, as long as the volume contains a mounted file system.

Example—Volume That Consists of Two Slices

Figure 3–2 shows a volume "containing" two slices, one each from Disk A and Disk B. An application or UFS will treat the volume as if it were one physical disk. Adding more slices to the volume will increase its capacity.

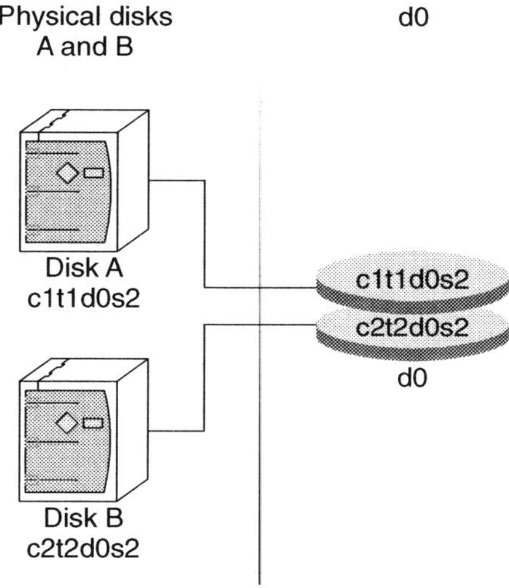

FIGURE 3–2 Relationship Among a Volume, Physical Disks, and Slices

Volume and Disk Space Expansion

Solaris Volume Manager enables you to expand a volume by adding additional slices. You can use either the Enhanced Storage tool within the Solaris Management Console or the command line interface to add a slice to an existing volume.

You can expand a mounted or unmounted UFS file system that is contained within a volume without having to halt or back up your system. (Nevertheless, backing up your data is always a good idea.) After you expand the volume, use the `growfs` command to grow the file system.

Note – After a file system has been expanded, it cannot be shrunk. Not shrinking the size of a file system is a UFS limitation. Similarly, after a Solaris Volume Manager partition has been increased in size, it cannot be reduced.

Applications and databases that use the raw volume must have their own method to "grow" the added space so that the application or database can recognize it. Solaris Volume Manager does not provide this capability.

You can expand the disk space in volumes in the following ways:

- Adding one or more slices to a RAID 0 volume
- Adding a slice or multiple slices to all submirrors of a RAID 1 volume
- Adding one or more slices to a RAID 5 volume
- Expanding a soft partition with additional space from the underlying component

The growfs Command

The growfs command expands a UFS file system without loss of service or data. However, write access to the volume is suspended while the growfs command is running. You can expand the file system to the size of the slice or the volume that contains the file system.

The file system can be expanded to use only part of the additional disk space by using the -s *size* option to the growfs command.

Note – When you expand a mirror, space is added to the mirror's underlying submirrors. Likewise, when you expand a transactional volume, space is added to the master device. The growfs command is then run on the RAID 1 volume or the transactional volume, respectively. The general rule is that space is added to the underlying devices, and the growfs command is run on the top-level device.

Volume Names

Volume Name Requirements

There are a few rules that you must follow when assigning names for volumes:

- Volume names must begin with the letter "d" followed by a number (for example, d0).
- Solaris Volume Manager has 128 default volume names from 0–127. The following table shows some example volume names.

TABLE 3–3 Example Volume Names

/dev/md/dsk/d0	Block volume d0
/dev/md/dsk/d1	Block volume d1
/dev/md/rdsk/d126	Raw volume d126
/dev/md/rdsk/d127	Raw volume d127

- Instead of specifying the full volume name, such as /dev/md/dsk/d1, you can often use an abbreviated volume name, such as d1, with any meta* command.

- Like physical slices, volumes have logical names that appear in the file system. Logical volume names have entries in the `/dev/md/dsk` directory (for block devices) and the `/dev/md/rdsk` directory (for raw devices).

- You can generally rename a volume, as long as the volume is not currently being used and the new name is not being used by another volume. For more information, see "Exchanging Volume Names" on page 222.

Volume Name Guidelines

The use of a standard for your volume names can simplify administration, and enable you at a glance to identify the volume type. Here are a few suggestions:

- Use ranges for each particular type of volume. For example, assign numbers 0–20 for RAID 1 volumes, 21–40 for RAID 0 volumes, and so on.

- Use a naming relationship for mirrors. For example, name mirrors with a number that ends in zero (0), and submirrors that end in one (1) and two (2). For example: mirror `d10`, submirrors `d11` and `d12`; mirror `d20`, submirrors `d21` and `d22`, and so on.

- Use a naming method that maps the slice number and disk number to volume numbers.

State Database and State Database Replicas

The *state database* is a database that stores information on disk about the state of your Solaris Volume Manager configuration. The state database records and tracks changes made to your configuration. Solaris Volume Manager automatically updates the state database when a configuration or state change occurs. Creating a new volume is an example of a configuration change. A submirror failure is an example of a state change.

The state database is actually a collection of multiple, replicated database copies. Each copy, referred to as a *state database replica*, ensures that the data in the database is always valid. Having copies of the state database protects against data loss from single points-of-failure. The state database tracks the location and status of all known state database replicas.

Solaris Volume Manager cannot operate until you have created the state database and its state database replicas. It is necessary that a Solaris Volume Manager configuration have an operating state database.

When you set up your configuration, you can locate the state database replicas on either of the following:

- On dedicated slices
- On slices that will later become part of volumes

Solaris Volume Manager recognizes when a slice contains a state database replica, and automatically skips over the portion of the slice reserved for the replica if the slice is used in a volume. The part of a slice reserved for the state database replica should not be used for any other purpose.

You can keep more than one copy of a state database on one slice. However, you might make the system more vulnerable to a single point-of-failure by doing so.

The system will continue to function correctly if all state database replicas are deleted. However, the system will lose all Solaris Volume Manager configuration data if a reboot occurs with no existing state database replicas on disk.

Hot Spare Pools

A *hot spare pool* is a collection of slices (*hot spares*) reserved by Solaris Volume Manager to be automatically substituted in case of a slice failure in either a submirror or RAID 5 volume. Hot spares provide increased data availability for RAID 1 and RAID 5 volumes. You can create a hot spare pool with either the Enhanced Storage tool within the Solaris Management Console or the command line interface.

When errors occur, Solaris Volume Manager checks the hot spare pool for the first available hot spare whose size is equal to or greater than the size of the slice being replaced. If found, Solaris Volume Manager automatically resynchronizes the data. If a slice of adequate size is not found in the list of hot spares, the submirror or RAID 5 volume is considered to have failed. For more information, see Chapter 15.

Disk Sets

A *shared disk set*, or simply *disk set*, is a set of disk drives that contain state database replicas, volumes, and hot spares that can be shared exclusively but not at the same time by multiple hosts.

A disk set provides for data availability in a clustered environment. If one host fails, another host can take over the failed host's disk set. (This type of configuration is known as a *failover configuration*.) Additionally, disk sets can be used to help manage the Solaris Volume Manager name space, and to provide ready access to network-attached storage devices.

For more information, see Chapter 19.

Solaris Volume Manager Configuration Guidelines

A poorly designed Solaris Volume Manager configuration can degrade performance. This section offers tips for achieving good performance from Solaris Volume Manager.

General Guidelines

- **Disk and controllers**–Place drives in a volume on separate drive paths. For SCSI drives, this means separate host adapters. Spreading the I/O load over several controllers improves volume performance and availability.

- **System files**–Never edit or remove the `/etc/lvm/mddb.cf` or `/etc/lvm/md.cf` files.

  Make sure these files are backed up on a regular basis.

- **Volume Integrity**–After a slice is defined as a volume and activated, do not use it for any other purpose.

- **Maximum volumes**–The maximum number of volumes supported in a disk set is 8192 (though the default number of volumes is 128). To increase the number of default volumes, edit the `/kernel/drv/md.conf` file. See "System Files and Startup Files" on page 277 for more information on this file.

- **Information about disks and partitions**–Have a copy of output from the `prtvtoc` and `metastat -p` command in case you need to reformat a bad disk or re-create your Solaris Volume Manager configuration.

File System Guidelines

- Do not mount file systems on a volume's underlying slice. If a slice is used for a volume of any kind, you must not mount that slice as a file system. If possible, unmount any physical device that you intend to use as a volume before you activate it. For example, if you create a transactional volume for a UFS, in the `/etc/vfstab` file, you would specify the transactional volume name as the device to mount and `fsck`.

Overview of Creating Solaris Volume Manager Elements

When you create a Solaris Volume Manager component, you assign physical slices to a logical Solaris Volume Manager name. The Solaris Volume Manager elements that you can create include the following:

- State database replicas
- Volumes (RAID 0 (stripes, concatenations), RAID 1 (mirrors), RAID 5, soft partitions, and transactional volumes)
- Hot spare pools
- Disk sets

Note – For suggestions on how to name volumes, see "Volume Names" on page 42.

Prerequisites for Creating Solaris Volume Manager Elements

The prerequisites for creating Solaris Volume Manager elements are as follows:

- Create initial state database replicas. If you have not done so, see "Creating State Database Replicas" on page 58.
- Identify slices that are available for use by Solaris Volume Manager. If necessary, use the `format` command, the `fmthard` command, or the Solaris Management Console to repartition existing disks.
- Make sure you have root privilege.
- Have a current backup of all data.
- If you are using the graphical user interface, start the Solaris Management Console and maneuver through it to get to the Solaris Volume Manager feature. For information, see "How to Access the Solaris Volume Manager Graphical User Interface" on page 37.

## CHAPTER 4

Configuring and Using Solaris Volume Manager (Scenario)

Throughout the *Solaris Volume Manager Administration Guide*, the examples generally relate to a single storage configuration, whenever that is possible. This chapter explains what that configuration is and provides information about this broad storage scenario for the rest of the book.

This chapter contains the following information:

- "Background" on page 47
- "Complete Solaris Volume Manager Configuration" on page 49

Background

Throughout this book, the scenarios and many examples relate to a single configuration. Although this configuration is small (to simplify the documentation), the concepts will scale to much larger storage environments.

Hardware Configuration

The hardware system is configured as follows:

- There are 3 physically separate controllers (c0 — IDE, c1—SCSI, and c2 — SCSI).
- Each SCSI controller connects to a MultiPack that contains 6 internal 9–Gbyte disks (c1t1 through c1t6 and c2t1 through c2t6).
- Each controller/terminator pair (c*n*t*n*) has 8.49 Gbytes of usable storage space.
- Storage space on the root (/) drive c0t0d0 is split into 6 partitions.

An alternative way to understand this configuration is shown in the following diagram.

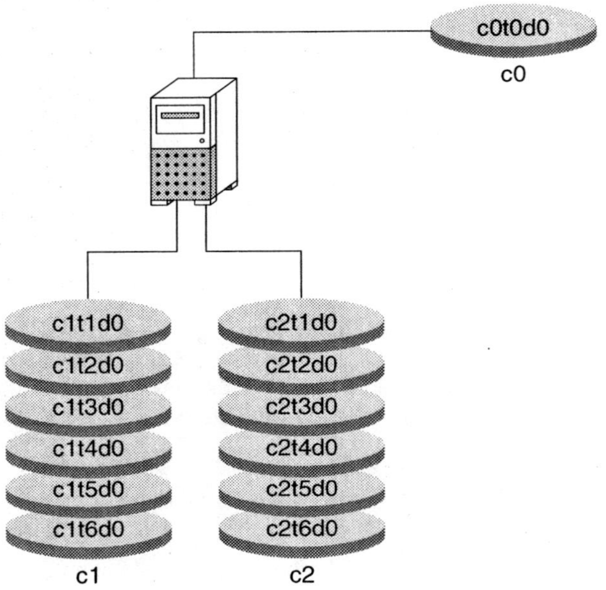

FIGURE 4–1 Basic Hardware Diagram

Storage Configuration

The storage configuration before Solaris Volume Manager is configured is as follows:

- The SCSI controller/terminator pairs (*cntn*) have approximately 20 Gbytes of storage space
- Storage space on each disk (for example, `c1t1d0`) is split into 7 partitions (*cntnd0s0* through *cntnd0s6*).

  To partition a disk, follow the procedures explained in "Formatting a Disk" in *System Administration Guide: Basic Administration*.

Complete Solaris Volume Manager Configuration

Throughout this book, specific scenarios are provided with specific tasks. However, so that you can better understand the examples throughout the book, the final configuration is approximately as follows (as displayed by the metastat(1M) command with the -p option):

```
[root@lexicon:/]$ metastat -p
d50 -r c1t4d0s5 c1t5d0s5 c2t4d0s5 c2t5d0s5 c1t1d0s5 c2t1d0s5 -k -i 32b
d1 1 1 c1t2d0s3
d2 1 1 c2t2d0s3
d12 1 1 c1t1d0s0
d13 1 1 c2t1d0s0
d16 1 1 c1t1d0s1
d17 1 1 c2t1d0s1
d25 2 2 c1t1d0s3 c2t1d0s3 -i 32b \
        1 c0t0d0s3
d31 1 2 c1t4d0s4 c2t4d0s4 -i 8192b
d80 -p d70 -o 1 -b 2097152
d81 -p d70 -o 2097154 -b 2097152
d82 -p d70 -o 4194307 -b 2097152
d83 -p d70 -o 6291460 -b 2097152
d84 -p d70 -o 8388613 -b 2097152
d85 -p d70 -o 10485766 -b 2097152
d70 -m d71 d72 1
d71 3 1 c1t3d0s3 \
        1 c1t3d0s4 \
        1 c1t3d0s5
d72 3 1 c2t3d0s3 \
        1 c2t3d0s4 \
        1 c2t3d0s5
d123 -p c1t3d0s6 -o 1 -b 204800
d124 -p c1t3d0s6 -o 204802 -b 204800
d125 -p c1t3d0s6 -o 409603 -b 204800
d126 -p c1t3d0s7 -o 3592 -b 20480
d127 -p c2t3d0s7 -o 3592 -b 1433600
hsp010
hsp014 c1t2d0s1 c2t2d0s1
hsp050 c1t2d0s5 c2t2d0s5
hsp070 c1t2d0s4 c2t2d0s4
```

## CHAPTER 5

State Database (Overview)

This chapter provides conceptual information about state database replicas. For information about performing related tasks, see Chapter 6.

This chapter contains the following information:

About the Solaris Volume Manager State Database and Replicas

The Solaris Volume Manager state database contains configuration and status information for all volumes, hot spares, and disk sets. Solaris Volume Manager maintains multiple copies (replicas) of the state database to provide redundancy and to prevent the database from being corrupted during a system crash (at most, only one database copy will be corrupted).

The state database replicas ensure that the data in the state database is always valid. When the state database is updated, each state database replica is also updated. The updates take place one at a time (to protect against corrupting all updates if the system crashes).

If your system loses a state database replica, Solaris Volume Manager must figure out which state database replicas still contain valid data. Solaris Volume Manager determines this information by using a *majority consensus algorithm*. This algorithm requires that a majority (half + 1) of the state database replicas be available and in agreement before any of them are considered valid. It is because of this majority consensus algorithm that you must create at least three state database replicas when you set up your disk configuration. A consensus can be reached as long as at least two of the three state database replicas are available.

During booting, Solaris Volume Manager ignores corrupted state database replicas. In some cases, Solaris Volume Manager tries to rewrite state database replicas that are corrupted. Otherwise, they are ignored until you repair them. If a state database replica becomes corrupted because its underlying slice encountered an error, you will need to repair or replace the slice and then enable the replica.

If all state database replicas are lost, you could, in theory, lose all data that is stored on your Solaris Volume Manager volumes. For this reason, it is good practice to create enough state database replicas on separate drives and across controllers to prevent catastrophic failure. It is also wise to save your initial Solaris Volume Manager configuration information, as well as your disk partition information.

See Chapter 6 for information on adding additional state database replicas to the system, and on recovering when state database replicas are lost.

State database replicas are also used for RAID 1 volume resynchronization regions. Too few state database replicas relative to the number of mirrors might cause replica I/O to impact RAID 1 volume performance. That is, if you have a large number of mirrors, make sure that you have a total of at least two state database replicas per RAID 1 volume, up to the maximum of 50 replicas per disk set.

Each state database replica occupies 4 Mbytes (8192 disk sectors) of disk storage by default. Replicas can be stored on the following devices:

- a dedicated disk partition
- a partition that will be part of a volume
- a partition that will be part of a UFS logging device

Note – Replicas cannot be stored on the root (/), `swap`, or `/usr` slices, or on slices that contain existing file systems or data. After the replicas have been stored, volumes or file systems can be placed on the same slice.

Understanding the Majority Consensus Algorithm

Replicated databases have an inherent problem in determining which database has valid and correct data. To solve this problem, Solaris Volume Manager uses a majority consensus algorithm. This algorithm requires that a majority of the database replicas agree with each other before any of them are declared valid. This algorithm requires the presence of at least three initial replicas which you create. A consensus can then be reached as long as at least two of the three replicas are available. If there is only one replica and the system crashes, it is possible that all volume configuration data will be lost.

To protect data, Solaris Volume Manager will not function unless half of all state database replicas are available. The algorithm, therefore, ensures against corrupt data.

The majority consensus algorithm provides the following:

- The system will stay running if at least half of the state database replicas are available.

- The system will panic if fewer than half of the state database replicas are available.

- The system will not reboot into multiuser mode unless a majority (half + 1) of the total number of state database replicas is available.

If insufficient state database replicas are available, you will have to boot into single-user mode and delete enough of the bad or missing replicas to achieve a quorum. See "How to Recover From Insufficient State Database Replicas" on page 265.

Note – When the number of state database replicas is odd, Solaris Volume Manager computes the majority by dividing the number in half, rounding down to the nearest integer, then adding 1 (one). For example, on a system with seven replicas, the majority would be four (seven divided by two is three and one-half, rounded down is three, plus one is four).

Background Information for Defining State Database Replicas

In general, it is best to distribute state database replicas across slices, drives, and controllers, to avoid single points-of-failure. You want a majority of replicas to survive a single component failure. If you lose a replica (for example, due to a device failure), it might cause problems with running Solaris Volume Manager or when rebooting the system. Solaris Volume Manager requires at least half of the replicas to be available to run, but a majority (half plus one) to reboot into multiuser mode.

When you work with state database replicas, consider the following "Recommendations for State Database Replicas" on page 54 and "Guidelines for State Database Replicas" on page 54.

Recommendations for State Database Replicas

- You should create state database replicas on a dedicated slice of at least 4 Mbytes per replica. If necessary, you could create state database replicas on a slice that will be used as part of a RAID 0, RAID 1, or RAID 5 volume, soft partitions, or transactional (master or log) volumes. You must create the replicas before you add the slice to the volume. Solaris Volume Manager reserves the starting part of the slice for the state database replica.

- You can create state database replicas on slices that are not in use.

- You cannot create state database replicas on existing file systems, or the root (/), /usr, and swap file systems. If necessary, you can create a new slice (provided a slice name is available) by allocating space from swap and then put state database replicas on that new slice.

- A minimum of 3 state database replicas are recommended, up to a maximum of 50 replicas per Solaris Volume Manager disk set. The following guidelines are recommended:

  - For a system with only a single drive: put all three replicas in one slice.

  - For a system with two to four drives: put two replicas on each drive.

  - For a system with five or more drives: put one replica on each drive.

- If you have a RAID 1 volume that will be used for small-sized random I/O (as in for a database), be sure that you have at least two extra replicas per RAID 1 volume on slices (and preferably disks and controllers)that are unconnected to the RAID 1 volume for best performance.

Guidelines for State Database Replicas

- You can add additional state database replicas to the system at any time. The additional state database replicas help ensure Solaris Volume Manager availability.

Caution – If you upgraded from Solstice DiskSuite™to Solaris Volume Manager and you have state database replicas sharing slices with file systems or logical volumes (as opposed to on separate slices), do not delete the existing replicas and replace them with new replicas in the same location.

The default state database replica size in Solaris Volume Manager is 8192 blocks, while the default size in Solstice DiskSuite was 1034 blocks. If you delete a default-sized state database replica from Solstice DiskSuite, then add a new default-sized replica with Solaris Volume Manager, you will overwrite the first 7158 blocks of any file system that occupies the rest of the shared slice, thus destroying the data.

- When a state database replica is placed on a slice that becomes part of a volume, the capacity of the volume is reduced by the space that is occupied by the replica(s). The space used by a replica is rounded up to the next cylinder boundary and this space is skipped by the volume.

- By default, the size of a state database replica is 4 Mbytes or 8192 disk blocks. Because your disk slices might not be that small, you might want to resize a slice to hold the state database replica. For information on resizing a slice, see "Administering Disks (Tasks)" in *System Administration Guide: Basic Administration.*

- If multiple controllers exist, replicas should be distributed as evenly as possible across all controllers. This strategy provides redundancy in case a controller fails and also helps balance the load. If multiple disks exist on a controller, at least two of the disks on each controller should store a replica.

Handling State Database Replica Errors

How does Solaris Volume Manager handle failed replicas?

The system will continue to run with at least half of the available replicas. The system will panic when fewer than half of the replicas are available.

The system can reboot multiuser when at least one more than half of the replicas are available. If fewer than a majority of replicas are available, you must reboot into single-user mode and delete the unavailable replicas (by using the `metadb` command).

For example, assume you have four replicas. The system will stay running as long as two replicas (half the total number) are available. However, to reboot the system, three replicas (half the total plus one) must be available.

In a two-disk configuration, you should always create at least two replicas on each disk. For example, assume you have a configuration with two disks, and you only create three replicas (two replicas on the first disk and one replica on the second disk). If the disk with two replicas fails, the system will panic because the remaining disk only has one replica and this is less than half the total number of replicas.

Note – If you create two replicas on each disk in a two-disk configuration, Solaris Volume Manager will still function if one disk fails. But because you must have one more than half of the total replicas available for the system to reboot, you will be unable to reboot.

What happens if a slice that contains a state database replica fails?
> The rest of your configuration should remain in operation. Solaris Volume Manager finds a valid state database during boot (as long as there are at least half plus one valid state database replicas).

What happens when state database replicas are repaired?
> When you manually repair or enable state database replicas, Solaris Volume Manager updates them with valid data.

Scenario—State Database Replicas

State database replicas provide redundant data about the overall Solaris Volume Manager configuration. The following example, drawing on the sample system provided in Chapter 4, describes how state database replicas can be distributed to provide adequate redundancy.

The sample system has one internal IDE controller and drive, plus two SCSI controllers, which each have six disks attached. With three controllers, the system can be configured to avoid any single point-of-failure. Any system with only two controllers cannot avoid a single point-of-failure relative to Solaris Volume Manager. By distributing replicas evenly across all three controllers and across at least one disk on each controller (across two disks if possible), the system can withstand any single hardware failure.

A minimal configuration could put a single state database replica on slice 7 of the root disk, then an additional replica on slice 7 of one disk on each of the other two controllers. To help protect against the admittedly remote possibility of media failure, using two replicas on the root disk and then two replicas on two different disks on each controller, for a total of six replicas, provides more than adequate security.

To round out the total, add 2 additional replicas for each of the 6 mirrors, on different disks than the mirrors. This configuration results in a total of 18 replicas with 2 on the root disk and 8 on each of the SCSI controllers, distributed across the disks on each controller.

## CHAPTER 6

State Database (Tasks)

This chapter provides information about performing tasks that are associated with Solaris Volume Manager state database replicas. For information about the concepts involved in these tasks, see Chapter 5.

State Database Replicas (Task Map)

The following task map identifies the procedures needed to manage Solaris Volume Manager state database replicas.

Task	Description	Instructions
Create state database replicas	Use the Solaris Volume Manager GUI or the `metadb -a` command to create state database replicas.	"How to Create State Database Replicas" on page 58
Check the status of state database replicas	Use the Solaris Volume Manager GUI or the `metadb` command to check the status of existing replicas.	"How to Check the Status of State Database Replicas" on page 60
Delete state database replicas.	Use the Solaris Volume Manager GUI or the `metadb -d` command to delete state database replicas.	"How to Delete State Database Replicas" on page 61

Creating State Database Replicas

Caution – If you upgraded from Solstice DiskSuite™to Solaris Volume Manager and you have state database replicas sharing slices with file systems or logical volumes (as opposed to on separate slices), do not delete existing replicas and replace them with new default replicas in the same location.

The default state database replica size in Solaris Volume Manager is 8192 blocks, while the default size in Solstice DiskSuite was 1034 blocks. If you delete a default-sized state database replica from Solstice DiskSuite, and then add a new default-sized replica with Solaris Volume Manager, you will overwrite the first 7158 blocks of any file system that occupies the rest of the shared slice, thus destroying the data.

▼ How to Create State Database Replicas

1. **Check "Prerequisites for Creating Solaris Volume Manager Elements" on page 46.**

2. **To create state database replicas, use one of the following methods:**

   - From the Enhanced Storage tool within the Solaris Management Console, open the State Database Replicas node. Choose Action->Create Replicas and follow the instructions. For more information, see the online help.

   - Use the following form of the `metadb` command. See the `metadb(1M)` man page for more information.

     `metadb -a -c` *n* `-l` *nnnn* `-f` *ctds-of-slice*

     - `-a` specifies to add a state database replica.

     - `-f` specifies to force the operation, even if no replicas exist.

     - `-c` *n* specifies the number of replicas to add to the specified slice.

     - `-l` *nnnn* specifies the size of the new replicas, in blocks.

     - *ctds-of-slice* specifies the name of the component that will hold the replica.

     Use the `-f` flag to force the addition of the initial replicas.

Note – The `metadb` command without options reports the status of all replicas.

Example—Creating the First State Database Replica

```
# metadb -a -f c0t0d0s7
# metadb
        flags           first blk       block count
...
     a        u         16              8192            /dev/dsk/c0t0d0s7
```

The -a option adds the additional state database replica to the system, and the -f option forces the creation of the first replica (and may be omitted when you add supplemental replicas to the system).

Example—Adding Two State Database Replicas to the Same Slice

```
# metadb -a -c 2 c1t3d0s1
# metadb
        flags           first blk       block count
...
     a        u         16              8192            /dev/dsk/c1t3d0s1
     a        u         8208            8192            /dev/dsk/c1t3d0s1
```

The -a option adds additional state database replicas to the system. The -c 2 option places two replicas on the specified slice. The metadb command checks that the replicas are active, as indicated by the -a.

You can also specify the size of the state database replica with the -l option, followed by the number of blocks. However, the default size of 8192 should be appropriate for virtually all configurations, including those configurations with thousands of logical volumes.

Example—Adding State Database Replicas of Specific Size

If you are replacing existing state database replicas, you might need to specify a replica size. Particularly if you have existing state database replicas (on a system upgraded from Solstice DiskSuite, perhaps) that share a slice with a file system, you must replace existing replicas with other replicas of the same size or add new replicas in a different location.

Caution – Do not replace default-sized (1034 block) state database replicas from Solstice DiskSuite with default-sized Solaris Volume Manager replicas on a slice shared with a file system. If you do, the new replicas will overwrite the beginning of your file system and corrupt it.

```
# metadb -a -c 3 -l 1034 c0t0d0s7
# metadb
        flags           first blk       block count
```

```
...
    a       u       16              1034            /dev/dsk/c0t0d0s7
    a       u       1050            1034            /dev/dsk/c0t0d0s7
    a       u       2084            1034            /dev/dsk/c0t0d0s7
```

The -a option adds the additional state database replica to the system, and the -l option specifies the length in blocks of the replica to add.

Maintaining State Database Replicas

▼ How to Check the Status of State Database Replicas

● **To check the status of state database replicas, use one of the following methods:**

■ From the Enhanced Storage tool within the Solaris Management Console, open the State Database Replicas node to view all existing state database replicas. For more information, see the online help.

■ Use the metadb command to view the status of state database replicas. Add the -i option to display a key to the status flags. See the metadb(1M) man page for more information.

Example—Checking the Status of All State Database Replicas

```
# metadb -i
    flags               first blk       block count
  a m  p  luo           16              8192            /dev/dsk/c0t0d0s7
  a    p  luo           8208            8192            /dev/dsk/c0t0d0s7
  a    p  luo           16400           8192            /dev/dsk/c0t0d0s7
  a    p  luo           16              8192            /dev/dsk/c1t3d0s1
    W  p  l             16              8192            /dev/dsk/c2t3d0s1
  a    p  luo           16              8192            /dev/dsk/c1t1d0s3
  a    p  luo           8208            8192            /dev/dsk/c1t1d0s3
  a    p  luo           16400           8192            /dev/dsk/c1t1d0s3
 r - replica does not have device relocation information
 o - replica active prior to last mddb configuration change
 u - replica is up to date
 l - locator for this replica was read successfully
 c - replica's location was in /etc/lvm/mddb.cf
 p - replica's location was patched in kernel
 m - replica is master, this is replica selected as input
 W - replica has device write errors
```

```
a - replica is active, commits are occurring to this replica
M - replica had problem with master blocks
D - replica had problem with data blocks
F - replica had format problems
S - replica is too small to hold current data base
R - replica had device read errcrs
```

A legend of all the flags follows the status. The characters in front of the device name represent the status. Uppercase letters indicate a problem status. Lowercase letters indicate an "Okay" status.

How to Delete State Database Replicas

You might need to delete state database replicas to maintain your Solaris Volume Manager configuration. For example, if you will be replacing disk drives, you would want to delete the state database replicas before you remove the drives so they are not considered to have errors by Solaris Volume Manager.

▼ How to Delete State Database Replicas

● **To remove state database replicas, use one of the following methods:**

■ From the Enhanced Storage tool within the Solaris Management Console, open the State Database Replicas node to view all existing state database replicas. Select replicas to delete, then choose Edit->Delete to remove them. For more information, see the online help.

■ Use the following form of the metadb command:

metadb -d -f *ctds-of-slice*

■ -d specifies to delete a state database replica.

■ -f specifies to force the operation, even if no replicas exist.

■ *ctds-of-slice* specifies the name of the component that holds the replica.

Note that you need to specify each slice from which you want to remove the state database replica. See the metadb(1M) man page for more information.

Example—Deleting State Database Replicas

```
# metadb -d -f c0t0d0s7
```

This example shows the last replica being deleted from a slice.

Note – You must add a -f option to force deletion of the last replica on the system.

## CHAPTER 7

RAID 0 (Stripe and Concatenation) Volumes (Overview)

This chapter describes RAID 0 volumes (both stripes and concatenations) that are available in Solaris Volume Manager. For information about related tasks, see Chapter 8.

This chapter provides the following information:

- "Overview of RAID 0 Volumes" on page 63
- "Background Information for Creating RAID 0 Volumes" on page 70
- "Scenario—RAID 0 Volumes" on page 71

Overview of RAID 0 Volumes

RAID 0 volumes, including both stripes and concatenations, are composed of slices or soft partitions and enable you to expand disk storage capacity. They can be used either directly or as the building blocks for RAID 1 (mirror) volumes, transactional volumes, and soft partitions. There are three kinds of RAID 0 volumes:

- Striped volumes (or *stripes*)
- Concatenated volumes (or *concatenations*)
- Concatenated striped volumes (or *concatenated stripes*)

Note – A *component* refers to any devices, from slices to soft partitions, used in another logical volume.

A stripe spreads data equally across all components in the stripe, while a concatenated volume writes data to the first available component until it is full, then moves to the next available component. A concatenated stripe is simply a stripe that has been expanded from its original configuration by adding additional components.

RAID 0 volumes allow you to quickly and simply expand disk storage capacity. The drawback is that these volumes do not provide any data redundancy, unlike RAID 1 or RAID 5 volumes. If a single component fails on a RAID 0 volume, data is lost.

You can use a RAID 0 volume containing a single slice for any file system.

You can use a RAID 0 volume that contains multiple components for any file system except the following:

- root (/)
- /usr
- swap
- /var
- /opt
- Any file system that is accessed during an operating system upgrade or installation

---

Note – When you mirror root (/), /usr, swap, /var, or /opt, you put the file system into a one-way concatenation or stripe (a concatenation of a single slice) that acts as a submirror. This one-way concatenation is mirrored by another submirror, which must also be a concatenation.

RAID 0 (Stripe) Volume

A RAID 0 (stripe) volume is a volume that arranges data across one or more components. Striping alternates equally-sized segments of data across two or more components, forming one logical storage unit. These segments are interleaved round-robin, so that the combined space is made alternately from each component, in effect, shuffled like a deck of cards.

Striping enables multiple controllers to access data at the same time, which is also called parallel access. Parallel access can increase I/O throughput because all disks in the volume are busy most of the time servicing I/O requests.

An existing file system cannot be converted directly to a stripe. To place an existing file system on a stripe, you must back up the file system, create the stripe, then restore the file system to the stripe.

For sequential I/O operations on a stripe, Solaris Volume Manager reads all the blocks in a segment of blocks (called an *interlace*) on the first component, then all the blocks in a segment of blocks on the second component, and so forth.

For sequential I/O operations on a concatenation, Solaris Volume Manager reads all the blocks on the first component, then all the blocks of the second component, and so forth.

On both a concatenation and a stripe, all I/O occurs in parallel.

Interlace Values for Stripes

An interlace is the size, in Kbytes, Mbytes, or blocks, of the logical data segments on a stripe. Depending on the application, different interlace values can increase performance for your configuration. The performance increase comes from having several disk arms doing I/O. When the I/O request is larger than the interlace size, you might get better performance.

Note – RAID 5 volumes also use an interlace value. See "Overview of RAID 5 Volumes" on page 131 for more information.

When you create a stripe, you can set the interlace value or use the Solaris Volume Manager default interlace value of 16 Kbytes. Once you have created the stripe, you cannot change the interlace value. However, you could back up the data on it, delete the stripe, create a new stripe with a new interlace value, and then restore the data.

Scenario—RAID 0 (Stripe) Volume

Figure 7–1 shows a stripe that is built from three components (disks).

When Solaris Volume Manager stripes data from the volume to the components, it writes data from chunk 1 to Disk A, from chunk 2 to Disk B, and from chunk 3 to Disk C. Solaris Volume Manager then writes chunk 4 to Disk A, chunk 5 to Disk B, chunk 6 to Disk C, and so forth.

The interlace value sets the size of each chunk. The total capacity of the stripe d2 equals the number of components multiplied by the size of the smallest component. (If each slice in the following example were 2 Gbytes, d2 would equal 6 Gbytes.)

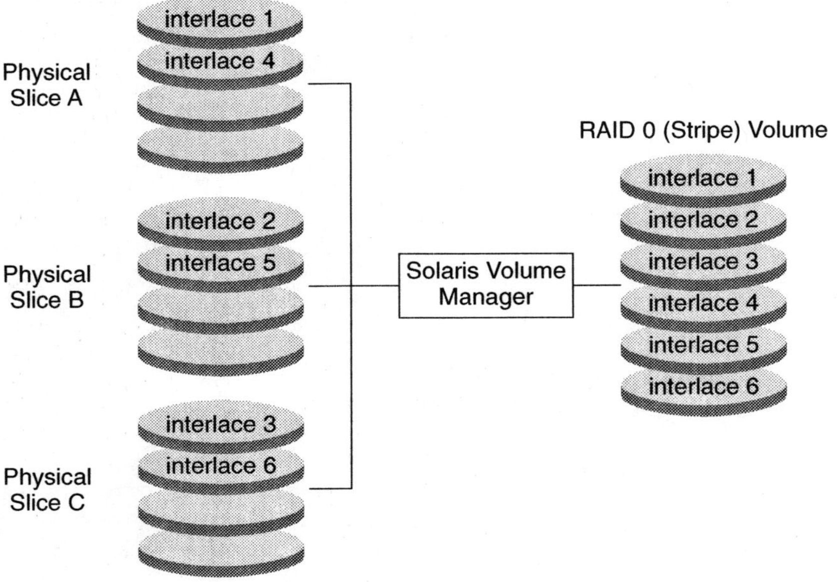

FIGURE 7–1 Stripe Example

RAID 0 (Concatenation) Volume

A concatenated volume, or concatenation, is a volume whose data is organized serially and adjacently across components, forming one logical storage unit.

Use a concatenation to get more storage capacity by combining the capacities of several components. You can add more components to the concatenation as the demand for storage grows.

A concatenation enables you to dynamically expand storage capacity and file system sizes online. With a concatenation you can add components even if the other components are currently active.

Note – To increase the capacity of a stripe, you need to build a concatenated stripe. See "RAID 0 (Concatenated Stripe) Volume" on page 67.

A concatenation can also expand any active and mounted UFS file system without having to bring down the system. In general, the total capacity of a concatenation is equal to the total size of all the components in the concatenation. If a concatenation contains a slice with a state database replica, the total capacity of the concatenation would be the sum of the components minus the space that is reserved for the replica.

You can also create a concatenation from a single component. Later, when you need more storage, you can add more components to the concatenation.

Note – You must use a concatenation to encapsulate root (/), swap, /usr, /opt, or /var when mirroring these file systems.

Scenario—RAID 0 (Concatenation)

Figure 7–2 illustrates a concatenation that is made of three components (slices).

The data blocks, or chunks, are written sequentially across the components, beginning with Disk A. Disk A can be envisioned as containing logical chunks 1 through 4. Logical chunk 5 would be written to Disk B, which would contain logical chunks 5 through 8. Logical chunk 9 would be written to Drive C, which would contain chunks 9 through 12. The total capacity of volume d1 would be the combined capacities of the three drives. If each drive were 2 Gbytes, volume d1 would have an overall capacity of 6 Gbytes.

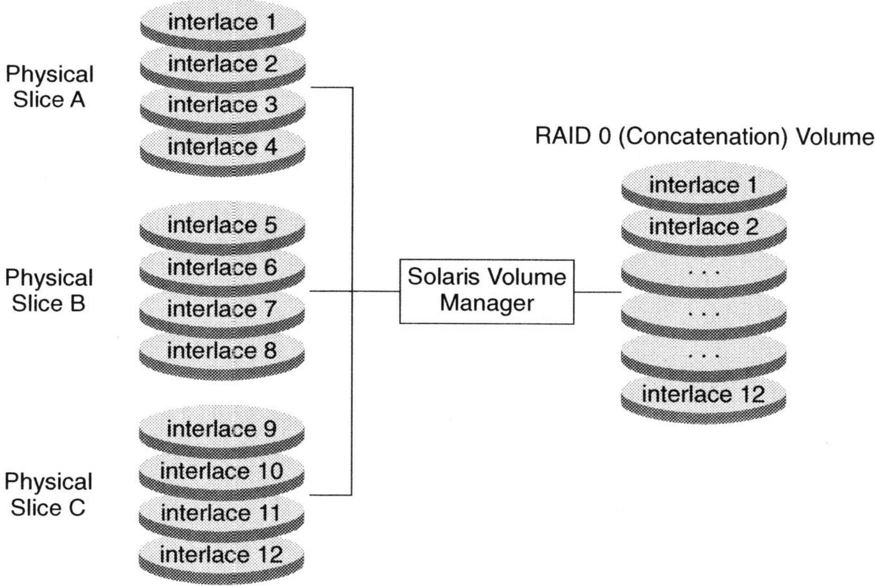

FIGURE 7–2 Concatenation Example

RAID 0 (Concatenated Stripe) Volume

A concatenated stripe is a stripe that has been expanded by adding additional components (stripes).

To set the interlace value for a concatenated stripe, at the stripe level, use either the Enhanced Storage tool within the Solaris Management Console, or the `metattach -i` command. Each stripe within the concatenated stripe can have its own interlace value. When you create a concatenated stripe from scratch, if you do not specify an interlace value for a particular stripe, it inherits the interlace value from the stripe before it.

Example—RAID 0 (Concatenated Stripe) Volume

Figure 7–3 illustrates that `d10` is a concatenation of three stripes.

The first stripe consists of three slices, Slice A through C, with an interlace value of 16 Kbytes. The second stripe consists of two slices Slice D and E, and uses an interlace value of 32 Kbytes. The last stripe consists of a two slices, Slice F and G. Because no interlace value is specified for the third stripe, it inherits the value from the stripe before it, which in this case is 32 Kbytes. Sequential data chunks are addressed to the first stripe until that stripe has no more space. Chunks are then addressed to the second stripe. When this stripe has no more space, chunks are addressed to the third stripe. Within each stripe, the data chunks are interleaved according to the specified interlace value.

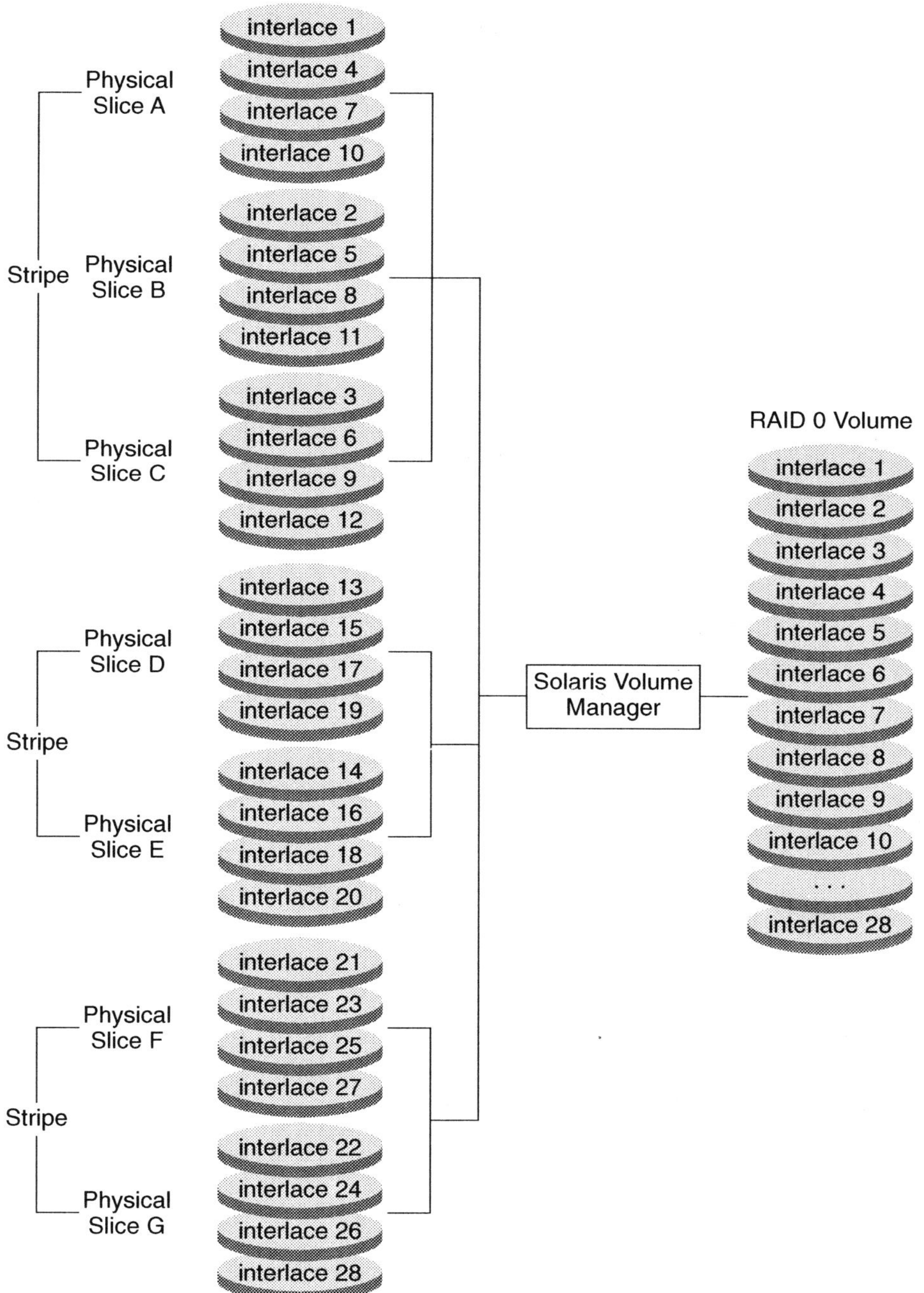

FIGURE 7–3 Concatenated Stripe Example

Background Information for Creating RAID 0 Volumes

Requirements for Stripes and Concatenations

When you are working with RAID 0 volumes, consider the following:

- Use components that are each on different controllers to increase the number of simultaneous reads and writes that can be performed.

- Do not create a stripe from an existing file system or data. Doing so will destroy data. Instead, use a concatenation. (You can create a stripe from existing data, but you must dump and restore the data to the volume.)

- Use the same size disk components for stripes. Striping different sized components results in wasted disk space.

- Set up a stripe's interlace value to better match the I/O requests made by the system or applications.

- Because a stripe or concatenation does not contain replicated data, when such a volume has a component failure you must replace the component, re-create the stripe or concatenation, and restore data from a backup.

- When you recreate a stripe or concatenation, use a replacement component that has at least the same size as the failed component.

Guidelines for Stripes and Concatenations

- Concatenation uses less CPU cycles than striping and performs well for small random I/O and for even I/O distribution.

- When possible, distribute the components of a stripe or concatenation across different controllers and busses. Using stripes that are each on different controllers increases the number of simultaneous reads and writes that can be performed.

- If a stripe is defined on a failing controller and there is another available controller on the system, you can "move" the stripe to the new controller by moving the disks to the controller and redefining the stripe.

- Number of stripes: Another way of looking at striping is to first determine the performance requirements. For example, you might need 10.4 Mbyte/sec performance for a selected application, and each disk might deliver approximately 4 Mbyte/sec. Based on this formula, then determine how many disk spindles you need to stripe across:

```
10.4 Mbyte/sec / 4 Mbyte/sec = 2.6
```

Therefore, you need 3 disks capable of performing I/O in parallel.

Scenario—RAID 0 Volumes

RAID 0 volumes provide the fundamental building blocks for aggregating storage or building mirrors. The following example, drawing on the sample system explained in Chapter 4, describes how RAID 0 volumes can provide larger storage spaces and allow you to construct a mirror of existing file systems, including root (/).

The sample system has a collection of relatively small (9 Gbyte) disks, and it is entirely possible that specific applications would require larger storage spaces. To create larger spaces (and improve performance), the system administrator can create a stripe that spans multiple disks. For example, each of `c1t1d0`, `c1t2d0`, `c1t3d0` and `c2t1d0`, `c2t2d0`, `c2t3d0` could be formatted with a slice 0 that spans the entire disk. Then, a stripe including all three of the disks from the same controller could provide approximately 27Gbytes of storage and allow faster access. The second stripe, from the second controller, can be used for redundancy, as described in Chapter 10 and specifically in the "Scenario—RAID 1 Volumes (Mirrors)" on page 90.

## CHAPTER 8

RAID 0 (Stripe and Concatenation) Volumes (Tasks)

This chapter contains information about tasks related to RAID 0 volumes. For information about related concepts, see Chapter 7.

RAID 0 Volumes (Task Map)

The following task map identifies the procedures needed to manage Solaris Volume Manager RAID 0 volumes.

Task	Description	Instructions
Create RAID 0 (stripe) volumes	Use the `metainit` command to create a new volume.	"How to Create a RAID 0 (Stripe) Volume" on page 74
Create RAID 0 (concatenation) volumes	Use the `metainit` command to create a new volume.	"How to Create a RAID 0 (Concatenation) Volume" on page 75
Expand storage space	Use the `metainit` command to expand an existing file system.	"How to Expand Space for Existing Data" on page 76
Expand an existing volume	Use the `metattach` command to expand an existing volume.	"How to Expand an Existing RAID 0 Volume" on page 78
Remove a RAID 0 volume	Use the `metaclear` command to delete a volume.	"How to Remove a Volume" on page 79

Creating RAID 0 (Stripe) Volumes

Caution – Do not create a stripe from an existing file system or data. Doing so will destroy data. To create a stripe from existing data, you must dump and restore the data to the volume.

▼ How to Create a RAID 0 (Stripe) Volume

1. **Check "Prerequisites for Creating Solaris Volume Manager Elements" on page 46 and "Background Information for Creating RAID 0 Volumes" on page 70.**

2. **To create the stripe, use one of the following methods:**

   - From the Enhanced Storage tool within the Solaris Management Console, open the Volumes node. Choose Action->Create Volume, then follow the instructions in the wizard. For more information, see the online help.

   - Use the following form of the `metainit` command:

     metainit {*volume-name*} {*number-of-stripes*} {*components-per-stripe*} {*component-names...*} [-i *interlace-value*]

     - *volume-name* is the name of the volume to create.
     - *number-of-stripes* specifies the number of stripes to create.
     - *components-per-stripe* specifies the number of components each stripe should have.
     - *component-names* specifies the names of the components that will be used.
     - -i*width* specifies the interlace width to use for the stripe.

     See the following examples and the `metainit`(1M) man page for more information.

Example—Creating a Stripe of Three Slices

```
# metainit d20 1 3 c0t1d0s2 c0t2d0s2 c0t3d0s2
d20: Concat/Stripe is setup
```

The stripe, d20, consists of a single stripe (the number 1) that is made of three slices (the number 3). Because no interlace value is specified, the stripe uses the default of 16 Kbytes. The system confirms that the volume has been set up.

Example—Creating a RAID 0 (Stripe) Volume of Two Slices With a 32–Kbyte Interlace Value

```
# metainit d10 1 2 c0t1d0s2 c0t2d0s2 -i 32k
d10: Concat/Stripe is setup
```

The stripe, d10, consists of a single stripe (the number 1) that is made of two slices (the number 2). The -i option sets the interlace value to 32 Kbytes. (The interlace value cannot be less than 8 Kbytes, nor greater than 100 Mbytes.) The system verifies that the volume has been set up.

Where to Go From Here

To prepare the newly created stripe for a file system, see "Creating File Systems (Tasks)" in *System Administration Guide: Basic Administration*. An application, such as a database, that uses the raw device must have its own way of accessing the raw device.

Creating RAID 0 (Concatenation) Volumes

▼ How to Create a RAID 0 (Concatenation) Volume

1. **Check "Prerequisites for Creating Solaris Volume Manager Elements" on page 46 and "Background Information for Creating RAID 0 Volumes" on page 70.**

2. **To create the concatenation use one of the following methods:**

   - From the Enhanced Storage tool within the Solaris Management Console, open the Volumes node. Choose Action->Create Volume, then follow the instructions in the wizard. For more information, see the online help.

   - Use the following form of the metainit command:

     metainit {*volume-name*} {*number-of-stripes*} { [*components-per-stripe*] | [*component-names*] ... }

     - *volume-name* is the name of the volume to create.

     - *number-of-stripes* specifies the number of stripes to create.

     - *components-per-stripe* specifies the number of components each stripe should have.

     - *component-names* specifies the names of the components that will be used.

For more information, see the following examples and the metainit(1M) man
page.

Example—Creating a Concatenation of One Slice

```
# metainit d25 1 1 c0t1d0s2
d25: Concat/Stripe is setup
```

This example shows the creation of a concatenation, d25, that consists of one stripe
(the first number 1) made of a single slice (the second number 1 in front of the slice).
The system verifies that the volume has been set up.

Note – This example shows a concatenation that can safely encapsulate existing data.

Example—Creating a Concatenation of Four Slices

```
# metainit d40 4 1 c0t1d0s2 1 c0t2d0s2 1 c0t2d0s3 1 c0t2d1s3
d40: Concat/Stripe is setup
```

This example creates a concatenation called d40 that consists of four "stripes" (the
number 4), each made of a single slice (the number 1 in front of each slice). The system
verifies that the volume has been set up.

Where to Go From Here

To prepare the newly created concatenation for a file system, see "Creating File
Systems (Tasks)" in *System Administration Guide: Basic Administration*.

Expanding Storage Space

To add space to a file system, create a concatenation. To add space to an existing stripe,
create a concatenated stripe.

▼ How to Expand Space for Existing Data

1. **Check "Prerequisites for Creating Solaris Volume Manager Elements" on page 46
   and "Background Information for Creating RAID 0 Volumes" on page 70.**

2. **Unmount the file system.**

```
# umount /filesystem
```

3. **To create a concatenation, use one of the following methods:**

   - From the Enhanced Storage tool within the Solaris Management Console, open the Volumes node. Choose Action->Create Volume, then follow the instructions in the wizard. For more information, see the online help.

   - Use the following form of the `metainit` command:

     `metainit` {*volume-name*} {*number-of-stripes*} { [*components-per-stripe*] | [*component-names*] ...}

     - *volume-name* is the name of the volume to create.

     - *number-of-stripes* specifies the number of stripes to create.

     - *components-per-stripe* specifies the number of components each stripe should have.

     - *components* specifies the names of the components that will be used.

     For more information, see the `metainit`(1M) man page.

4. **Edit the** `/etc/vfstab` **file so that the file system references the name of the concatenation.**

5. **Remount the file system.**

   ```
   # mount /filesystem
   ```

Example—Expanding a File System By Creating a Concatenation

```
# umount /docs
# metainit d25 2 1 c0t1d0s2 1 c0t2d0s2
d25: Concat/Stripe is setup
     (Edit the /etc/vfstab file so that the file system references the volume d25 instead of slice c0t1d0s2)
# mount /docs
```

This example shows the creation of a concatenation called `d25` out of two slices, `/dev/dsk/c0t1d0s2` (which contains a file system mounted on `/docs`) and `/dev/dsk/c0t2d0s2`. The file system must first be unmounted.

Caution – The first slice in the `metainit` command must be the slice that contains the file system. If not, you will corrupt your data.

Next, the entry for the file system in the `/etc/vfstab` file is changed (or entered for the first time) to reference the concatenation. For example, the following line:

```
/dev/dsk/c0t1d0s2 /dev/rdsk/c0t1d0s2 /docs ufs 2 yes -
```

should be changed to:

```
/dev/md/dsk/d25 /dev/md/rdsk/d25 /docs ufs 2 yes -
```

Finally, the file system is remounted.

Where to Go From Here

For a UFS file system, run the `growfs` command on the concatenation. See "How to Grow a File System" on page 229.

An application, such as a database, that uses the raw concatenation must have its own way of recognizing the concatenation, or of growing the added space.

▼ How to Expand an Existing RAID 0 Volume

A concatenated stripe enables you to expand an existing stripe. For example, if a stripe has run out of space, you can make it into a concatenated stripe, and expand it without having to back up and restore data.

This procedure assumes that you are adding an additional stripe to an existing stripe.

1. **Check "Prerequisites for Creating Solaris Volume Manager Elements" on page 46 and "Background Information for Creating RAID 0 Volumes" on page 70.**

2. **To create a concatenated stripe, use one of the following methods:**

   - From the Enhanced Storage tool within the Solaris Management Console, open the Volumes node. Choose Action->Create Volume, then follow the instructions in the wizard. For more information, see the online help.

   - To concatenate existing stripes from the command line, use the following form of the `metattach` command:

     metattach {*volume-name*} {*component-names...*}

     - *volume-name* is the name of the volume to expand.
     - *components* specifies the names of the components that will be used.

     See "Example—Creating a Concatenated Stripe By Attaching a Single Slice" on page 78, "Example—Creating a Concatenated Stripe By Adding Several Slices" on page 79, and the `metattach`(1M) man page for more information.

Example—Creating a Concatenated Stripe By Attaching a Single Slice

```
# metattach d2 c1t2d0s2
d2: components are attached
```

This example illustrates how to attach a slice to an existing stripe, d2. The system confirms that the slice is attached.

Example—Creating a Concatenated Stripe By Adding Several Slices

```
# metattach d25 c1t2d0s2 c1t2d1s2 c1t2d3s2
d25: components are attached
```

This example takes an existing three-way stripe, d25, and concatenates another three-way stripe. Because no interlace value is given for the attached slices, they inherit the interlace value configured for d25. The system verifies that the volume has been set up.

Where To Go From Here

For a UFS, run the `growfs` command on the volume. See "How to Grow a File System" on page 229.

An application, such as a database, that uses the raw volume must have its own way of recognizing the volume, or of growing the added space.

To prepare a newly created concatenated stripe for a file system, see "Creating File Systems (Tasks)" in *System Administration Guide: Basic Administration*.

Removing a Volume

▼ How to Remove a Volume

1. **Make sure you have a current backup of all data and that you have root privilege.**

2. **Make sure you no longer need the volume.**

   If you delete a stripe or concatenation and reuse the slices that were part of the deleted volume, all data on the volume is gone from the system.

3. **Unmount the file system, if needed.**

   ```
   # umount /filesystem
   ```

4. **To remove a volume, use one of the following methods:**

- From the Enhanced Storage tool within the Solaris Management Console, open the Volumes node. Choose Edit->Delete, then follow the instructions. For more information, see the online help.

- Use the following format of the `metaclear` command to delete the volume:

  metaclear {*volume-name*}

  See the following example and the `metaclear`(1M) man page for more information.

Example—Removing a Concatenation

```
# umount d8
# metaclear d8
d8: Concat/Stripe is cleared
    (Edit the /etc/vfstab file)
```

This example illustrated clearing the concatenation d8 that also contains a mounted file system. The file system must be unmounted before the volume can be cleared. The system displays a confirmation message that the concatenation is cleared. If there is an entry in the `/etc/vfstab` file for this volume, delete that entry. You do not want to confuse the system by asking it to mount a file system on a nonexistent volume.

## CHAPTER 9

RAID 1 (Mirror) Volumes (Overview)

This chapter explains essential Solaris Volume Manager concepts related to mirrors and submirrors. For information about performing related tasks, see Chapter 10.

This chapter contains the following information:

- "Overview of RAID 1 (Mirror) Volumes" on page 81
- "RAID 1 Volume (Mirror) Resynchronization" on page 87
- "Background Information for RAID 1 Volumes" on page 88
- "How Booting Into Single-User Mode Affects RAID 1 Volumes" on page 90

Overview of RAID 1 (Mirror) Volumes

A RAID 1 volume, or *mirror*, is a volume that maintains identical copies of the data in RAID 0 (stripe or concatenation) volumes. Mirroring requires an investment in disks. You need at least twice as much disk space as the amount of data you have to mirror. Because Solaris Volume Manager must write to all submirrors, mirroring can also increase the amount of time it takes for write requests to be written to disk.

After you configure a mirror, it can be used just as if it were a physical slice.

You can mirror any file system, including existing file systems. You can also use a mirror for any application, such as a database.

Tip – Use Solaris Volume Manager's hot spare feature with mirrors to keep data safe and available. For information on hot spares, see Chapter 15 and Chapter 16.

Overview of Submirrors

The RAID 0 volumes that are *mirrored* are called *submirrors*. A mirror is made of one or more RAID 0 volumes (stripes or concatenations).

A mirror can consist of up to three submirrors. Practically, a two-way mirror is usually sufficient. A third submirror enables you to make online backups without losing data redundancy while one submirror is offline for the backup.

If you take a submirror "offline," the mirror stops reading and writing to the submirror. At this point, you could access the submirror itself, for example, to perform a backup. However, the submirror is in a read-only state. While a submirror is offline, Solaris Volume Manager keeps track of all writes to the mirror. When the submirror is brought back online, only the portions of the mirror that were written while the submirror was offline (*resynchronization regions*) are resynchronized. Submirrors can also be taken offline to troubleshoot or repair physical devices which have errors.

Submirrors can be attached or detached from a mirror at any time, though at least one submirror must remain attached at all times.

Normally, you create a mirror with only a single submirror. Then, you attach a second submirror after you create the mirror.

Scenario—RAID 1 (Mirror) Volume

Figure 9–1 illustrates a mirror, d2, that is made of two volumes (submirrors) d20 and d21.

Solaris Volume Manager software makes duplicate copies of the data on multiple physical disks, and presents one virtual disk to the application. All disk writes are duplicated; disk reads come from one of the underlying submirrors. The total capacity of mirror d2 is the size of the smallest of the submirrors (if they are not of equal size).

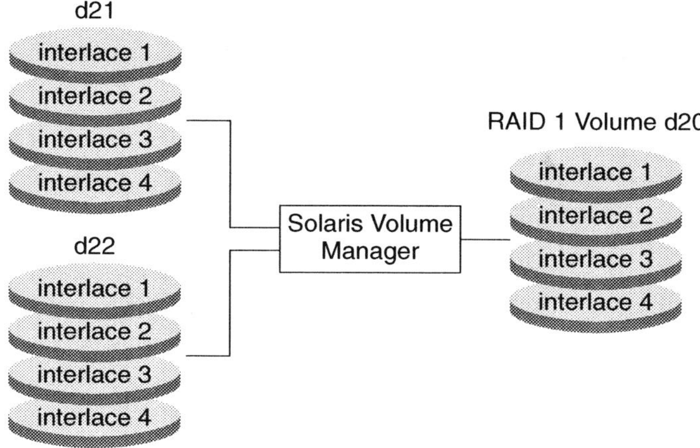

FIGURE 9–1 Mirror Example

Providing RAID 1+0 and RAID 0+1

Solaris Volume Manager supports both RAID 1+0 (which is like having mirrors that are then striped) and RAID 0+1 (stripes that are then mirrored) redundancy, depending on the context. The Solaris Volume Manager interface makes it appear that all RAID 1 devices are strictly RAID 0+1, but Solaris Volume Manager recognizes the underlying components and mirrors each individually, when possible.

Note – Solaris Volume Manager cannot always provide RAID 1+0 functionality. However, in a best practices environment, where both submirrors are identical to each other and are made up of disk slices (and not soft partitions), RAID 1+0 will be possible.

For example, with a pure RAID 0+1 implementation and a two-way mirror that consists of three striped slices, a single slice failure could fail one side of the mirror. And, assuming that no hot spares were in use, a second slice failure would fail the mirror. Using Solaris Volume Manager, up to three slices could potentially fail without failing the mirror, because each of the three striped slices are individually mirrored to their counterparts on the other half of the mirror.

Consider this example:

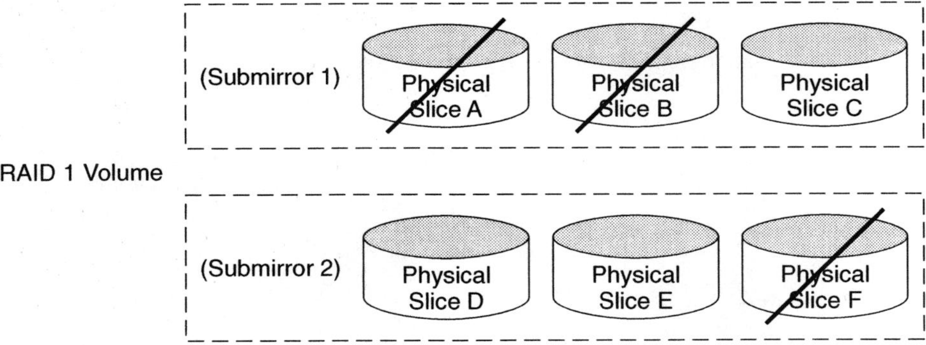

FIGURE 9–2 RAID 1+ 0 Example

Mirror d1 consists of two submirrors, each of which consists of three identical physical disks and the same interlace value. A failure of three disks, A, B, and F can be tolerated because the entire logical block range of the mirror is still contained on at least one good disk.

If, however, disks A and D fail, a portion of the mirror's data is no longer available on any disk and access to these logical blocks will fail.

When a portion of a mirror's data is unavailable due to multiple slice errors, access to portions of the mirror where data is still available will succeed. Under this situation, the mirror acts like a single disk that has developed bad blocks. The damaged portions are unavailable, but the rest is available.

Frequently Asked Questions About RAID 1 (Mirror) Volumes

Why would I use a mirror?
For maximum data availability. The trade-off is that a mirror requires twice the number of slices (disks) as the amount of data to be mirrored.

How many submirrors can a mirror contain?
Solaris Volume Manager allows you to create up to a three-way mirror (a mirror of three submirrors). However, two-way mirrors usually provide sufficient data redundancy for most applications, and are less expensive in terms of disk drive costs.

Why should I create a one-way mirror then attach additional submirrors?
If you have existing data that you are mirroring, you must create the primary submirror, then attach additional submirrors so they can be updated with the data that is contained in the primary submirror.

When should I create a two-way or three-way mirror with a single command? If you have no existing data that you are mirroring and you are comfortable destroying all data on all submirrors, you can speed the creation process by creating all submirrors with a single command.

RAID 1 Volume Configuration Guidelines

- Keep the slices of different submirrors on different disks and controllers. Data protection is diminished considerably if slices of two or more submirrors of the same mirror are on the same disk. Likewise, organize submirrors across separate controllers, because controllers and associated cables tends to fail more often than disks. This practice also improves mirror performance.

- Use the same type of disks and controllers in a single mirror. Particularly in old SCSI storage devices, different models or brands of disk or controller can have widely varying performance. Mixing the different performance levels in a single mirror can cause performance to degrade significantly.

- Use the same size submirrors. Submirrors of different sizes result in unused disk space.

- Only mount the mirror device directly. Do not try to mount a submirror directly, unless it is offline and mounted read-only. Do not mount a slice that is part of a submirror. This process could destroy data and crash the system.

- Mirroring might improve read performance, but write performance is always degraded. Mirroring improves read performance only in threaded or asynchronous I/O situations. No performance gain results if there is only a single thread reading from the volume.

- Experimenting with the mirror read policies can improve performance. For example, the default read mode is to alternate reads in a round-robin fashion among the disks. This policy is the default because it tends to work best for UFS multiuser, multiprocess activity.

  In some cases, the `geometric` read option improves performance by minimizing head motion and access time. This option is most effective when there is only one slice per disk, when only one process at a time is using the slice/file system, and when I/O patterns are highly sequential or when all accesses are read.

  To change mirror options, see "How to Change RAID 1 Volume Options" on page 110.

- Use the `swap -l` command to check for all `swap` devices. Each slice that is specified as `swap` must be mirrored independently from the remaining swap slices.

- Use only similarly configured submirrors within a mirror. In particular, if you create a mirror with an unlabeled submirror, you will be unable to attach any submirrors that contain disk labels.

RAID 1 Volume Options

The following options are available to optimize mirror performance:

- Mirror read policy
- Mirror write policy
- The order in which mirrors are resynchronized (pass number)

You can define mirror options when you initially create the mirror, or after a mirror has been set up. For tasks related to changing these options, see "How to Change RAID 1 Volume Options" on page 110.

RAID 1 Volume Read and Write Policies

Solaris Volume Manager enables different read and write policies to be configured for a mirror. Properly set read and write policies can improve performance for a given configuration.

TABLE 9–1 Mirror Read Policies

Read Policy	Description
Round Robin (Default)	Attempts to balance the load across the submirrors. All reads are made in a round-robin order (one after another) from all submirrors in a mirror.
Geometric	Enables reads to be divided among submirrors on the basis of a logical disk block address. For instance, with a two-way submirror, the disk space on the mirror is divided into two equally-sized logical address ranges. Reads from one submirror are restricted to one half of the logical range, and reads from the other submirror are restricted to the other half. The geometric read policy effectively reduces the seek time necessary for reads. The performance gained by this mode depends on the system I/O load and the access patterns of the applications.
First	Directs all reads to the first submirror. This policy should be used only when the device or devices that comprise the first submirror are substantially faster than those of the second submirror.

TABLE 9–2 Mirror Write Policies

Write Policy	Description
Parallel (Default)	A write to a mirror is replicated and dispatched to all of the submirrors simultaneously.

Write Policy	Description
Serial	Performs writes to submirrors serially (that is, the first submirror write completes before the second is started). The serial option specifies that writes to one submirror must complete before the next submirror write is initiated. The serial option is provided in case a submirror becomes unreadable, for example, due to a power failure.

RAID 1 Volume (Mirror) Resynchronization

RAID 1 volume (mirror) resynchronization is the process of copying data from one submirror to another after submirror failures, system crashes, when a submirror has been taken offline and brought back online, or after the addition of a new submirror.

While the resynchronization takes place, the mirror remains readable and writable by users.

A mirror resynchronization ensures proper mirror operation by maintaining all submirrors with identical data, with the exception of writes in progress.

Note – A mirror resynchronization is mandatory, and cannot be omitted. You do not need to manually initiate a mirror resynchronization. This process occurs automatically.

Full Resynchronization

When a new submirror is attached (added) to a mirror, all the data from another submirror in the mirror is automatically written to the newly attached submirror. Once the mirror resynchronization is done, the new submirror is readable. A submirror remains attached to a mirror until it is explicitly detached.

If the system crashes while a resynchronization is in progress, the resynchronization is restarted when the system finishes rebooting.

Optimized Resynchronization

During a reboot following a system failure, or when a submirror that was offline is brought back online, Solaris Volume Manager performs an *optimized mirror resynchronization*. The metadisk driver tracks submirror regions and knows which submirror regions might be out-of-sync after a failure. An optimized mirror resynchronization is performed only on the out-of-sync regions. You can specify the order in which mirrors are resynchronized during reboot, and you can omit a mirror resynchronization by setting submirror pass numbers to 0 (zero). (See "Pass Number" on page 88 for information.)

Caution – A pass number of 0 (zero) should only be used on mirrors that are mounted as read-only.

Partial Resynchronization

Following a replacement of a slice within a submirror, Solaris Volume Manager performs a *partial mirror resynchronization* of data. Solaris Volume Manager copies the data from the remaining good slices of another submirror to the replaced slice.

Pass Number

The pass number, a number in the range 0–9, determines the order in which a particular mirror is resynchronized during a system reboot. The default pass number is 1. Smaller pass numbers are resynchronized first. If 0 is used, the mirror resynchronization is skipped. A pass number of 0 should be used only for mirrors that are mounted as read-only. Mirrors with the same pass number are resynchronized at the same time.

Background Information for RAID 1 Volumes

- **Unmirroring** – The Enhanced Storage tool within the Solaris Management Console does not support unmirroring root (/), `/opt`, `/usr`, or `swap`, or any other file system that cannot be unmounted while the system is running. Instead, use the command-line procedure for these file systems.

- **Attaching** – You can attach a submirror to a mirror without interrupting service. You attach submirrors to mirrors to create two-way and three-way mirrors.

- **Detach vs. Offline** – When you place a submirror offline, you prevent the mirror from reading from and writing to the submirror, but you preserve the submirror's logical association to the mirror. While the submirror is offline, Solaris Volume Manager keeps track of all writes to the mirror and they are written to the submirror when it is brought back online. By performing an optimized resynchronization, Solaris Volume Manager only has to resynchronize data that has changed, not the entire submirror. When you detach a submirror, you sever its logical association to the mirror. Typically, you place a submirror offline to perform maintenance. You detach a submirror to remove it.

Background Information for Creating RAID 1 Volumes

- Before you create a mirror, create the RAID 0 (stripe or concatenation) volumes that will make up the mirror.

- Any file system including root (/), `swap`, and `/usr`, or any application such as a database, can use a mirror.

Caution – When you create a mirror for an existing file system, be sure that the initial submirror contains the existing file system.

- When creating a mirror, first create a one-way mirror, then attach a second submirror. This strategy starts a resynchronization operation and ensures that data is not corrupted.

- You can create a one-way mirror for a future two-way or three-way mirror.

- You can create up to a three-way mirror. However, two-way mirrors usually provide sufficient data redundancy for most applications, and are less expensive in terms of disk drive costs. A three-way mirror enables you to take a submirror offline and perform a backup while maintaining a two-way mirror for continued data redundancy.

- Use components of identical size when creating submirrors. Using components of different sizes leaves wasted space in the mirror.

- Adding additional state database replicas before you create a mirror can improve the mirror's performance. As a general rule, add two additional replicas for each mirror you add to the system. Solaris Volume Manager uses these additional replicas to store the dirty region log (DRL), used to provide optimized resynchronization. By providing adequate numbers of replicas to prevent contention or using replicas on the same disks or controllers as the mirror they log, you will improve overall performance.

Background Information for Changing RAID 1 Volume Options

- You can change a mirror's pass number, and its read and write policies.

- Mirror options can be changed while the mirror is running.

How Booting Into Single-User Mode Affects RAID 1 Volumes

If a system with mirrors for root (/), /usr, and swap, the so-called "boot" file systems, is booted into single-user mode (by using the boot -s command), these mirrors and possibly all mirrors on the system will appear in the "Needing Maintenance" state when viewed with the metastat command. Furthermore, if writes occur to these slices, the metastat command shows an increase in dirty regions on the mirrors.

Though this situation appears to be potentially dangerous, there is no need for concern. The metasync -r command, which normally occurs during boot to resynchronize mirrors, is interrupted when the system is booted into single-user mode. Once the system is rebooted, the metasync -r command will run and resynchronize all mirrors.

If this is a concern, run the metasync -r command manually.

Scenario—RAID 1 Volumes (Mirrors)

RAID 1 volumes provide a means of constructing redundant volumes, in which a partial or complete failure of one of the underlying RAID 0 volumes does not cause data loss or interruption of access to the file systems. The following example, drawing on the sample system explained in Chapter 4, describes how RAID 1 volumes can provide redundant storage.

As described in "Interlace Values for Stripes" on page 65, the sample system has two RAID 0 volumes, each of which is approximately 27Gbytes in size and spans three disks. By creating a RAID 1 volume to mirror these two RAID 0 volumes, a fully redundant storage space can provide resilient data storage.

Within this RAID 1 volume, the failure of either of the disk controllers will not interrupt access to the volume. Similarly, failure of up to three individual disks might be tolerated without access interruption.

To provide additional protection against problems that could interrupt access, use hot spares, as described in Chapter 15 and specifically in "How Hot Spares Work" on page 148.

## CHAPTER 10

RAID 1 (Mirror) Volumes (Tasks)

This chapter explains how to perform Solaris Volume Manager tasks related to RAID 1 volumes. For information about related concepts, see Chapter 9.

RAID 1 Volumes (Task Map)

The following task map identifies the procedures needed to manage Solaris Volume Manager RAID 1 volumes.

Task	Description	Instructions
Create a mirror from unused slices	Use the Solaris Volume Manager GUI or the `metainit` command to create a mirror from unused slices.	"How to Create a RAID 1 Volume From Unused Slices" on page 95
Create a mirror from an existing file system	Use the Solaris Volume Manager GUI or the `metainit` command to create a mirror from an existing file system.	"How to Create a RAID 1 Volume From a File System" on page 97
Record the path to the alternate boot device for a mirrored root	Find the path to the alternative book device and enter it in the boot instructions.	"How to Record the Path to the Alternate Boot Device" on page 102
Attach a submirror	Use the Solaris Volume Manager GUI or the `metattach` command to attach a submirror.	"How to Attach a Submirror" on page 103
Detach a submirror	Use the Solaris Volume Manager GUI or the `metadetach` command to detach the submirror.	"How to Detach a Submirror" on page 104

Task	Description	Instructions
Place a submirror online or take a submirror offline	Use the Solaris Volume Manager GUI or the `metaonline` command to put a submirror online. Use the Solaris Volume Manager GUI or the `metaoffline` command to take a submirror offline..	"How to Place a Submirror Offline and Online" on page 105
Enable a component within a submirror	Use the Solaris Volume Manager GUI or the `metareplace` command to enable a slice in a submirror.	"How to Enable a Slice in a Submirror" on page 106
Check mirror status	Use the Solaris Volume Manager GUI or the `metastat` command to check the status of RAID 1 volumes.	"How to Check the Status of Mirrors and Submirrors" on page 108
Change mirror options	Use the Solaris Volume Manager GUI or the `metaparam` command to change the options for a specific RAID 1 volume.	"How to Change RAID 1 Volume Options" on page 110
Expand a mirror	Use the Solaris Volume Manager GUI or the `metattach` command to expand the capacity of a mirror.	"How to Expand a RAID 1 Volume" on page 111
Replace a slice within a submirror	Use the Solaris Volume Manager GUI or the `metareplace` command to replace a slice in a submirror.	"How to Replace a Slice in a Submirror" on page 112
Replace a submirror	Use the Solaris Volume Manager GUI or the `metattach` command to replace a submirror.	"How to Replace a Submirror" on page 113
Remove a mirror (unmirror)	Use the Solaris Volume Manager GUI or the `metadetach` command or the `metaclear` command to unmirror a file system.	"How to Unmirror a File System" on page 115
Remove a mirror (unmirror) of a file system that cannot be unmounted	Use the Solaris Volume Manager GUI or the `metadetach` command or the `metaclear` command to unmirror a file system that cannot be unmounted.	"How to Unmirror a File System That Cannot Be Unmounted" on page 116
Use a mirror to perform backups	Use the Solaris Volume Manager GUI or the `metaonline` command and the `metaoffline` commands to perform backups with mirrors.	"How to Use a RAID 1 Volume to Make an Online Backup" on page 118

Creating a RAID 1 Volume

▼ How to Create a RAID 1 Volume From Unused Slices

1. **Check "Prerequisites for Creating Solaris Volume Manager Elements" on page 46 and "Background Information for Creating RAID 1 Volumes" on page 89.**

2. **Create two stripes or concatenations, which will be the submirrors.**

   See "How to Create a RAID 0 (Stripe) Volume" on page 74 or "How to Create a RAID 0 (Concatenation) Volume" on page 75.

3. **To create the mirror, use one of the following methods:**

   - From the Enhanced Storage tool within the Solaris Management Console, open the Volumes node, then choose Action->Create Volume and follow the instructions on screen. For more information, see the online help.

   - Use the following form of the `metainit` command to create a one-way mirror:

     `metainit` {*volume-name*} [-m] {*submirror-name...*}

     - *volume-name* is the name of the volume to create.

     - -m specifies to create a mirror.

     - *submirror-name* specifies the name of the component that will be the first submirror in the mirror.

     See the following examples and the `metainit`(1M) man page for more information.

4. **To add the second submirror, use one of the following methods:**

   - From the Enhanced Storage tool within the Solaris Management Console, open the Volumes node, then choose the mirror you want to modify. Choose Action->Properties, then the Submirrors tab and follow the instructions on screen to Attach Submirror. For more information, see the online help.

   - Use the following form of the `metattach` command:

     `metattach` {*mirror-name*} {*new-submirror-name...*}

     - *volume-name* is the name of the RAID 1 volume to modify.

     - *submirror-name* specifies the name of the component that will be the next submirror in the mirror.

     See the following examples and the `metattach`(1M) man page for more information.

Example—Creating a Two-Way Mirror

```
# metainit d51 1 1 c0t0d0s2
d51: Concat/Stripe is setup
# metainit d52 1 1 c1t0d0s2
d52: Concat/Stripe is setup
# metainit d50 -m d51
d50: Mirror is setup
# metattach d50 d52
d50: Submirror d52 is attached
```

This example shows the creation of a two-way mirror, d50. The metainit command creates two submirrors (d51 and d52), which are RAID 0 volumes. The metainit -m command creates the one-way mirror from the d51 RAID 0 volume. The metattach command attaches d52, creating a two-way mirror and causing a resynchronization. (Any data on the attached submirror is overwritten by the other submirror during the resynchronization.) The system verifies that the objects are defined.

Example—Creating a Two-Way Mirror Without Resynchronization

```
# metainit d51 1 1 c0t0d0s2
d51: Concat/Stripe is setup
# metainit d52 1 1 c1t0d0s2
d52: Concat/Stripe is setup
# metainit d50 -m d51 d52
metainit: d50: WARNING: This form of metainit is not recommended.
The submirrors may not have the same data.
Please see ERRORS in metainit(1M) for additional information.
d50: Mirror is setup
```

This example creates a two-way mirror, d50. The metainit command creates two submirrors (d51 and d52), which are RAID 0 volumes. The metainit -m command with both submirrors creates the mirror from the d51 RAID 0 volume and avoids resynchronization. It is assumed that all information on the mirror is considered invalid and will be regenerated (for example, through a newfs operation) before the mirror is used.

Where to Go From Here

To prepare a newly created mirror for a file system, see "Creating File Systems (Tasks)" in *System Administration Guide: Basic Administration*. An application, such as a database, that uses the raw volume must have its own way of recognizing the volume.

▼ How to Create a RAID 1 Volume From a File System

Use this procedure to mirror an existing file system. If the file system can be unmounted, the entire procedure can be completed without a reboot. For file systems (such as root (/)) that cannot be unmounted, the system will have to be rebooted to complete the procedure.

Note – When mirroring root (/), it is essential that you record the secondary root slice name to reboot the system if the primary submirror fails. This information should be written down, not recorded on the system, which might not be available. See Chapter 24 for details on recording the alternate boot device, and on booting from the alternate boot device.

If you are mirroring root on an IA system, install the boot information on the alternate boot disk before you create the RAID 0 or RAID 1 devices. See "SPARC: Booting a System (Tasks)" in *System Administration Guide: Basic Administration*.

In this procedure, an existing device is `c1t0d0s0`. A second device, `c1t1d0s0`, is available for the second half of the mirror. The submirrors will be `d1` and `d2`, respectively, and the mirror will be `d0`.

1. **Check "Prerequisites for Creating Solaris Volume Manager Elements" on page 46 and "Background Information for Creating RAID 1 Volumes" on page 89.**

2. **Identify the slice that contains the existing file system to be mirrored (`c1t0d0s0` in this example).**

3. **Create a new RAID 0 volume on the slice from the previous step by using one of the following methods:**

   - From the Enhanced Storage tool within the Solaris Management Console, open the Volumes node, then choose Action->Create Volume and follow the instructions on screen. For more information, see the online help.

   - Use the `metainit` *raid-0-volume-name* `-f 1 1` *ctds-of-slice* command.

     ```
     # metainit d1 -f 1 1 c1t0d0s0
     ```

4. **Create a second RAID 0 volume (concatenation) on an unused slice (`c1t1d0s0` in this example) to act as the second submirror. The second submirror must be the same size as the original submirror or larger. Use one of the following methods:**

   - From the Enhanced Storage tool within the Solaris Management Console, open the Volumes node, then choose Action->Create Volume and follow the instructions on screen. For more information, see the online help.

   - Use the `metainit` *second-raid-0-volume-name* `1 1` *ctds-of-slice* command.

```
# metainit d2 1 1 c1t1d0s0
```

5. **Create a one-way mirror by using one of the following methods:**

   - From the Enhanced Storage tool within the Solaris Management Console, open the Volumes node, then choose Action->Create Volume and follow the instructions on screen. For more information, see the online help.

   - Use the `metainit` *mirror-name* `-m` *raid-0-volume-name* command.

   ```
   # metainit d0 -m d1
   ```

   See the `metainit`(1M) man page for more information.

Note – When you create a mirror from an existing file system, you must follow the next two steps precisely to avoid data corruption.

If you are mirroring any file system other than the root (/) file system, then edit the `/etc/vfstab` file so that the file system mount instructions refer to the mirror, not to the block device.

For more information about the `/etc/vfstab` file, see "Mounting File Systems ()" in *System Administration Guide: Basic Administration*.

6. **Remount your newly mirrored file system according to one of the following procedures:**

   - If you are mirroring your root (/) file system, run the `metaroot` *d0* command, replacing `d0` with the name of the mirror you just created, then reboot your system.

     For more information, see the `metaroot`(1M) man page.

   - If you are mirroring a file system that can be unmounted, then unmount and remount the file system.

   - If you are mirroring a file system other than root (/) that cannot be unmounted, then reboot your system.

7. **Use the `metattach` command to attach the second submirror.**

   ```
   # metattach d0 d2
   ```

   See the `metattach`(1M) man page for more information.

8. **If you mirrored your root file system, record the alternate boot path.**

   See "How to Record the Path to the Alternate Boot Device" on page 102.

Caution – Be sure to create a one-way mirror with the `metainit` command then attach the additional submirrors with the `metattach` command. When the `metattach` command is not used, no resynchronization operations occur. As a result, data could become corrupted when Solaris Volume Manager assumes that both sides of the mirror are identical and can be used interchangably.

Example—Creating a Two-Way Mirror (Unmountable File System)

```
# metainit -f d1 1 1 c1t0d0s0
d1: Concat/Stripe is setup
# metainit d2 1 1 c1t1d0s0
d2: Concat/Stripe is setup
# metainit d0 -m d1
d0: Mirror is setup
# umount /master
     (Edit the /etc/vfstab file so that the file system references the mirror)
# mount /master
# metattach d0 d2
d0: Submirror d2 is attached
```

The `-f` option forces the creation of the first concatenation, d1, which contains the mounted file system /master on /dev/dsk/c1t0d0s0. The second concatenation, d2, is created from /dev/dsk/c1t1d0s0. (This slice must be the same size or greater than that of d1.) The `metainit` command with the `-m` option creates the one-way mirror, d0, from d1.

Next, the entry for the file system should be changed in the /etc/vfstab file to reference the mirror. For example, the following line:

```
/dev/dsk/c1t0d0s0 /dev/rdsk/c1t0d0s0 /var ufs 2 yes -
```

should be changed to:

```
/dev/md/dsk/d0 /dev/md/rdsk/d0 /var ufs 2 yes -
```

Finally, the file system is remounted and submirror d2 is attached to the mirror, causing a mirror resynchronization. The system confirms that the RAID 0 and RAID 1 volumes are set up, and that submirror d2 is attached.

Example—Creating a Mirror From root (/)

```
# metainit -f d1 1 1 c0t0d0s0
d11: Concat/Stripe is setup
# metainit d2 1 1 c0t1d0s0
d12: Concat/Stripe is setup
# metainit d0 -m d1
```

```
d10: Mirror is setup
# metaroot d0
# lockfs -fa
# reboot
...
# metattach d0 d2
d10: Submirror d12 is attached
# ls -l /dev/rdsk/c0t1d0s0
lrwxrwxrwx   1 root        root              88 Feb  8 15:51 /dev/rdsk/c1t3d0s0 ->
../../devices/iommu@f,e0000000/vme@f,df010000/SUNW,pn@4d,1080000/ipi3sc@0,0/i
d@3,0:a,raw
```

Note – Do not attach the second submirror before the system is rebooted. You must reboot between running the `metaroot` command and attaching the second submirror.

The `-f` option forces the creation of the first RAID 0 volume, d1, which contains the mounted file system root (/) on `/dev/dsk/c0t0d0s0`. The second concatenation, d2, is created from `/dev/dsk/c0t1d0s0`. (This slice must be the same size or greater than that of d1.) The `metainit` command with the `-m` option creates the one-way mirror d0 using the concatenation that contains root (/).

Next, the `metaroot` command edits the `/etc/vfstab` and `/etc/system` files so that the system can be booted with the root file system (/) on a volume. (It is a good idea to run the `lockfs -fa` command before rebooting.) After a reboot, the submirror d2 is attached to the mirror, causing a mirror resynchronization. (The system confirms that the concatenations and the mirror are set up, and that submirror d2 is attached.) The `ls -l` command is run on the root raw device to determine the path to the alternate root device in case the system might later need to be booted from it.

Example—Creating a Two-way Mirror (File System That Cannot Be Unmounted—/usr)

```
# metainit -f d12 1 1 c0t3d0s6
d12: Concat/Stripe is setup
# metainit d22 1 1 c1t0d0s6
d22: Concat/Stripe is setup
# metainit d2 -m d12
d2: Mirror is setup
      (Edit the /etc/vfstab file so that /usr references the mirror)
# reboot
...
# metattach d2 d22
d2: Submirror d22 is attached
```

The `-f` option forces the creation of the first concatenation, d12, which contains the mounted file system /usr on `/dev/dsk/c0t3d0s6`. The second concatenation, d22, is created from `/dev/dsk/c1t0d0s6`. (This slice must be the same size or greater than that of d12.) The metainit command with the -m option creates the one-way mirror d2 using the concatenation containing /usr. Next, the /etc/vfstab file must be edited to change the entry for /usr to reference the mirror. For example, the following line:

```
/dev/dsk/c0t3d0s6 /dev/rdsk/c0t3d0s6 /usr ufs 1 yes -
```

should be changed to:

```
/dev/md/dsk/d2 /dev/md/rdsk/d2 /usr ufs 1 yes -
```

After a reboot, the second submirror d22 is attached to the mirror, causing a mirror resynchronization. (The system confirms that the concatenation and the mirror are set up, and that submirror d22 is attached.

Example—Creating a Mirror From swap

```
# metainit -f d11 1 1 c0t0d0s1
d11: Concat/Stripe is setup
# metainit d21 1 1 c1t0d0s1
d21: Concat/Stripe is setup
# metainit d1 -m d11
d1: Mirror is setup
      (Edit the /etc/vfstab file so that swap references the mirror)
# reboot
. . .
# metattach d1 d21
d1: Submirror d21 is attached
```

The -f option forces the creation of the first concatenation, d11, which contains the mounted file system swap on /dev/dsk/c0t0d0s1. The second concatenation, d21, is created from /dev/dsk/c1t0d0s1. (This slice must be the same size or greater than that of d11.) The metainit command with the -m option creates the one-way mirror d1 using the concatenation that contains swap. Next, if there is an entry for swap in the /etc/vfstab file, it must be edited to reference the mirror. For example, the following line:

```
/dev/dsk/c0t0d0s1 - - swap - no -
```

should be changed to:

```
/dev/md/dsk/d1 - - swap - no -
```

After a reboot, the second submirror d21 is attached to the mirror, causing a mirror resynchronization. (The system confirms that the concatenations and the mirror are set up, and that submirror d21 is attached.

To save the crash dump when you have mirrored swap, use the dumpadm command to configure the dump device as a volume. For instance, if the swap device is named /dev/md/dsk/d2, use the dumpadm command to set this device as the dump device.

Mirroring root (/) Special Considerations

The process for mirroring root (/) is the same as in mirroring any other file system that you cannot unmount, with the exception that you run the `metaroot` command instead of manually editing the `/etc/vfstab` file. See "How to Create a RAID 1 Volume From a File System" on page 97. The following sections outline special considerations and issues for mirroring root (/) file systems.

How to Record the Path to the Alternate Boot Device

When you are mirroring root (/), you might need the path to the alternate boot device later if the primary device fails. The process for finding and recording the alternate boot device differs, depending on your system's architecture. See "SPARC: Example—Recording the Alternate Boot Device Path" on page 102 or "IA: Example—Recording the Alternate Boot Device Path" on page 103.

SPARC: Example—Recording the Alternate Boot Device Path

In this example, you determine the path to the alternate root device by using the `ls -l` command on the slice that is being attached as the second submirror to the root (/) mirror.

```
# ls -l /dev/rdsk/c1t3d0s0
lrwxrwxrwx 1  root root   55 Mar 5 12:54  /dev/rdsk/c1t3d0s0 -> \
../../devices/sbus@1,f8000000/esp@1,200000/sd@3,0:a
```

Here you would record the string that follows the `/devices` directory: `/sbus@1,f8000000/esp@1,200000/sd@3,0:a`.

Solaris Volume Manager users who are using a system with OpenBoot™ Prom can use the OpenBoot `nvalias` command to define a "backup root" device alias for the secondary root (/) mirror. For example:

```
ok  nvalias backup_root /sbus@1,f8000000/esp@1,200000/sd@3,0:a
```

Then, redefine the `boot-device` alias to reference both the primary and secondary submirrors, in the order in which you want them to be used, and store the configuration.

```
ok printenv boot-device
boot-device =           disk net
```

```
ok setenv boot-device disk backup-root net
boot-device =           disk backup-root net
ok nvstore
```

In the event of primary root disk failure, the system would automatically boot to the second submirror. Or, if you boot manually, rather than using auto boot, you would only enter:

```
ok  boot backup_root
```

IA: Example—Recording the Alternate Boot Device Path

In this example, you would determine the path to the alternate boot device by using the `ls -l` command on the slice that is being attached as the second submirror to the root (/) mirror.

```
# ls -l /dev/rdsk/c1t0d0s0
lrwxrwxrwx 1  root root  55 Mar 5 12:54  /dev/rdsk/c1t0d0s0 -> ../.
./devices/eisa/eha@1000,0/cmdk@1,0:a
```

Here, you would record the string that follows the `/devices` directory:
`/eisa/eha@1000,0/cmdk@1,0:a`

Booting From Alternate Boot Devices

If your primary submirror on a mirrored root (/) fails, you will need to initiate the boot from the other submirror. You can either configure the system to boot automatically from the second side of the mirror, or can manually boot from the second side.

See "SPARC: Booting a System (Tasks)" in *System Administration Guide: Basic Administration*

Working with Submirrors

▼ How to Attach a Submirror

1. **Identify the component (concatenation or stripe) to be used as a submirror.**

   It must be the same size (or larger) as the existing submirror in the mirror. If you have not yet created a volume to be a submirror, see "Creating RAID 0 (Stripe) Volumes" on page 74 or "Creating RAID 0 (Concatenation) Volumes" on page 75.

2. **Make sure that you have root privilege and that you have a current backup of all data.**

3. **Use one of the following methods to attach a submirror.**

   - From the Enhanced Storage tool within the Solaris Management Console, open the Volumes node, choose the mirror, then choose Action->Properties and click the Components tab. Follow the instructions on screen. For more information, see the online help.

   - Use the `metattach` *mirror submirror* command.

     ```
     # metattach mirror submirror
     ```

See the `metattach`(1M) man page for more information.

Example—Attaching a Submirror

```
# metastat d30
d30: mirror
    Submirror 0: d60
      State: Okay
...
# metattach d30 d70
d30: submirror d70 is attached
# metastat d30
d30: mirror
    Submirror 0: d60
      State: Okay
    Submirror 1: d70
      State: Resyncing
    Resync in progress: 41 % done
    Pass: 1
    Read option: roundrobin (default)
    Write option: parallel (default)
    Size: 2006130 blocks
...
```

This example shows the attaching of a submirror, d70, to a one-way mirror, d30, creating a two-way mirror. The mirror d30 initially consists of submirror d60. The submirror d70 is a RAID 0 volume. You verify that the status of the mirror is "Okay" with the `metastat` command, then attach the submirror. When the `metattach` command is run, the new submirror is resynchronized with the existing mirror. When you attach an additional submirror to the mirror, the system displays a message. To verify that the mirror is resynchronizing, use the `metastat` command.

▼ How to Detach a Submirror

1. **Make sure that you have root privilege and that you have a current backup of all data.**

2. **Read "Background Information for RAID 1 Volumes" on page 88.**

3. **Use one of the following methods to detach a submirror.**

- From the Enhanced Storage tool within the Solaris Management Console, open the Volumes node, choose the mirror, then choose Action->Properties and click the Components tab. Follow the instructions on screen. For more information, see the online help.

- Use the `metadetach` command to detach a submirror from a mirror.

  ```
  # metadetach mirror submirror
  ```
  See the `metadetach(1M)` man page for more information.

Example—Detaching a Submirror

```
# metastat
d5: mirror
    Submirror 0: d50
...
# metadetach d5 d50
d5: submirror d50 is detached
```

In this example, mirror d5 has a submirror, d50, which is detached with the `metadetach` command. The underlying slices from d50 are going to be reused elsewhere. When you detach a submirror from a mirror, the system displays a confirmation message.

▼ How to Place a Submirror Offline and Online

The `metaonline` command can only be used when a submirror was taken offline by the `metaoffline` command. After the `metaonline` command runs, Solaris Volume Manager automatically begins resynchronizing the submirror with the mirror.

Note – The `metaoffline` command's capabilities are similar to that offered by the `metadetach` command. However, the `metaoffline` command does not sever the logical association between the submirror and the mirror.

---

1. **Make sure that you have root privilege and that you have a current backup of all data.**

2. **Read "Background Information for RAID 1 Volumes" on page 88.**

3. **Use one of the following methods to place a submirror online or offline.**

- From the Enhanced Storage tool within the Solaris Management Console, open the Volumes node, choose the mirror, then choose Action->Properties and click the Components tab. Follow the instructions on screen. For more information, see the online help.

- Use the `metaoffline` command to take offline a submirror.

  # **metaoffline** *mirror submirror*

  See the `metaoffline`(1M) man page for more information.

- Use the `metaonline` command to bring a submirror online.

  # **metaonline** *mirror submirror*

  See the `metaonline`(1M) man page for more information.

Example—Placing a Submirror Offline

```
# metaoffline d10 d11
d10: submirror d11 is offlined
```

In this example, submirror `d11` is taken offline from mirror `d10`. Reads will continue to be made from the other submirror. The mirror will be out of sync as soon as the first write is made. This inconsistency is corrected when the offlined submirror is brought back online.

Example—Placing a Submirror Online

```
# metaonline d10 d11
d10: submirror d11 is onlined
```

In this example, submirror `d11` is brought back online in mirror `d10`.

▼ How to Enable a Slice in a Submirror

1. **Make sure that you have root privilege and that you have a current backup of all data.**

2. **Read "Overview of Replacing and Enabling Components in RAID 1 and RAID 5 Volumes" on page 230 and "Background Information for RAID 1 Volumes" on page 88.**

3. **Use one of the following methods to enable a slice in a submirror.**

   - From the Enhanced Storage tool within the Solaris Management Console, open the Volumes node, choose the mirror, then choose Action->Properties and click the Components tab. Follow the instructions on screen. For more information, see the online help.

   - Use the `metareplace` command to enable a failed slice in a submirror.

     # **metareplace -e** *mirror failed-slice*

     The `metareplace` command automatically starts a resynchronization to synchronize the repaired or replaced slice with the rest of the mirror.

See the `metareplace`(1M) man page for more information.

Example—Enabling a Slice in a Submirror

```
# metareplace -e d11 c1t4d0s7
d11: device c1t4d0s7 is enabled
```

In this example, the mirror `d11` has a submirror that contains slice, `c1t4d0s7`, which had a soft error. The `metareplace` command with the `-e` option enables the failed slice.

Note – If a physical disk is defective, you can either replace it with another available disk (and its slices) on the system as documented in "How to Replace a Slice in a Submirror" on page 112. Alternatively, you can repair/replace the disk, format it, and run the `metareplace` command with the `-e` option as shown in this example.

Maintaining RAID 1 Volumes

Solaris Volume Manager reports status information on RAID 1 volumes and submirrors so a system administrator can determine what, if any, maintenance action is required. The following table explains mirror states.

TABLE 10–1 Submirror States

State	Meaning
Okay	The submirror has no errors and is functioning correctly.
Resyncing	The submirror is actively being resynchronized. An error has occurred and been corrected, the submirror has just been brought back online, or a new submirror has been added.
Needs Maintenance	A slice (or slices) in the submirror has encountered an I/O error or an open error. All reads and writes to and from this slice in the submirror have been discontinued.

Additionally, for each slice in a submirror, the `metastat` command shows the "Device" (device name of the slice in the stripe); "Start Block" on which the slice begins; "Dbase" to show if the slice contains a state database replica; "State" of the slice; and "Hot Spare" to show the slice being used to hot spare a failed slice.

The slice state is perhaps the most important information when you are troubleshooting mirror errors. The submirror state only provides general status information, such as "Okay" or "Needs Maintenance." If the submirror reports a

"Needs Maintenance" state, refer to the slice state. You take a different recovery action if the slice is in the "Maintenance" or "Last Erred" state. If you only have slices in the "Maintenance" state, they can be repaired in any order. If you have a slices in the "Maintenance" state and a slice in the "Last Erred" state, you must fix the slices in the "Maintenance" state first then the "Last Erred" slice. See "Overview of Replacing and Enabling Components in RAID 1 and RAID 5 Volumes" on page 230.

The following table explains the slice states for submirrors and possible actions to take.

TABLE 10–2 Submirror Slice States

State	Meaning	Action
Okay	The component has no errors and is functioning correctly.	None.
Resyncing	The component is actively being resynchronized. An error has occurred and been corrected, the submirror has just been brought back online, or a new submirror has been added.	If desired, monitor the submirror status until the resynchronization is done.
Maintenance	The component has encountered an I/O error or an open error. All reads and writes to and from this component have been discontinued.	Enable or replace the failed component. See "How to Enable a Slice in a Submirror" on page 106, or "How to Replace a Slice in a Submirror" on page 112. The `metastat` command will show an `invoke` recovery message with the appropriate action to take with the `metareplace` command. You can also use the `metareplace -e` command.
Last Erred	The component has encountered an I/O error or an open error. However, the data is not replicated elsewhere due to another slice failure. I/O is still performed on the slice. If I/O errors result, the mirror I/O will fail.	First, enable or replace components in the "Maintenance" state. See "How to Enable a Slice in a Submirror" on page 106, or "How to Replace a Slice in a Submirror" on page 112. Usually, this error results in some data loss, so validate the mirror after it is fixed. For a file system, use the `fsck` command, then check the data. An application or database must have its own method of validating the device.

▼ How to Check the Status of Mirrors and Submirrors

● **Use one of the following methods to check mirror or submirror status.**

- From the Enhanced Storage tool within the Solaris Management Console, open the Volumes node, choose the mirror, then choose Action->Properties. Follow the instructions on screen. For more information, see the online help.

- Run the `metastat` command on a mirror to see the state of each submirror, the pass number, the read option, the write option, and the size of the total number of blocks in mirror. For example, to check the status of the one-way mirror d70, use:

```
# metastat d70
d70: Mirror
    Submirror 0: d71
      State: Okay
    Pass: 1
    Read option: roundrobin (default)
    Write option: parallel (default)
    Size: 12593637 blocks

d71: Submirror of d70
    State: Okay
    Size: 12593637 blocks
    Stripe 0:
        Device                    Start Block  Dbase State        Reloc  Hot Spare
        c1t3d0s3                            0   No    Okay         Yes
    Stripe 1:
        Device                    Start Block  Dbase State        Reloc  Hot Spare
        c1t3d0s4                            0   No    Okay         Yes
    Stripe 2:
        Device                    Start Block  Dbase State        Reloc  Hot Spare
        c1t3d0s5                            0   No    Okay         Yes
```

See "How to Change RAID 1 Volume Options" on page 110 to change a mirror's pass number, read option, or write option.

See `metastat`(1M) for more information about checking device status.

Example—Checking Status of RAID 1 Volumes

Here is sample output from the `metastat` command.

```
# metastat
d0: Mirror
    Submirror 0: d1
      State: Okay
    Submirror 1: d2
      State: Okay
    Pass: 1
    Read option: roundrobin (default)
    Write option: parallel (default)
    Size: 5600 blocks

d1: Submirror of d0
    State: Okay
    Size: 5600 blocks
```

```
    Stripe 0:
        Device                      Start Block   Dbase State        Hot Spare
        c0t2d0s7                             0     No    Okay
```

...

For each submirror in the mirror, the `metastat` command shows the state, an
"invoke" line if there is an error, the assigned hot spare pool (if any), size in blocks,
and information about each slice in the submirror.

▼ How to Change RAID 1 Volume Options

1. **Make sure that you have root privilege and that you have a current backup of all
   data.**

2. **Check "Background Information for Changing RAID 1 Volume Options"
   on page 90.**

3. **Use one of the following methods to change mirror options.**

   - From the Enhanced Storage tool within the Solaris Management Console, open the
     Volumes node, choose the mirror, then choose Action->Properties. Follow the
     instructions on screen. For more information, see the online help.

   - Use the `metaparam` command to display and change a mirror's options. For
     example, to change a mirror to "first", rather than round-robin, for reading, use the
     following:

     ```
     # metaparam -r first mirror
     ```

     See "RAID 1 Volume Options" on page 86 for a description of mirror options. Also
     see the `metaparam`(1M) man page.

Example—Changing a RAID 1 Volume's Read Policy

```
# metaparam -r geometric d30
# metaparam d30
d30: mirror current parameters are:
    Pass: 1
    Read option: geometric (-g)
    Write option: parallel (default)
```

In this example, the `-r` option changes a mirror's read policy to `geometric`.

Example—Changing a RAID 1 Volume's Write Policy

```
# metaparam -w serial d40
# metaparam d40
d40: mirror current parameters are:
```

```
Pass: 1
Read option: roundrobin (default)
Write option: serial (-S)
```

In this example, the `-w` option changes a mirror's write policy to `serial`.

Example—Changing a RAID 1 Volume's Pass Number

```
# metaparam -p 5 d50
# metaparam d50
d50: mirror current parameters are:
    Pass: 5
    Read option: roundrobin (default)
    Write option: parallel (default)
```

In this example, the `-p` option changes a mirror's pass number to 5.

▼ How to Expand a RAID 1 Volume

1. **Make sure that you have root privilege and that you have a current backup of all data.**

2. **Read "Background Information for RAID 1 Volumes" on page 88.**

3. **Use one of the following methods to expand a mirror.**

   - From the Enhanced Storage tool within the Solaris Management Console, open the Volumes node, choose the mirror, then choose Action->Properties and click the Components tab. Follow the instructions on screen. For more information, see the online help.

   - Use the `metattach` command to attach additional slices to each submirror. For example, to attach a component to a submirror, use the following:

     ```
     # metattach submirror component
     ```

     Each submirror in a mirror must be expanded. See the `metattach`(1M) man page for more information.

Example—Expanding a Two-Way Mirror That Contains a Mounted File System

```
# metastat
d8: Mirror
    Submirror 0: d9
      State: Okay
    Submirror 1: d10
      State: Okay
```

```
. . .
# metattach d9 c0t2d0s5
d9: component is attached
# metattach d10 c0t3d0s5
d10: component is attached
```

This example shows how to expand a mirrored mounted file system by concatenating
two disk drives to the mirror's two submirrors. The mirror is named d8 and contains
two submirrors named d9 and d10.

Where to Go From Here

For a UFS, run the growfs(1M) command on the mirror volume. See "How to Grow a
File System" on page 229.

An application, such as a database, that uses the raw volume must have its own way
of growing the added space.

Responding to RAID 1 Volume Component Failures

▼ How to Replace a Slice in a Submirror

1. **Make sure that you have root privilege and that you have a current backup of all
   data.**

2. **Read "Overview of Replacing and Enabling Components in RAID 1 and RAID 5
   Volumes" on page 230 and "Background Information for RAID 1 Volumes"
   on page 88.**

3. **Use one of the following methods to replace a slice in a mirror.**

   - From the Enhanced Storage tool within the Solaris Management Console, open the
     Volumes node, choose the mirror, then choose Action->Properties and click the
     Components tab. Follow the instructions on screen. For more information, see the
     online help.

   - Use the following form of the metareplace command to replace a slice in a
     submirror:

     metareplace {*mirror-name*} {*component-name...*}

     - *mirror-name* is the name of the volume to create.

- *component-name* specifies the name of the component that is to be replaced.

See the following examples and the `metainit`(1M) man page for more information.

Example—Replacing a Failed Slice in a Mirror

The following example illustrates how to replace a failed slice when the system is not configured to use hot spare pools for the automatic replacement of failed disks. See Chapter 15 for more information about using hot spare pools.

```
# metastat d6
d6: Mirror
    Submirror 0: d16
      State: Okay
    Submirror 1: d26
      State: Needs maintenance
...
d26: Submirror of d6
    State: Needs maintenance
    Invoke: metareplace d6 c0t2d0s2 <new device>
...
# metareplace d6 c0t2d0s2 c0t2d2s2
d6: device c0t2d0s2 is replaced with c0t2d2s2
```

The `metastat` command confirms that mirror d6 has a submirror, d26, with a slice in the "Needs maintenance" state. The `metareplace` command replaces the slice as specified in the "Invoke" line of the `metastat` output with another available slice on the system. The system confirms that the slice is replaced, and starts resynchronizing the submirror.

▼ How to Replace a Submirror

1. **Make sure that you have root privilege and that you have a current backup of all data.**

2. **Read "Overview of Replacing and Enabling Components in RAID 1 and RAID 5 Volumes" on page 230 and "Background Information for RAID 1 Volumes" on page 88.**

3. **Use one of the following methods to replace a submirror.**

   - From the Enhanced Storage tool within the Solaris Management Console, open the Volumes node, choose the mirror, then choose Action->Properties and click the Components tab. Follow the instructions on screen. For more information, see the online help.

   - Use the `metadetach`, `metaclear`, `metatinit`, and `metattach` commands to replace an entire submirror.

Example—Replacing a Submirror in a Mirror

The following example illustrates how to replace a submirror in an active mirror.

Note – The specific configuration of the new volume d22 will depend on the component you are replacing. A concatenation, as shown here, would be fine to replace a concatenation, but would not be an ideal replacement for a stripe as it could impact performance.

```
# metastat d20
d20: Mirror
    Submirror 0: d21
      State: Okay
    Submirror 1: d22
      State: Needs maintenance
. . .
# metadetach -f d20 d22
d20: submirror d22 is detached
# metaclear -f d22
d22: Concat/Stripe is cleared
# metainit d22 2 1 c1t0d0s2 1 c1t0d1s2
d22: Concat/Stripe is setup
# metattach d20 d22
d20: components are attached
```

The metastat command confirms that the two-way mirror d20 has a submirror, d22, in the "Needs maintenance" state. In this case, the entire submirror will be cleared and recreated. The metadetach command detaches the failed submirror from the mirror by using the -f option, which forces the detach to occur. The metaclear command clears the submirror. The metainit command recreates submirror d22, with new slices. The metattach command attaches the rebuilt submirror, and a mirror resynchronization begins automatically.

Note – You temporarily lose the capability for data redundancy while the mirror is a one-way mirror.

Removing RAID 1 Volumes (Unmirroring)

▼ How to Unmirror a File System

Use this procedure to unmirror a file system that can be unmounted while the system is running. To unmirror root (/), /var, /usr, or swap, or any other file system that cannot be unmounted while the system is running. see "How to Unmirror a File System That Cannot Be Unmounted" on page 116.

1. **Make sure that you have root privilege and that you have a current backup of all data.**

2. **Read "Background Information for RAID 1 Volumes" on page 88.**

3. **Verify that at least one submirror is in the Okay state.**

   ```
   # metastat
   ```

4. **Unmount the file system.**

   ```
   # umount /home
   ```

5. **Detach the submirror that will continue to be used for the file system**

   For more information, see the metadetach(1M) man page.

   ```
   # metadetach d1 d10
   ```

6. **Clear the mirror and remaining subcomponents.**

   For more information, see the metaclear(1M)

   ```
   # metaclear -r d1
   ```

7. **Edit the /etc/vfstab file to use the component detached in Step 5, if necessary.**

8. **Remount the file system.**

Example—Unmirroring the /opt File System

```
# metastat d4
d4: Mirror
    Submirror 0: d2
      State: Okay
    Submirror 1: d3
```

```
      State: Okay
. . .
# umount /opt
# metadetach d4 d2
d4: submirror d2 is detached
# metaclear -r d4
d4: Mirror is cleared
d3: Concat/Stripe is cleared
```
   (Edit the /etc/vfstab file so that the entry for /opt is changed from d4 to the underlying slice or volume)
```
# mount /opt
```

In this example, the `/opt` filesystem is made of a two-way mirror named d4; its
submirrors are d2 and d3, made of slices `/dev/dsk/c0t0d0s0` and
`/dev/dsk/c1t0d0s0`, respectively. The `metastat` command verifies that at least
one submirror is in the "Okay" state. (A mirror with no submirrors in the "Okay" state
must be repaired first.) The file system is unmounted then submirror d2 is detached.
The `metaclear -r` command deletes the mirror and the other submirror, d3.

Next, the entry for `/opt` in the `/etc/vfstab` file is changed to reference the
underlying slice. For example, if d4 were the mirror and d2 the submirror, the
following line:

```
/dev/md/dsk/d4   /dev/md/rdsk/d4   /var ufs   2   yes -
```

should be changed to:

```
/dev/md/dsk/d2   /dev/md/rdsk/d2   /var ufs   2   yes -
```

By using the submirror name, you can continue to have the file system mounted on a
volume. Finally, the `/opt` file system is remounted.

Note – By using d2 instead of d4 in the `/etc/vfstab` file, you have unmirrored the
mirror. Because d2 consists of a single slice, you can mount the file system on the slice
name (`/dev/dsk/c0t0d0s0`) if you do not want the device to support a volume.

▼ How to Unmirror a File System That Cannot Be Unmounted

Use this task to unmirror file systems that cannot be unmounted during normal
system operation, including root (`/`), `/usr`, `/opt`, and `swap`.

1. **Run the `metastat` command to verify that at least one submirror is in the "Okay"
   state.**

2. **Run the `metadetach` command on the mirror that contains root (`/`), `/usr`, `/opt`, or
   `swap` to make a one-way mirror.**

3. **For** /usr, /opt, **and** swap: **change the file system entry in the** /etc/vfstab **file to use a non-Solaris Volume Manager device (slice).**

4. **For root (/) only: running the** metaroot **command.**

5. **Reboot the system.**

6. **Run the** metaclear **command to clear the mirror and submirrors.**

Example—Unmirroring root (/)

```
# metadetach d0 d20
d0: submirror d20 is detached
# metaroot /dev/dsk/c0t3d0s0
# reboot
...
# metaclear -r d0
d0: Mirror is cleared
d10: Concat/Stripe is cleared
# metaclear d20
d20: Concat/Stripe is cleared
```

In this example, root (/) is a two-way mirror named d0; its submirrors are d10 and d20, which are made of slices /dev/dsk/c0t3d0s0 and /dev/dsk/c1t3d0s0, respectively. The metastat command verifies that at least one submirror is in the "Okay" state. (A mirror with no submirrors in the "Okay" state must first be repaired.) Submirror d20 is detached to make d0 a one-way mirror. The metaroot command is then run, using the *rootslice* from which the system is going to boot. This command edits the /etc/system and /etc/vfstab files to remove information that specifies the mirroring of root (/). After a reboot, the metaclear -r command deletes the mirror and the other submirror, d10. The last metaclear command clears submirror d20.

Example—Unmirroring swap

```
# metastat d1
d1: Mirror
    Submirror 0: d11
      State: Okay
    Submirror 1: d21
      State: Okay
...
# metadetach d1 d21
d1: submirror d21 is detached
    (Edit the /etc/vfstab file to change the entry for swap from metadevice to slice name)
# reboot
...
# metaclear -r d1
d1: Mirror is cleared
```

```
d11: Concat/Stripe is cleared
# metaclear d21
d21: Concat/stripe is cleared
```

In this example, swap is made of a two-way mirror named d1; its submirrors are d11 and d21, which are made of slices /dev/dsk/c0t3d0s1 and /dev/dsk/c1t3d0s1, respectively. The metastat command verifies that at least one submirror is in the "Okay" state. (A mirror with no submirrors in the "Okay" state must first be repaired.) Submirror d21 is detached to make d1 a one-way mirror. Next, the /etc/vfstab file must be edited to change the entry for swap to reference the slice that is in submirror d21. For example, if d1 was the mirror, and d21 the submirror containing slice /dev/dsk/c0t3d0s1, the following line:

```
/dev/md/dsk/d1 - - swap - no -
```

should be changed to:

```
/dev/dsk/c0t3d0s1 - - swap - no -
```

After a reboot, the metaclear -r command deletes the mirror and the other submirror, d11. The final metaclear command clears submirror d21.

Using a Mirror to Back Up Data

Although Solaris Volume Manager is not meant to be a "backup product," it does provide a means for backing up mirrored data without unmounting the mirror or taking the entire mirror offline, and without halting the system or denying users access to data. This process happens as follows: one of the submirrors is taken offline, temporarily losing the mirroring, and backed up. That submirror is then placed online and resynchronized as soon as the backup is complete.

▼ How to Use a RAID 1 Volume to Make an Online Backup

You can use this procedure on any file system except root (/). Be aware that this type of backup creates a "snapshot" of an active file system. Depending on how the file system is being used when it is write-locked, some files and file content on the backup might not correspond to the actual files on disk.

The following limitations apply to this procedure:

- If you use this procedure on a two-way mirror, be aware that data redundancy is lost while one submirror is offline for backup. A three-way mirror does not have this problem.

- There is some overhead on the system when the offlined submirror is brought back online after the backup is complete.

The high-level steps in this procedure are as follows:

- Write-locking the file system (UFS only). Do not lock root (/).
- Using the `metaoffline` command to take one submirror offline from the mirror
- Unlocking the file system
- Backing up the data on the offlined submirror
- Using the `metaonline` command to place the offlined submirror back online

---

Note – If you use these procedures regularly, put them into a script for ease of use.

---

1. **Run the `metastat` command to make sure the mirror is in the "Okay" state.**

   A mirror that is in the "Maintenance" state should be repaired first.

2. **For all file systems except root (/), lock the file system from writes.**

   ```
   # /usr/sbin/lockfs -w mount point
   ```

   Only a UFS needs to be write-locked. If the volume is set up as a raw device for database management software or some other application, running `lockfs` is not necessary. (You might, however, want to run the appropriate vendor-supplied utility to flush any buffers and lock access.)

Caution – Write-locking root (/) causes the system to hang, so it should never be performed.

---

3. **Take one submirror offline from the mirror.**

   ```
   # metaoffline mirror submirror
   ```

   In this command:

   mirror   Is the volume name of the mirror.

   submirror   Is the volume name of the submirror (volume) being taken offline.

   Reads will continue to be made from the other submirror. The mirror will be out of sync as soon as the first write is made. This inconsistency is corrected when the offlined submirror is brought back online in Step 6.

   There is no need to run the `fsck` command on the offlined file system.

4. **Unlock the file system and allow writes to continue.**

   ```
   # /usr/sbin/lockfs -u mount-point
   ```

You might need to perform necessary unlocking procedures based on
vendor-dependent utilities used in Step 2 above.

5. **Perform a backup of the offlined submirror.**

   Use the `ufsdump` command or your usual backup utility.

Note – To ensure a proper backup, use the *raw* volume, for example,
`/dev/md/rdsk/d4`. Using "rdsk" allows greater than 2 Gbyte access.

---

6. **Place the submirror back online.**

   ```
   # metaonline mirror submirror
   ```

   Solaris Volume Manager automatically begins resynchronizing the submirror with the
   mirror.

Example—Using a Mirror to Make an Online Backup

This example uses a mirror named d1, consisting of submirrors d2 and d3. The
submirror d3 is taken offline and backed up while submirror d2 stays online. The file
system on the mirror is /home1.

```
# /usr/sbin/lockfs -w /home1
# metaoffline d1 d3
d1: submirror d3 is offlined
# /usr/sbin/lockfs -u /home1
(Perform backup using /dev/md/rdsk/d3)
# metaonline d1 d3
d1: submirror d3 is onlined
```

## CHAPTER 11

Soft Partitions (Overview)

This chapter provides information about Solaris Volume Manager soft partitions. For information about related tasks, see Chapter 12.

This chapter contains the following information:

- "Overview of Soft Partitions" on page 121
- "Background Information About Soft Partitions" on page 122

Overview of Soft Partitions

As disks become larger, and disk arrays present ever larger logical devices to Solaris systems, users need to be able to subdivide disks or logical volumes into more than eight partitions, often to create manageable file systems or partition sizes. Solaris Volume Manager's soft partition feature addresses this need.

Solaris Volume Manager can support up to 8192 logical volumes per disk set (including the local, or unspecified, disk set), but is configured for 128 (d0–d127) by default. To increase the number of logical volumes, see "Changing Solaris Volume Manager Defaults" on page 226.

Note – Do not increase the number of possible logical volumes far beyond the number that you will actually use. Solaris Volume Manager creates a device node (/dev/dsk/md/*) and associated data structures for every logical volume that is permitted by the maximum value. These additional possible volumes can result in a substantial performance impact.

You use soft partitions to divide a disk slice or logical volume into as many partitions as needed. You must provide a name for each division or *soft partition*, just like you do for other storage volumes, such as stripes or mirrors. A soft partition, once named, can be accessed by applications, including file systems, as long as it is not included in another volume. Once included in a volume, the soft partition should no longer be directly accessed.

Soft partitions can be placed directly above a disk slice, or on top of a mirror, stripe or RAID 5 volume. Nesting of a soft partition between volumes is not allowed. For example, a soft partition built on a stripe with a mirror built on the soft partition is not allowed.

Although a soft partition appears, to file systems and other applications, to be a single contiguous logical volume, it actually comprises a series of *extents* that could be located at arbitrary locations on the underlying media. In addition to the soft partitions, extent headers (also called system recovery data areas) on disk record information about the soft partitions to facilitate recovery in the event of a catastrophic system failure.

Background Information About Soft Partitions

Requirements for Soft Partitions

Slices that are used for soft partitions cannot be used for other purposes.

When you partition a disk and build file systems on the resulting slices, you cannot later extend a slice without modifying or destroying the disk format. With soft partitions, you can extend the soft partitions up to the amount of space on the underlying device without moving or destroying data on other soft partitions.

Guidelines for Soft Partitions

- While it is technically possible to manually place extents of soft partitions at arbitrary locations on disk (as you can see in the output of `metastat -p`, described in "Viewing the Solaris Volume Manager Configuration" on page 218), you should allow the system to place them automatically.

- Although you can build soft partitions on any slice, creating a single slice that occupies the entire disk and then creating soft partitions on that slice is the most efficient way to use soft partitions at the disk level.

- Because the maximum size of a soft partition is limited to the size of the slice or logical volume on which it is built, you should build a volume on top of your disk slices, then build soft partitions on top of the volume. This strategy allows you to add components to the volume later, then expand the soft partitions as needed.

- For maximum flexibility and high availability, build RAID 1 (mirror) or RAID 5 volumes on disk slices, then create soft partitions on the mirror or RAID 5 volume.

Scenario—Soft Partitions

Soft partitions provide tools with which to subdivide larger storage spaces into more managable spaces. For example, in other scenarios ("Scenario—RAID 1 Volumes (Mirrors)" on page 90 or "Scenario—RAID 5 Volumes" on page 136), large storage aggregations provided redundant storage of many Gigabytes. However, many possible scenarios would not require so much space—at least at first. Soft partitions allow you to subdivide that storage space into more manageable sections, each of which can have a complete file system. For example, you could create 1000 soft partitions on top of a RAID 1 or RAID 5 volume so that each of your users can have a home directory on a separate file system. If a user needs more space, simply expand the soft partition.

## CHAPTER 12

Soft Partitions (Tasks)

This chapter provides information about performing tasks that are associated with Solaris Volume Manager soft partitions. For information about the concepts involved in these tasks, see Chapter 11.

Soft Partitions (Task Map)

The following task map identifies the procedures needed to manage Solaris Volume Manager soft partitions.

Task	Description	Instructions
Create soft partitions	Use the Solaris Volume Manager GUI or the `metainit` command to create soft partitions.	"How to Create a Soft Partition" on page 126
Check the status of soft partitions	Use the Solaris Volume Manager GUI or the `metastat` command to check the status of soft partitions.	"How to Check the Status of a Soft Partition" on page 127
Expand soft partitions	Use the Solaris Volume Manager GUI or the `metattach` command to expand soft partitions.	"How to Expand a Soft Partition" on page 128
Remove soft partitions	Use the Solaris Volume Manager GUI or the `metaclear` command to remove soft partitions.	"How to Remove a Soft Partition" on page 129

Creating Soft Partitions

▼ How to Create a Soft Partition

1. **Check the "Background Information About Soft Partitions" on page 122.**

2. **Use one of the following methods to create a soft partition:**

   - From the Enhanced Storage tool within the Solaris Management Console, open the Volumes node. Choose Action->Create Volume, then follow the instructions in the wizard. For more information, see the online help.

   - To create a soft partition, use the following form of the `metainit` command:

     `metainit [-s set] soft-partition -p [-e] component size`

     `-s` is used to specify which set is being used. If `-s` isn't specified, the local (default) disk set is used.

     `-e` is used to specify that the entire disk should be reformatted to provide a slice 0, taking most of the disk, and a slice 7 of a minimum of 4 Mbytes in size to contain a state database replica.

     soft-partition is the name of the soft partition. The name is of the form d*nnn*, where *nnn* is a number in the range of 0 to 8192.

     component is the disk, slice, or (logical) volume from which to create the soft partition. All *existing data on the component is destroyed* because the soft partition headers are written at the beginning of the component.

     size is the size of the soft partition, and is specified as a number followed by one of the following:

     - `M` or `m` for megabytes
     - `G` or `g` for gigabytes
     - `T` or `t` for terabyte
     - `B` or `b` for blocks (sectors)

   See the following examples and the `metainit`(1M) man page for more information.

Example—Creating a Soft Partition

```
# metainit d20 -p c1t3d0s2 4g
```
In this example, a 4 Gbyte soft partition called d20 is created on c1t3d0s2.

Example—Taking a Whole Disk for Soft Partitions

This example shows repartitioning disk c1t2d0, thus destroying any data on that disk, and creating a new soft partition on slice 0. The command looks like the following:

```
metainit d7 -p -e c1t2d0 1G
```

Maintaining Soft Partitions

Maintaining soft partitions is no different from maintaining other logical volumes. The following outlines the procedure.

▼ How to Check the Status of a Soft Partition

1. **Read the "Background Information About Soft Partitions" on page 122.**

2. **Use one of the following methods to check the status of a soft partition:**

   - From the Enhanced Storage tool within the Solaris Management Console, open the Volumes node. Choose the soft partition you want to monitor, then choose Action->Properties, then follow the instructions on screen. For more information, see the online help.

   - To view the existing configuration, use the following format of the metastat command:

     ```
     metastat soft-partition
     ```

     soft-partition is the name of the partition you want to check.

   See "Viewing the Solaris Volume Manager Configuration" on page 218 for more information.

Example—Checking the Status of a Soft Partition

This example shows checking the status of soft partition d1, which includes two extents and is built on the RAID 1 volume d100.

```
# metastat d1
d1: soft partition
    component:  d100
    state: OKAY
    size:  42674285 blocks
```

```
          Extent                    Start Block              Block Count
            0                            10234                 40674285
            1                         89377263                  2000000
d100: Mirror
    Submirror 0: d10
    State: OKAY
    Read option: roundrobin (default)
    Write option: parallel (default)
    Size: 426742857 blocks

d10: Submirror of d100
    State:  OKAY
    Hot spare pool: hsp002
    Size: 426742857 blocks
    Stripe 0: (interlace: 32 blocks)
        Device              Start Block  Dbase State      Hot Spare
        c3t3d0s0                0               No    Okay
```

▼ How to Expand a Soft Partition

When no other logical volumes have been built on a soft partition, you can add space to the soft partition. Free space is located and used to extend the partition. Existing data is not moved.

1. **Read the "Background Information About Soft Partitions" on page 122.**

2. **Use one of the following methods to expand a soft partition:**

   - From the Enhanced Storage tool within the Solaris Management Console, open the Volumes node. Choose the soft partition you want to expand, then choose Action->Properties, then follow the instructions on screen. For more information, see the online help.

   - To add space to a soft partition, use the following form of the `metattach` command:

     `metattach [-s` *disk-set*`]` *soft-partition size*

     disk-set is the name of the disk set in which the soft partition exists.

     soft-partition is the name of an existing soft partition.

     size is the amount of space to add.

Example—Expanding a Soft Partition

This example shows how you can attach space to a soft partition and then expand the file system that sits on it while the soft partition is online and mounted is online:

```
# mount /dev/md/dsk/d20 /home2
# metattach d20 10g
# growfs -M /home2 /dev/md/rdsk/d20
```

How to Remove a Soft Partition

1. **Read the "Background Information About Soft Partitions" on page 122.**

2. **Use one of the following methods to delete a soft partition:**

   - From the Enhanced Storage tool within the Solaris Management Console, open the Volumes node. Choose the soft partition you want to expand, then choose Action->Properties, then follow the instructions on screen. For more information, see the online help.

   - To delete a soft partition, use one of the following forms of the `metaclear` command:

     ```
     metaclear  [-s disk-set]  component
     metaclear  [-s disk-set]  -r soft-partition
     metaclear  [-s disk-set]  -p component
     ```

     where:

     - *disk-set* is the disk set in which the soft partition exists.

     - *soft-partition* is the soft partition to delete.

     - *r* specifies to recursively delete logical volumes, but not volumes on which others depend.

     - *p* specifies to purge all soft partitions on the specified component, except those soft partitions that are open.

     - *component* is the component from which to clear all of the soft partitions.

Example—Removing a Soft Partition

This example shows how to delete all soft partitions on `c1t4d2s0`.

```
# metaclear -p c1t4d2s0
```

## CHAPTER 13

RAID 5 Volumes (Overview)

This chapter provides conceptual information about Solaris Volume Manager RAID 5 volumes. For information about performing related tasks, see Chapter 14.

This chapter contains the following:

- "Overview of RAID 5 Volumes" on page 131
- "Background Information for Creating RAID 5 Volumes" on page 134
- "Overview of Replacing and Enabling Slices in RAID 5 Volumes" on page 136

Overview of RAID 5 Volumes

RAID level 5 is similar to striping, but with parity data distributed across all components (disk or logical volume). If a component fails, the data on the failed component can be rebuilt from the distributed data and parity information on the other components. In Solaris Volume Manager, a *RAID 5 volume* is a volume that supports RAID level 5.

A RAID 5 volume uses storage capacity equivalent to one component in the volume to store redundant information (parity) about user data stored on the remainder of the RAID 5 volume's components. That is, if you have three components, the equivalent of one will be used for the parity information. If you have five components, then the equivalent of one will be used for parity information. The parity is distributed across all components in the volume. Like a mirror, a RAID 5 volume increases data availability, but with a minimum of cost in terms of hardware and only a moderate penalty for write operations. However, you cannot use a RAID 5 volume for root (/), /usr, and swap, or for existing file systems.

Solaris Volume Manager automatically resynchronizes a RAID 5 volume when you replace an existing component. Solaris Volume Manager also resynchronizes RAID 5 volumes during rebooting if a system failure or panic took place.

Example—RAID 5 Volume

Figure 13–1 shows a RAID 5 volume, d40.

The first three data chunks are written to Disks A through C. The next chunk that is written is a parity chunk, written to Drive D, which consists of an exclusive OR of the first three chunks of data. This pattern of writing data and parity chunks results in both data and parity being spread across all disks in the RAID 5 volume. Each drive can be read independently. The parity protects against a single disk failure. If each disk in this example were 2 Gbytes, the total capacity of d40 would be 6 Gbytes. (One drive's worth of space is allocated to parity.)

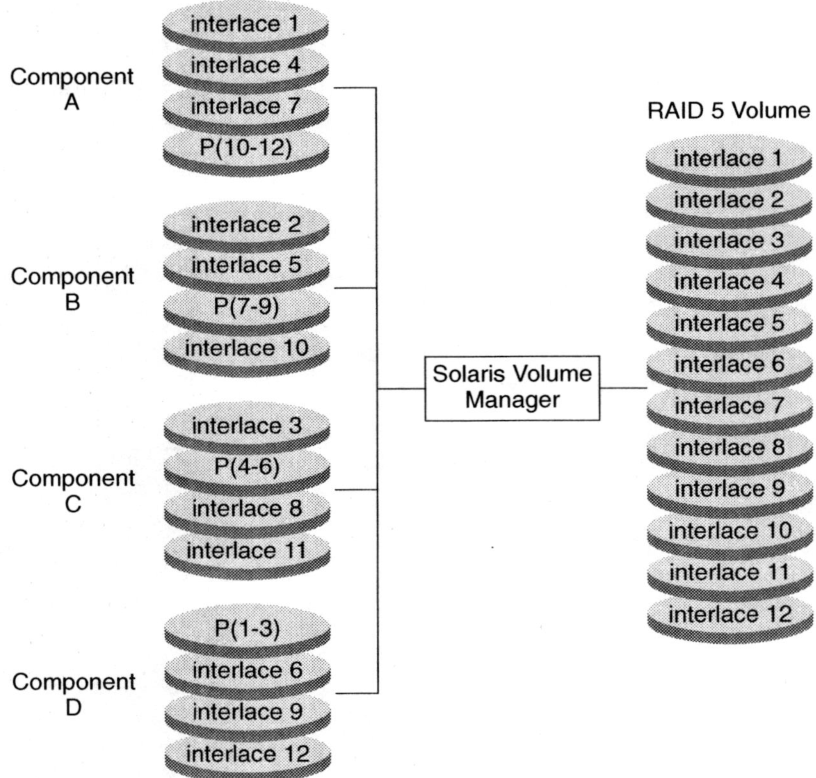

FIGURE 13–1 RAID 5 Volume Example

Example—Concatenated (Expanded) RAID 5 Volume

The following figure shows an example of an RAID 5 volume that initially consisted of four disks (components). A fifth disk has been dynamically concatenated to the volume to expand the RAID 5 volume.

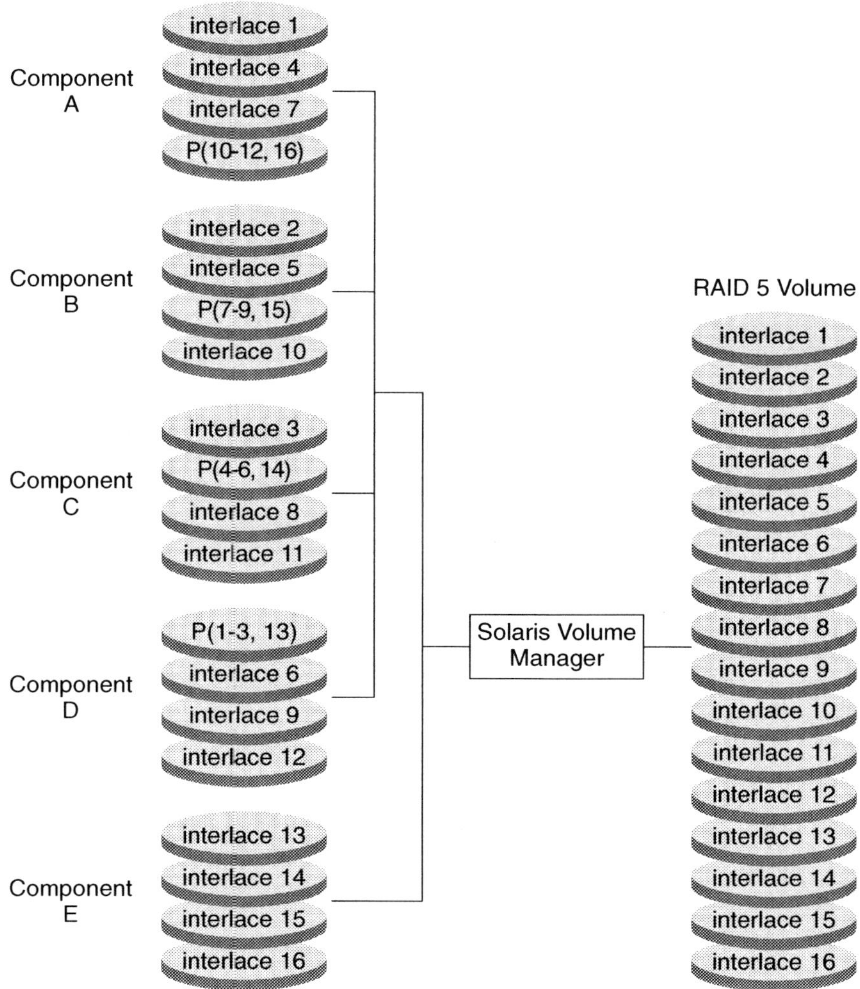

FIGURE 13–2 Expanded RAID 5 Volume Example

The parity areas are allocated when the initial RAID 5 volume is created. One component's worth of space is allocated to parity, although the actual parity blocks are distributed across all of the original components to distribute I/O. When you concatenate additional components to the RAID, the additional space is devoted entirely to data. No new parity blocks are allocated. The data on the concatenated components is, however, included in the parity calculations, so it is protected against single device failures.

Concatenated RAID 5 volumes are not suited for long-term use. Use a concatenated RAID 5 volume until it is possible to reconfigure a larger RAID 5 volume and copy the data to the larger volume.

Note – When you add a new component to a RAID 5 volume, Solaris Volume Manager "zeros" all the blocks in that component. This process ensures that the parity will protect the new data. As data is written to the additional space, Solaris Volume Manager includes it in the parity calculations.

Background Information for Creating RAID 5 Volumes

When you work with RAID 5 volumes, consider the "Requirements for RAID 5 Volumes" on page 134 and "Guidelines for RAID 5 Volumes" on page 135. Many striping guidelines also apply to RAID 5 volume configurations. See "Requirements for Stripes and Concatenations" on page 70.

Requirements for RAID 5 Volumes

- A RAID 5 volume must consist of at least three components. The more components a RAID 5 volume contains, however, the longer read and write operations take when a component fails.

- RAID 5 volumes cannot be striped, concatenated, or mirrored.

- Do not create a RAID 5 volume from a component that contains an existing file system. Doing so will erase the data during the RAID 5 initialization process.

- When you create a RAID 5 volume, you can define the interlace value. If not specified, the interlace value is 16 Kbytes. This value is reasonable for most applications.

- A RAID 5 volume (with no hot spares) can only handle a single component failure.

- When you create RAID 5 volumes, use components across separate controllers, because controllers and associated cables tend to fail more often than disks.

- Use components of the same size. Creating a RAID 5 volume with components of different sizes results in unused disk space.

Guidelines for RAID 5 Volumes

- Because of the complexity of parity calculations, volumes with greater than about 20 percent writes should probably not be RAID 5 volumes. If data redundancy on a write-heavy volume is needed, consider mirroring.

- If the different components in the RAID 5 volume reside on different controllers and the accesses to the volume are primarily large sequential accesses, then setting the interlace value to 32 Kbytes might improve performance.

- You can expand a RAID 5 volume by concatenating additional components to the volume. Concatenating a new component to an existing RAID 5 decreases the overall performance of the volume because the data on concatenations is sequential. Data is not striped across all components. The original components of the volume have data and parity striped across all components. This striping is lost for the concatenated component, although the data is still recoverable from errors because the parity is used during the component I/O. The resulting RAID 5 volume continues to handle a single component failure.

  Concatenated components also differ in the sense that they do not have parity striped on any of the regions. Thus, the entire contents of the component are available for data.

  Any performance enhancements for large or sequential writes are lost when components are concatenated.

- You can create a RAID 5 volume without having to "zero out" the data blocks. To do so, do one of the following:

  - Use the `metainit` command with the `-k` option. The `-k` option recreates the RAID 5 volume without initializing it, and sets the disk blocks to the OK state. This option is potentially dangerous, as any errors that exist on disk blocks within the volume will cause unpredictable behavior from Solaris Volume Manager, including the possibility of fabricated data.

  - Initialize the device and restore data from tape. See the `metainit`(1M) man page for more information.

Overview of Replacing and Enabling Slices in RAID 5 Volumes

Solaris Volume Manager has the capability to *replace* and *enable* components within mirrors and RAID 5 volumes. The issues and requirements for doing so are the same for mirrors and RAID 5 volumes. For more information, see "Overview of Replacing and Enabling Components in RAID 1 and RAID 5 Volumes" on page 230.

Scenario—RAID 5 Volumes

RAID 5 volumes allow you to have redundant storage without the overhead of RAID 1 volumes, which require two times the total storage space to provide data redundancy. By setting up a RAID 5 volume, you can provide redundant storage of greater capacity than you could achieve with RAID 1 on the same set of disk components, and, with the help of hot spares (see Chapter 15 and specifically "How Hot Spares Work" on page 148), nearly the same level of safety. The drawbacks are increased write time and markedly impaired performance in the event of a component failure, but those tradeoffs might be insignificant for many situations. The following example, drawing on the sample system explained in Chapter 4, describes how RAID 5 volumes can provide extra storage capacity.

Other scenarios for RAID 0 and RAID 1 volumes used 6 slices (c1t1d0, c1t2d0, c1t3d0, c2t1d0, c2t2d0, c2t3d0) on six disks, spread over two controllers, to provide 27 Gbytes of redundant storage. By using the same slices in a RAID 5 configuration, 45 Gbytes of storage is available, and the configuration can withstand a single component failure without data loss or access interruption. By adding hot spares to the configuration, the RAID 5 volume can withstand additional component failures. The most significant drawback to this approach is that a controller failure would result in data loss to this RAID 5 volume, while it would not with the RAID 1 volume described in "Scenario—RAID 1 Volumes (Mirrors)" on page 90.

## CHAPTER 14

RAID 5 Volumes (Tasks)

This chapter provides information about performing Solaris Volume Manager tasks that are associated with RAID 5 volumes. For information about the concepts involved in these tasks, see Chapter 13.

RAID 5 Volumes (Task Map)

The following task map identifies the procedures needed to manage Solaris Volume Manager RAID 5 volumes.

Task	Description	Instructions
Create RAID 5 volumes	Use the Solaris Volume Manager GUI or the `metainit` command to create RAID 5 volumes.	"How to Create a RAID 5 Volume" on page 138
Check the status of RAID 5 volumes	Use the Solaris Volume Manager GUI or the `metastat` command to check the status of RAID 5 volumes.	"How to Check the Status of RAID 5 Volumes" on page 139
Expand a RAID 5 volume	Use the Solaris Volume Manager GUI or the `metattach` command to expand RAID 5 volumes.	"How to Expand a RAID 5 Volume" on page 142
Enable a slice in a RAID 5 volume	Use the Solaris Volume Manager GUI or the `metareplace` command to enable slices in RAID 5 volumes.	"How to Enable a Component in a RAID 5 Volume" on page 142
Replace a slice in a RAID 5 volume	Use the Solaris Volume Manager GUI or the `metareplace` command to enable slices in RAID 5 volumes.	"How to Replace a Component in a RAID 5 Volume" on page 143

Creating RAID 5 Volumes

▼ How to Create a RAID 5 Volume

1. Check "Prerequisites for Creating Solaris Volume Manager Elements" on page 46 and "Background Information for Creating RAID 5 Volumes" on page 134.

2. To create the RAID 5 volume, use one of the following methods:

- From the Enhanced Storage tool within the Solaris Management Console, open the Volumes node, then choose Action->Create Volume and follow the steps in the wizard. For more information, see the online help.

- Use the following form of the `metainit` command:

  `metainit` *name* `-r` *component component component*

  - *name* is the name for the volume to create.

  - *r* specifies to create a RAID 5 volume.

  - *component* specifies a slice or soft partition to include in the RAID 5 volume.

  To specify an interlace value, add the `-i` *interlace-value* option. For more information, see the `metainit`(1M) man page.

Example—Creating a RAID 5 Volume of Three Slices

```
# metainit d45 -r c2t3d0s2 c3t0d0s2 c4t0d0s2
d45: RAID is setup
```

In this example, the RAID 5 volume d45 is created with the `-r` option from three slices. Because no interlace value is specified, d45 uses the default of 16 Kbytes. The system verifies that the RAID 5 volume has been set up, and begins initializing the volume.

Note – You must wait for the initialization to finish before you can use the RAID 5 volume.

Where to Go From Here

To prepare the newly created RAID 5 volume for a file system, see "Creating File Systems (Tasks)" in *System Administration Guide: Basic Administration*. An application, such as a database, that uses the raw volume must have its own way of recognizing the volume.

To associate a hot spare pool with a RAID 5 volume, see "How to Associate a Hot Spare Pool With a Volume" on page 156.

Maintaining RAID 5 Volumes

▼ How to Check the Status of RAID 5 Volumes

● **To check status on a RAID 5 volume, use one of the following methods:**

- From the Enhanced Storage tool within the Solaris Management Console, open the Volumes node and view the status of the volumes. Choose a volume, then choose Action->Properties to see more detailed information. For more information, see the online help.

- Use the `metastat` command.

  For each slice in the RAID 5 volume, the `metastat` command shows the following:

  - "Device" (device name of the slice in the stripe)

  - "Start Block" on which the slice begins

  - "Dbase" to show if the slice contains a state database replica

  - "State" of the slice

  - "Hot Spare" to show the slice being used to hot spare a failed slice

Example—Viewing RAID 5 Volume Status

Here is sample RAID 5 volume output from the `metastat` command.

```
# metastat
d10: RAID
    State: Okay
    Interlace: 32 blocks
    Size: 10080 blocks
Original device:
    Size: 10496 blocks
        Device            Start Block  Dbase State          Hot Spare
        c0t0d0s1                  330  No    Okay
        c1t2d0s1                  330  No    Okay
        c2t3d0s1                  330  No    Okay
```

The `metastat` command output identifies the volume as a RAID 5 volume. For each slice in the RAID 5 volume, it shows the name of the slice in the stripe, the block on which the slice begins, an indicator that none of these slices contain a state database replica, that all the slices are okay, and that none of the slices are hot spare replacements for a failed slice.

RAID 5 Volume Status Information

The following table explains RAID 5 volume states.

TABLE 14–1 RAID 5 States

State	Meaning
Initializing	Slices are in the process of having all disk blocks zeroed. This process is necessary due to the nature of RAID 5 volumes with respect to data and parity interlace striping.
	Once the state changes to "Okay," the initialization process is complete and you are able to open the device. Up to this point, applications receive error messages.
Okay	The device is ready for use and is currently free from errors.
Maintenance	A slice has been marked as failed due to I/O or open errors that were encountered during a read or write operation.

The slice state is perhaps the most important information when you are troubleshooting RAID 5 volume errors. The RAID 5 state only provides general status information, such as "Okay" or "Needs Maintenance." If the RAID 5 reports a "Needs Maintenance" state, refer to the slice state. You take a different recovery action if the slice is in the "Maintenance" or "Last Erred" state. If you only have a slice in the "Maintenance" state, it can be repaired without loss of data. If you have a slice in the "Maintenance" state and a slice in the "Last Erred" state, data has probably been corrupted. You must fix the slice in the "Maintenance" state first then the "Last Erred" slice. See "Overview of Replacing and Enabling Components in RAID 1 and RAID 5 Volumes" on page 230.

The following table explains the slice states for a RAID 5 volume and possible actions to take.

State	Meaning	Action
Initializing	Slices are in the process of having all disk blocks zeroed. This process is necessary due to the nature of RAID 5 volumes with respect to data and parity interlace striping.	Normally none. If an I/O error occurs during this process, the device goes into the "Maintenance" state. If the initialization fails, the volume is in the "Initialization Failed" state, and the slice is in the "Maintenance" state. If this happens, clear the volume and re-create it.
Okay	The device is ready for use and is currently free from errors.	None. Slices can be added or replaced, if necessary.
Resyncing	The slice is actively being resynchronized. An error has occurred and been corrected, a slice has been enabled, or a slice has been added.	If desired, monitor the RAID 5 volume status until the resynchronization is done.
Maintenance	A single slice has been marked as failed due to I/O or open errors that were encountered during a read or write operation.	Enable or replace the failed slice. See "How to Enable a Component in a RAID 5 Volume" on page 142, or "How to Replace a Component in a RAID 5 Volume" on page 143. The `metastat` command will show an `invoke` recovery message with the appropriate action to take with the `metareplace` command.
Maintenance/ Last Erred	Multiple slices have encountered errors. The state of the failed slices is either "Maintenance" or "Last Erred." In this state, no I/O is attempted on the slice that is in the "Maintenance" state, but I/O is attempted to the slice marked "Last Erred" with the outcome being the overall status of the I/O request.	Enable or replace the failed slices. See "How to Enable a Component in a RAID 5 Volume" on page 142, or "How to Replace a Component in a RAID 5 Volume" on page 143. The `metastat` command will show an `invoke` recovery message with the appropriate action to take with the `metareplace` command, which must be run with the `-f` flag. This state indicates that data might be fabricated due to multiple failed slices.

Note – RAID 5 volume initialization or resynchronization cannot be interrupted.

▼ How to Expand a RAID 5 Volume

1. **Make sure that you have a current backup of all data and that you have root access.**

2. **Read "Background Information for Creating RAID 5 Volumes" on page 134.**

3. **To attach additional components to a RAID 5 volume, use one of the following methods:**

   - From the Enhanced Storage tool within the Solaris Management Console, open the Volumes node, then open the RAID 5 volume. Choose the Components pane, then choose Attach Component and follow the instructions. For more information, see the online help.

   - Use the following form of the `metattach` command:

     `metattach` *volume-name* *name-of-component-to-add*

     - *volume-name* is the name for the volume to expand.

     - *name-of-component-to-add* specifies the name of the component to attach to the RAID 5 volume.

     See the `metattach`(1M) man page for more information.

Note – In general, attaching components is a short-term solution to a RAID 5 volume that is running out of space. For performance reasons, it is best to have a "pure" RAID 5 volume.

Example—Adding a Component to a RAID 5 Volume

```
# metattach d2 c2t1d0s2
d2: column is attached
```

This example shows the addition of slice `c2t1d0s2` to an existing RAID 5 volume named `d2`.

Where to Go From Here

For a UFS, run the `growfs` command on the RAID 5 volume. See "Volume and Disk Space Expansion" on page 41.

An application, such as a database, that uses the raw volume must have its own way of growing the added space.

▼ How to Enable a Component in a RAID 5 Volume

1. **Make sure that you have a current backup of all data and that you have root access.**

2. **To enable a failed component in a RAID 5 volume, use one of the following methods:**

  - From the Enhanced Storage tool within the Solaris Management Console, open the Volumes node, then open the RAID 5 volume. Choose the Components pane, then choose the failed component. Click Enable Component and follow the instructions. For more information, see the online help.

  - Use the following form of the `metareplace` command:

    `metareplace -e` *volume-name* *component-name*

    - `-e` specifies to replace the failed component with a component at the same location (perhaps after physically replacing a disk).
    - *volume-name* is the name of the volume with a failed component.
    - *component-name* specifies the name of the component to replace.

    `metareplace` automatically starts resynchronizing the new component with the rest of the RAID 5 volume.

Example—Enabling a Component in a RAID 5 Volume

```
# metareplace -e d20 c2t0d0s2
```

In this example, the RAID 5 volume `d20` has a slice, `c2t0d0s2`, which had a soft error. The `metareplace` command with the `-e` option enables the slice.

Note – If a disk drive is defective, you can either replace it with another available disk (and its slices) on the system as documented in "How to Replace a Component in a RAID 5 Volume" on page 143. Alternatively, you can repair/replace the disk, label it, and run the `metareplace` command with the `-e` option.

▼ How to Replace a Component in a RAID 5 Volume

This task replaces a failed slice of a RAID 5 volume in which only one slice has failed.

Caution – Replacing a failed slice when multiple slices are in error might cause data to be fabricated. The integrity of the data in this instance would be questionable.

---

1. **Make sure that you have a current backup of all data and that you have root access.**

2. **Use one of the following methods to determine which slice of the RAID 5 volume needs to be replaced:**

- From the Enhanced Storage tool within the Solaris Management Console, open the Volumes node, then open the RAID 5 volume. Choose the Components pane, then view the status of the individual components. For more information, see the online help.

- Use the `metastat` command.

Look for the keyword "Maintenance" to identify the failed slice.

3. **Use one of the following methods to replace the failed slice with another slice:**

- From the Enhanced Storage tool within the Solaris Management Console, open the Volumes node, then open the RAID 5 volume. Choose the Components pane, then choose the failed component. Click Replace Component and follow the instructions. For more information, see the online help.

- Use the following form of the `metareplace` command:

    `metareplace` *volume-name failed-component new-component*

    - *volume-name* is the name of the volume with a failed component.
    - *failed-component* specifies the name of the component to replace.
    - *new-component* specifies the name of the component to add to the volume in place of the failed component.

    See the `metareplace`(1M) man page for more information.

4. **To verify the status of the replacement slice, use one of the methods described in Step 2.**

    The state of the replaced slice should be "Resyncing" or "Okay".

Example—Replacing a RAID 5 Component

```
# metastat d1
d1: RAID
State: Needs Maintenance
    Invoke: metareplace d1 c0t14d0s6 <new device>
    Interlace: 32 blocks
    Size: 8087040 blocks
Original device:
    Size: 8087520 blocks
    Device                  Start Block   Dbase State           Hot Spare
    c0t9d0s6                        330   No    Okay
    c0t13d0s6                       330   No    Okay
    c0t10d0s6                       330   No    Okay
    c0t11d0s6                       330   No    Okay
    c0t12d0s6                       330   No    Okay
    c0t14d0s6                       330   No    Maintenance

# metareplace d1 c0t14d0s6 c0t4d0s6
d1: device c0t14d0s6 is replaced with c0t4d0s6
# metastat d1
```

```
d1: RAID
    State: Resyncing
    Resync in progress: 98% done
    Interlace: 32 blocks
    Size: 8087040 blocks
Original device:
    Size: 8087520 blocks
    Device                  Start Block  Dbase State        Hot Spare
    c0t9d0s6                        330  No    Okay
    c0t13d0s6                       330  No    Okay
    c0t10d0s6                       330  No    Okay
    c0t11d0s6                       330  No    Okay
    c0t12d0s6                       330  No    Okay
    c0t4d0s6                        330  No    Resyncing
```

In this example, the `metastat` command displays the action to take to recover from the failed slice in the `d1` RAID 5 volume. After locating an available slice, the `metareplace` command is run, specifying the failed slice first, then the replacement slice. (If no other slices are available, run the `metareplace` command with the `-e` option to attempt to recover from possible soft errors by resynchronizing the failed device.) If multiple errors exist, the slice in the "Maintenance" state must first be replaced or enabled. Then the slice in the "Last Erred" state can be repaired. After the `metareplace` command, the `metastat` command monitors the progress of the resynchronization. During the replacement, the state of the volume and the new slice will is "Resyncing." You can continue to use the volume while it is in this state.

Note – You can use the `metareplace` command on non-failed devices to change a disk slice or other component. This procedure can be useful for tuning the performance of RAID 5 volumes.

## CHAPTER 15

Hot Spare Pools (Overview)

This chapter explains how Solaris Volume Manager uses hot spare pools. For information about performing related tasks, see Chapter 16.

This chapter contains the following information:

Overview of Hot Spares and Hot Spare Pools

A *hot spare pool* is collection of slices (*hot spares*) that Solaris Volume Manager uses to provide increased data availability for RAID 1 (mirror) and RAID 5 volumes. In the event of a slice failure in either a submirror or a RAID 5 volume, Solaris Volume Manager automatically substitutes the hot spare for the failed slice.

Note – Hot spares do not apply to RAID 0 volumes or one-way mirrors. For automatic substitution to work, redundant data must be available.

A hot spare cannot be used to hold data or state database replicas while it is idle. A hot spare must remain ready for immediate use in the event of a slice failure in the volume with which it is associated. To use hot spares, you must invest in additional disks beyond those disks that the system actually requires to function.

Hot Spares

A hot spare is a slice (not a volume) that is functional and available, but not in use. A hot spare is reserved, meaning that it stands ready to substitute for a failed slice in a submirror or RAID 5 volume.

Hot spares provide protection from hardware failure because slices from RAID 1 or RAID 5 volumes are automatically replaced and resynchronized when they fail. The hot spare can be used temporarily until a failed submirror or RAID 5 volume slice can be either fixed or replaced.

You create hot spares within hot spare pools. Individual hot spares can be included in one or more hot spare pools. For example, you might have two submirrors and two hot spares. The hot spares can be arranged as two hot spare pools, with each pool having the two hot spares in a different order of preference. This strategy enables you to specify which hot spare is used first, and it improves availability by having more hot spares available.

A submirror or RAID 5 volume can use only a hot spare whose size is equal to or greater than the size of the failed slice in the submirror or RAID 5 volume. If, for example, you have a submirror made of 1 Gbyte drives, a hot spare for the submirror must be 1 Gbyte or greater.

How Hot Spares Work

When a slice in a submirror or RAID 5 volume fails, a slice from the associated hot spare pool is used to replace it. Solaris Volume Manager searches the hot spare pool for a hot spare based on the order in which hot spares were added to the hot spare pool. The first hot spare found that is large enough is used as a replacement. The order of hot spares in the hot spare pools is not changed when a replacement occurs.

Tip – When you add hot spares to a hot spare pool, add them from smallest to largest. This strategy avoids potentially wasting "large" hot spares as replacements for small slices.

When the slice experiences an I/O error, the failed slice is placed in the "Broken" state. To fix this condition, first repair or replace the failed slice. Then, bring the slice back to the "Available" state by using the Enhanced Storage tool within the Solaris Management Console or the `metahs -e` command.

When a submirror or RAID 5 volume is using a hot spare in place of an failed slice and that failed slice is enabled or replaced, the hot spare is then marked "Available" in the hot spare pool, and is again ready for use.

Hot Spare Pools

A hot spare pool is an ordered list (collection) of hot spares.

You can place hot spares into one or more pools to get the most flexibility and protection from the fewest slices. That is, you could put a single slice designated for use as a hot spare into multiple pools, each hot spare pool having different slices and characteristics. Then, you could assign a hot spare pool to any number of submirror volumes or RAID 5 volumes.

Note – You can assign a single hot spare pool to multiple submirrors or RAID 5 volumes. On the other hand, a submirror or a RAID 5 volume can be associated with only one hot spare pool.

When I/O errors occur, Solaris Volume Manager checks the hot spare pool for the first available hot spare whose size is equal to or greater than the size of the slice that is being replaced. If found, Solaris Volume Manager changes the hot spare's status to "In-Use" and automatically resynchronizes the data. In the case of a mirror, the hot spare is resynchronized with data from a good submirror. In the case of a RAID 5 volume, the hot spare is resynchronized with the other slices in the volume. If a slice of adequate size is not found in the list of hot spares, the submirror or RAID 5 volume that failed goes into a failed state and the hot spares remain unused. In the case of the submirror, the submirror no longer replicates the data completely. In the case of the RAID 5 volume, data redundancy is no longer available.

Example—Hot Spare Pool

Figure 15–1 illustrates a hot spare pool, hsp000, that is associated with submirrors d11 and d12 in mirror d1. If a slice in either submirror were to fail, a hot spare would automatically be substituted for the failed slice. The hot spare pool itself is associated with each submirror volume, not the mirror. The hot spare pool could also be associated with other submirrors or RAID 5 volumes, if desired.

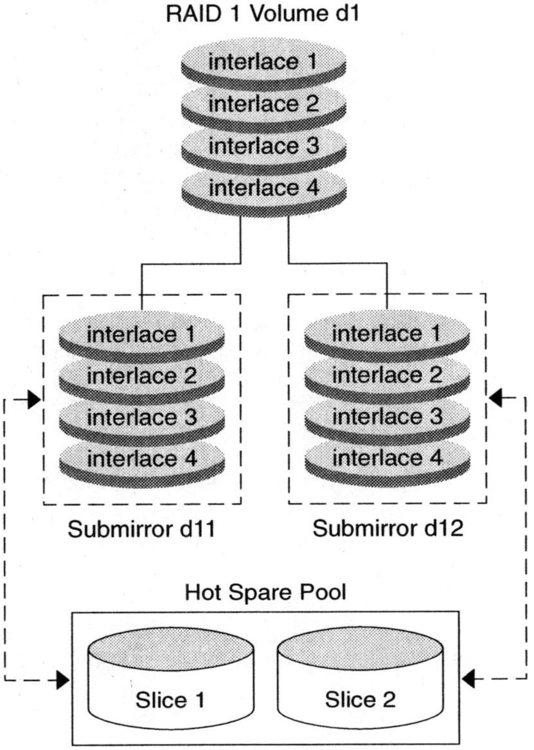

FIGURE 15–1 Hot Spare Pool Example

Administering Hot Spare Pools

Solaris Volume Manager enables you to dynamically add, delete, replace, and enable hot spares within hot spare pools. You can use either the Solaris Management Console or the command-line utilities to administer hot spares and hot spare pools. See Chapter 16 for details on these tasks.

Scenario—Hot Spares

Hot spares provide extra protection for redundant volumes (RAID 1 and RAID 5) to help guard against data loss. By associating hot spares with the underlying slices that comprise your RAID 0 submirrors or RAID 5 configuration, you can have the system automatically replace failed slices with good slices from the hot spare pool. Those slices that were swapped into use are updated with the information they should have, then can continue to function just like the original. You can replace them at your convenience.

## CHAPTER 16

Hot Spare Pools (Tasks)

This chapter explains how to work with Solaris Volume Manager's hot spares and hot spare pools. For information about related concepts, see Chapter 15.

Hot Spare Pools (Task Map)

The following task map identifies the procedures needed to manage Solaris Volume Manager hot spare pools.

Task	Description	Instructions
Create a hot spare pool	Use the Solaris Volume Manager GUI or the `metainit` command to create a hot spare pool.	"How to Create a Hot Spare Pool" on page 154
Add slices to a hot spare pool	Use the Solaris Volume Manager GUI or the `metahs` command to add slices to a hot spare pool.	"How to Add Additional Slices to a Hot Spare Pool" on page 155
Associate a hot spare pool with a volume	Use the Solaris Volume Manager GUI or the `metaparam` command to associate a hot spare pool with a volume.	"How to Associate a Hot Spare Pool With a Volume" on page 156
Change which hot spare pool is associated with a volume	Use the Solaris Volume Manager GUI or the `metaparam` command to change which hot spare pool is associated with a volume.	"How to Change the Associated Hot Spare Pool" on page 157

Task	Description	Instructions
Check the status of hot spares and hot spare pools	Use the Solaris Volume Manager GUI, or the `metastat` or `metahs -i` commands to check the status of a hot spare or hot spare pool.	"How to Check Status of Hot Spares and Hot Spare Pools" on page 159
Replace a hot spare in a hot spare pool	Use the Solaris Volume Manager GUI or the `metahs` command to replace a hot spare in a hot spare pool.	"How to Replace a Hot Spare in a Hot Spare Pool" on page 160
Delete a hot spare from a hot spare pool	Use the Solaris Volume Manager GUI or the `metahs` command to delete a hot spare from a hot spare pool.	"How to Delete a Hot Spare from a Hot Spare Pool" on page 161
Enable a hot spare	Use the Solaris Volume Manager GUI or the `metahs` command to enable a hot spare in a hot spare pool.	"How to Enable a Hot Spare" on page 162

Creating a Hot Spare Pool

▼ How to Create a Hot Spare Pool

1. **Check "Prerequisites for Creating Solaris Volume Manager Elements" on page 46.**

2. **To create a hot spare pool, use one of the following methods:**

   - From the Enhanced Storage tool within the Solaris Management Console, open the Hot Spare Pools node, then choose Action->Create Hot Spare Pool. For more information, see the online help.

   - Use the following form of the `metainit` command:

     `metainit` *hot-spare-pool-name ctds-for-slice*

     where *ctds-for-slice* is repeated for each slice in the hot spare pool. See the `metainit`(1M) man page for more information.

Note – The `metahs` command can also be used to create hot spare pools.

Example—Creating a Hot Spare Pool

```
# metainit hsp001 c2t2d0s2 c3t2d0s2
hsp001: Hotspare pool is setup
```

In this example, the hot spare pool hsp001 contains two disks as the hot spares. The system confirms that the hot spare pool has been set up.

Caution – Solaris Volume Manager will not warn you if you create a hot spare that is not large enough. If the hot spare is not equal to, or larger than, the volume to which it is attached, the hot spare will not work.

Where to Go From Here

To add more hot spares to the hot spare pool, see "How to Add Additional Slices to a Hot Spare Pool" on page 155. After you create the hot spare pool, you need to associate it with a submirror or RAID 5 volume. See "How to Associate a Hot Spare Pool With a Volume" on page 156.

▼ How to Add Additional Slices to a Hot Spare Pool

1. **Check "Prerequisites for Creating Solaris Volume Manager Elements" on page 46.**

2. **To add a slice to an existing hot spare pool, use one of the following methods:**

   - From the Enhanced Storage tool within the Solaris Management Console, open the Hot Spare Pools node, then choose the hot spare pool you want to change. Choose Action->Properties, then choose the Components panel. For more information, see the online help.

   - Use the following form of the metahs command:

     metahs -a *hot-spare-pool-name slice-to-add*

     Use -a for *hot-spare-pool-name* to add the slice to the specified hot spare pool.

     Use -all for *hot-spare-pool-name* to add the slice to all hot spare pools. See the metahs(1M) man page for more information.

Note – You can add a hot spare to one or more hot spare pools. When you add a hot spare to a hot spare pool, it is added to the end of the list of slices in the hot spare pool.

Example—Adding a Hot Spare Slice to One Hot Spare Pool

```
# metahs -a hsp001 /dev/dsk/c3t0d0s2
hsp001: Hotspare is added
```

In this example, the -a option adds the slice /dev/dsk/c3t0d0s2 to hot spare pool
hsp001. The system verifies that the slice has been added to the hot spare pool.

Example—Adding a Hot Spare Slice to All Hot Spare Pools

```
# metahs -a -all /dev/dsk/c3t0d0s2
hsp001: Hotspare is added
hsp002: Hotspare is added
hsp003: Hotspare is added
```

In this example, the -a and -all options add the slice /dev/dsk/c3t0d0s2 to all
hot spare pools configured on the system. The system verifies that the slice has been
added to all hot spare pools.

Associating a Hot Spare Pool With Volumes

▼ How to Associate a Hot Spare Pool With a Volume

1. **Check "Prerequisites for Creating Solaris Volume Manager Elements" on page 46.**

2. **To associate a hot spare pool with a RAID 5 volume or submirror, use one of the following methods:**

   - From the Enhanced Storage tool within the Solaris Management Console, open the
     Volumes and choose a volume. Choose Action->Properties, then choose the Hot
     Spare Pool panel and Attach HSP. For more information, see the online help.

   - Use the following form of the metaparam command:

     metaparam -h *hot-spare-pool* *component*

-h	Specifies to modify the hot spare pool named.
hot-spare-pool	Is the name of the hot spare pool.
component	Is the name of the submirror or RAID 5 volume to which the hot spare pool is being attached.

     See the metaparam(1M) man page for more information.

Example—Associating a Hot Spare Pool With Submirrors

```
# metaparam -h hsp100 d10
# metaparam -h hsp100 d11
# metastat d0
d0: Mirror
    Submirror 0: d10
      State: Okay
    Submirror 1: d11
      State: Okay
...


d10: Submirror of d0
    State: Okay
    Hot spare pool: hsp100
...


d11: Submirror of d0
    State: Okay
    Hot spare pool: hsp100
...
```

The -h option associates a hot spare pool, hsp100, with two submirrors, d10 and d11, of mirror, d0. The metastat command shows that the hot spare pool is associated with the submirrors.

Example—Associating a Hot Spare Pool With a RAID 5 Volume

```
# metaparam -h hsp001 d10
# metastat d10
d10: RAID
    State: Okay
    Hot spare pool: hsp001
...
```

The -h option associates a hot spare pool named hsp001 with a RAID 5 volume named d10. The metastat command shows that the hot spare pool is associated with the RAID 5 volume.

▼ How to Change the Associated Hot Spare Pool

1. **Check "Prerequisites for Creating Solaris Volume Manager Elements" on page 46.**

2. **To change a volume's associated hot spare pool, use one of the following methods:**

- From the Enhanced Storage tool within the Solaris Management Console, open the Volumes node and choose the volume. Choose Action->Properties, then choose the Hot Spare Pool panel. Detach the unwanted hot spare pool and detach the new hot spare pool by following the instructions. For more information, see the online help.

- Use the following form of the `metaparam` command:

  `metaparam -h` *hot-spare-pool-name RAID5-volume-or-submirror-name*

`-h`	Specifies to modify the hot spare pool named.
hot-spare-pool	Is the name of the new hot spare pool, or the special keyword `none` to remove hot spare pool associations.
component	Is the name of the submirror or RAID 5 volume to which the hot spare pool is being attached.

  See the `metaparam`(1M) man page for more information.

Example—Changing the Hot Spare Pool Association

```
# metastat d4
d4: RAID
    State: Okay
    Hot spare pool: hsp001
. . .
# metaparam -h hsp002 d4
# metastat d4
d4: RAID
    State: Okay
    Hot spare pool: hsp002
. . .
```

In this example, the hot spare pool `hsp001` is initially associated with a RAID 5 volume named d4. The hot spare pool association is changed to `hsp002`. The `metastat` command shows the hot spare pool association before and after this change.

Example—Removing the Hot Spare Pool Association

```
# metastat d4
d4: RAID
    State: Okay
    Hot spare pool: hsp001
. . .
# metaparam -h none d4
# metastat d4
d4: RAID
    State: Okay
    Hot spare pool:
```

. . .

In this example, the hot spare pool hsp001 is initially associated with a RAID 5 volume named d4. The hot spare pool association is changed to none, which indicates that no hot spare pool should be associated with this device. The metastat command shows the hot spare pool association before and after this change.

Maintaining Hot Spare Pools

▼ How to Check Status of Hot Spares and Hot Spare Pools

● **To view the status of a hot spare pool and its hot spares, use one of the following methods:**

- From the Enhanced Storage tool within the Solaris Management Console, open the Hot Spare Pools node and select a hot spare pool. Choose Action->Properties to get detailed status information. For more information, see the online help.

- Run the following form of the metastat command:

  metastat *hot-spare-pool-name*

Note – The metahs command can also be used to check the status of hot spare pool.

Example—Viewing Hot Spare Pool Status

Here is sample output from the metastat command on a hot spare pool.

```
# metastat hsp001
hsp001: 1 hot spare
        c1t3d0s2                Available       16800 blocks
```

Hot Spare Pool States

The following table explains hot spare pool states and possible actions to take.

TABLE 16-1 Hot Spare Pool States (Command Line)

State	Meaning	Action
Available	The hot spares are running and ready to accept data, but are not currently being written to or read from.	None.
In-use	This hot spare pool includes slices that have been used to replace failed components in a redundant volume.	Diagnose how the hot spares are being used. Then, repair the slice in the volume for which the hot spare is being used.
Broken	There is a problem with a hot spare or hot spare pool, but there is no immediate danger of losing data. This status is also displayed if all the hot spares are in use or if any hot spares are broken.	Diagnose how the hot spares are being used or why they are broken. You can add more hot spares to the hot spare pool, if desired.

▼ How to Replace a Hot Spare in a Hot Spare Pool

1. **Verify whether the hot spare is currently being used by using one of the following methods:**

   - From the Enhanced Storage tool within the Solaris Management Console, open the Hot Spare Pools node and select a hot spare pool. Choose Action->Properties, then choose the Hot Spares panel and follow the instructions. For more information, see the online help.

   - Use the following form of the `metastat` command:

     `metastat` *hot-spare-pool-name*

     See the `metastat`(1M) man page.

2. **To replace the hot spare, use one of the following methods:**

   - From the Enhanced Storage tool within the Solaris Management Console, open the Hot Spare Pools node and select a hot spare pool. Choose Action->Properties, then choose the Hot Spares panel and follow the instructions. For more information, see the online help.

   - Use the following form of the `metahs` command:

     `metahs -r` *hot-spare-pool-name current-hot-spare replacement-hot-spare*

`-r`	Specifies to replace disks in the hot spare pool named.
hot-spare-pool	Is the name of the hot spare pool, or the special keyword `all` to change all hot spare pool associations.
current-hot-spare	Is the name of the current hot spare that will be replaced.

replacement-hot-spare Is the name of the slice to take the place of the current hot spare in the named pools.

See the `metahs`(1M) man page for more information.

Example—Replacing a Hot Spare in One Hot Spare Pool

```
# metastat hsp003
hsp003: 1 hot spare
        c0t2d0s2                      Broken          5600 blocks
# metahs -r hsp003 c0t2d0s2 c3t1d0s2
hsp003: Hotspare c0t2d0s2 is replaced with c3t1d0s2
```

In this example, the `metastat` command makes sure that the hot spare is not in use. The `metahs -r` command replaces hot spare `/dev/dsk/c0t2d0s2` with `/dev/dsk/c3t1d0s2` in the hot spare pool `hsp003`.

Example—Replacing a Hot Spare in All Associated Hot Spare Pools

```
# metahs -r all c1t0d0s2 c3t1d0s2
hsp001: Hotspare c1t0d0s2 is replaced with c3t1d0s2
hsp002: Hotspare c1t0d0s2 is replaced with c3t1d0s2
hsp003: Hotspare c1t0d0s2 is replaced with c3t1d0s2
```

In this example, the keyword `all` replaces hot spare `/dev/dsk/c1t0d0s2` with `/dev/dsk/c3t1d0s2` in all its associated hot spare pools.

▼ How to Delete a Hot Spare from a Hot Spare Pool

1. **Verify whether the hot spare is currently being used by using one of the following methods:**

   - From the Enhanced Storage tool within the Solaris Management Console, open the Hot Spare Pools node and select a hot spare pool. Choose Action->Properties, then choose the Hot Spares panel and follow the instructions. For more information, see the online help.

   - Use the following form of the `metastat` command:

     `metastat` *hot-spare-pool-name*

     See the `metastat`(1M) man page.

2. **To delete the hot spare, use one of the following methods:**

- From the Enhanced Storage tool within the Solaris Management Console, open the Hot Spare Pools node and select a hot spare pool. Choose Action->Properties, then choose the Hot Spares panel and follow the instructions. For more information, see the online help.

- Use the following form of the `metahs` command:

  `metahs -d` *hot-spare-pool-name current-hot-spare*

`-d`	Specifies to delete a hot spare from the hot spare pool named.
hot-spare-pool	Is the name of the hot spare pool, or the special keyword `all` to delete from all hot spare pools.
current-hot-spare	Is the name of the current hot spare that will be deleted.

  See the `metahs`(1M) man page for more information.

Example—Deleting a Hot Spare from One Hot Spare Pool

```
# metastat hsp003
hsp003: 1 hot spare
        c0t2d0s2                        Broken          5600 blocks
# metahs -d hsp003 c0t2d0s2
```

In this example, the `metastat` command makes sure that the hot spare is not in use. The `metahs -d` command deletes hot spare `/dev/dsk/c0t2d0s2` in the hot spare pool `hsp003`.

▼ How to Enable a Hot Spare

- **To return a hot spare to the "available" state, use one of the following methods:**

  - From the Enhanced Storage tool within the Solaris Management Console, open the Hot Spare Pools node and select a hot spare pool. Choose Action->Properties, then the Hot Spares panel and follow the instructions. For more information, see the online help.

  - Use the following form of the `metahs` command:

    `metahs -e` *hot-spare-slice*

`-e`	Specifies to enable a hot spare.
hot-spare-slice	Is the name of the slice to enable.

    For more information, see the `metahs`(1M) man page.

Example—Enabling a Hot Spare

```
# metahs -e c0t0d0s2
```

In this example, the command places the hot spare /dev/dsk/c0t0d0s2 in the "Available" state after it has been repaired. It is unnecessary to specify a hot spare pool.

## CHAPTER 17

Transactional Volumes (Overview)

This chapter provides conceptual information about two types of file system logging, transactional volumes and UFS logging. For information about performing tasks related to transactional volumes, see Chapter 18. For more information about UFS logging, see "Mounting and Unmounting File Systems (Tasks)" in *System Administration Guide: Basic Administration*.

This chapter includes the following information:

Note – Transactional volumes are scheduled to be removed from the Solaris operating environment in an upcoming Solaris release. UFS logging, available since the Solaris 8 release, provides the same capabilities but superior performance, as well as lower system administration requirements and overhead. These benefits provide a clear choice for optimal performance and capabilities.

About File System Logging

Transactional volumes and UFS logging are two types of file system logging.

File system logging describes writing file system updates to a log before applying the updates to a UFS file system. Once a transaction is recorded in the log, the transaction information can be applied to the file system later. For example, if a user creates a new directory, the `mkdir` command will be logged, then applied to the file system.

At reboot, the system discards incomplete transactions, but applies the transactions for completed operations. The file system remains consistent because only completed transactions are ever applied. Because the file system is never inconsistent, it does not need checking by the `fsck` command.

A system crash can interrupt current system calls and introduce inconsistencies into an unlogged UFS. If you mount a UFS without running the `fsck` command, these inconsistencies can cause panics or corrupt data.

Checking large file systems takes a long time, because it requires reading and verifying the file system data. With UFS logging, UFS file systems do not have to be checked at boot time because the changes from unfinished system calls are discarded.

Choosing a Logging Method

UFS logging and *transactional volumes* provide the same capability of keeping a log of file system information. The only significant differences between the two methods are the following:

- Transactional volumes can write log information onto physically separate devices, while UFS logging combines logs and file systems on the same volume.
- UFS logging offers superior performance to transactional volumes in all cases.
- UFS logging allows logging of all UFS file systems, including root (/), while transactional volumes cannot log the root (/) file system.

Note – Transactional volumes are scheduled to be removed from the Solaris operating environment in an upcoming Solaris release. UFS logging, available since the Solaris 8 release, provides the same capabilities but superior performance, as well as lower system administration requirements and overhead. These benefits provide a clear choice for optimal performance and capabilities.

To enable UFS logging, use the `mount_ufs -logging` option on the file system, or add `logging` to the mount options for the file system in the `/etc/vfstab` file. For more information about mounting file systems with UFS logging enabled, see "Mounting and Unmounting File Systems (Tasks)" in *System Administration Guide: Basic Administration* and the `mount_ufs`(1M) man page.

To learn more about using transactional volumes, continue reading this document.

Note – If you are not currently logging UFS file systems but want to use this feature, choose UFS logging, rather than transactional volumes.

Transactional Volumes

A *transactional volume* is a volume that is used to manage file system logging, which is essentially the same as UFS logging. Both methods record UFS updates in a log before the updates are applied to the file system.

A transactional volume consists of two devices:

- The *master device* is a slice or volume that contains the file system that is being logged.

- The *log device* is a slice or volume that contains the log and can be shared by several file systems. The log is a sequence of records, each of which describes a change to a file system.

Caution – A log device or a master device can be a physical slice or a volume. However, to improve reliability and availability, use RAID 1 volumes (mirrors) for log devices. A device error on a physical log device could cause data loss. You can also use RAID 1 or RAID 5 volumes as master devices.

Logging begins automatically when the transactional volume is mounted, provided the transactional volume has a log device. The master device can contain an existing UFS file system (because creating a transactional volume does not alter the master device). Or, you can create a file system on the transactional volume later. Likewise, clearing a transactional volume leaves the UFS file system on the master device intact.

After you configure a transactional volume, you can use it as though it were a physical slice or another logical volume. For information about creating a transactional volume, see "Creating Transactional Volumes" on page 175.

Example—Transactional Volume

The following figure shows a transactional volume, d1, which consists of a master device, d3, and a mirrored log device, d30.

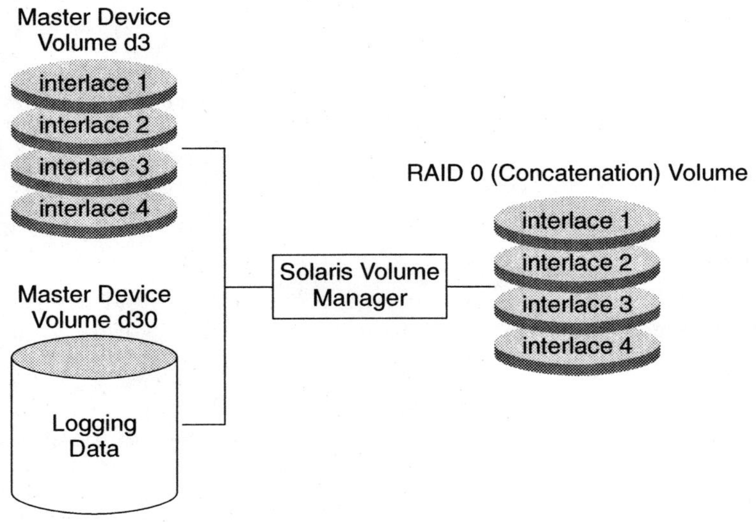

FIGURE 17–1 Transactional Volume Example

Example—Shared Log Device

The following figure shows two transactional volumes, d1 and d2, sharing a mirrored log device, d30. Each master device is also a RAID 1 volume, as is the shared log device.

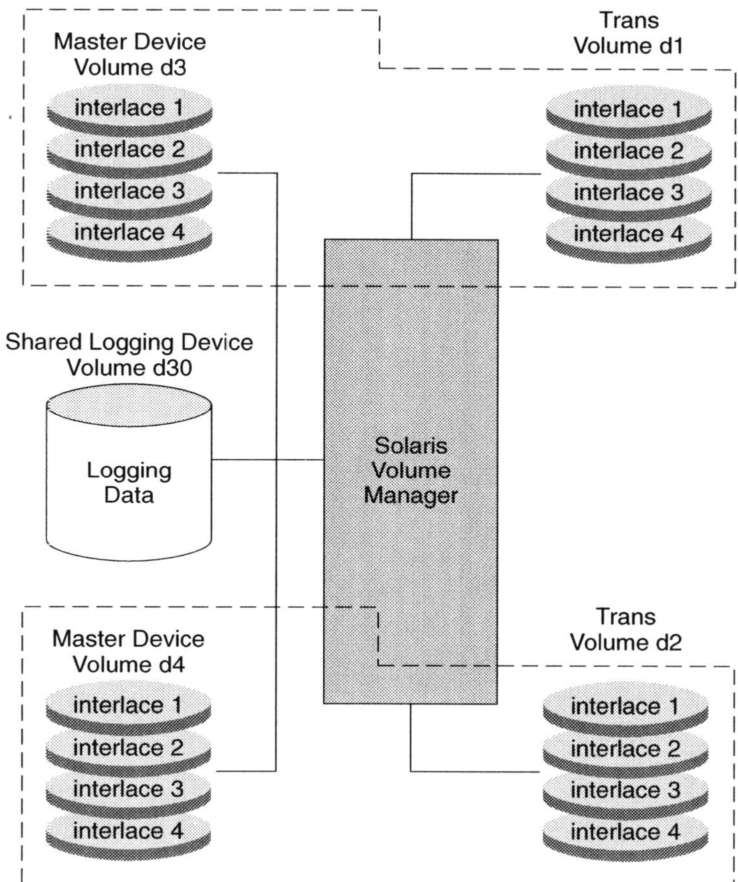

FIGURE 17–2 Shared Log Transactional Volume Example

Background Information for Transactional Volumes

When you are working with transactional volumes, consider the following "Requirements for Working with Transactional Volumes" on page 170 and "Guidelines for Working with Transactional Volumes" on page 170.

Requirements for Working with Transactional Volumes

Before you can work with transactional volumes, note the following requirements:

- Before you create transactional volumes, identify the slices or volume to be used as the master devices and log devices.

- Log any UFS file system except root (/).

- Use a mirrored log device for data redundancy.

- Do not place logs on heavily used disks.

- Plan for a minimum of 1 Mbyte of storage space for logs. (Larger logs permit more simultaneous file system transactions.) Plan on using an additional 1 Mbyte of log space per 100 Mbytes of file system data, up to a maximum recommended log size of 64 Mbytes. Although the maximum possible log size is 1 Gbyte, logs larger than 64 Mbytes are rarely fully used and often waste storage space.

- The log device and the master device of the same transactional volume should be located on separate drives and possibly separate controllers to help balance the I/O load.

- Transactional volumes can share log devices. However, heavily used file systems should have separate logs. The disadvantage of sharing a log device is that certain errors require that all file systems that share the log device must be checked with the `fsck` command.

- Once you set up a transactional volume, you can share the log device among file systems.

- Logs (log devices) are typically accessed frequently. For best performance, avoid placing logs on disks with high usage. You might also want to place logs in the middle of a disk, to minimize the average seek times when accessing the log.

- The larger the log size, the better the performance. Larger logs allow for greater concurrency (more simultaneous file system operations per second).

Note – Mirroring log devices is strongly recommended. Losing the data in a log device because of device errors can leave a file system in an inconsistent state that `fsck` might be unable to fix without user intervention. Using a RAID 1 volume for the master device is a good idea to ensure data redundancy.

Guidelines for Working with Transactional Volumes

- Generally, you should log your largest UFS file systems and the UFS file system whose data changes most often. It is probably not necessary to log small file systems with mostly read-only activity.

- If no slice is available for the log device, you can still configure a transactional volume. This strategy might be useful if you plan to log exported file systems when you do not have a spare slice for the log device. When a slice is available, you only need to attach it as a log device.

- Consider sharing a log device among file systems if your system does not have many available slices, or if the file systems sharing the log device are primarily read, not written.

Caution – When one master device of a shared log device goes into a failed state, the log device is unable to roll its changes forward. This problem causes all master devices sharing the log device to go into the hard error state.

Scenario—Transactional Volumes

Transactional volumes provide logging capabilities for UFS file systems, similar to UFS Logging. The following example, drawing on the sample system explained in Chapter 4, describes how transactional volumes can help speed reboot by providing file system logging.

Note – Unless your situation requires the special capabilities of transactional volumes, specifically the ability to log to a different device than the logged device, consider using UFS logging instead. UFS logging provides superior performance to transactional volumes.

The sample system has several logical volumes that should be logged to provide maximum uptime and availability, including the root (/) and /var mirrors. By configuring transactional volumes to log to a third RAID 1 volume, you can provide redundancy and speed the reboot process.

## CHAPTER 18

Transactional Volumes (Tasks)

This chapter provides information about performing tasks that are associated with transactional volumes. For information about the concepts involved in these tasks, see Chapter 17.

Note – Transactional volumes are scheduled to be removed from the Solaris operating environment in an upcoming Solaris release. UFS logging, available since the Solaris 8 release, provides the same capabilities but superior performance, as well as lower system administration requirements and overhead. These benefits provide a clear choice for optimal performance and capabilities.

Transactional Volumes (Task Map)

The following task map identifies the procedures needed to manage Solaris Volume Manager transactional volumes.

Task	Description	Instructions
Create a transactional volume	Use the Solaris Volume Manager GUI or the `metainit` command to create a transactional volume.	"How to Create a Transactional Volume" on page 175
Convert transactional volumes to UFS logging	Use the `metaclear` and `mount` commands to clear a transactional volume and mount the file system with UFS logging.	"How to Convert a Transactional Volume to UFS Logging" on page 178

Task	Description	Instructions
Check the status of transactional volumes	Use the Solaris Volume Manager GUI or the `metastat` command to check the status of a transactional volume.	"How to Check the State of Transactional Volumes " on page 182
Attach a log device to a transactional volume	Use the Solaris Volume Manager GUI or the `metattach` command to attach a log device.	"How to Attach a Log Device to a Transactional Volume" on page 184
Detach a log device from a transactional volume	Use the Solaris Volume Manager GUI or the `metadetach` command to detach a log device.	"How to Detach a Log Device from a Transactional Volume" on page 185
Expand a transactional volume	Use the Solaris Volume Manager GUI or the `metattach` command to expand a transactional volume.	"How to Expand a Transactional Volume" on page 186
Delete a transactional volume	Use the Solaris Volume Manager GUI, the `metadetach` command, or the `metarename` command to delete a transactional volume.	"How to Remove a Transactional Volume" on page 187
Delete a transactional volume and retain the mount point	Use the Solaris Volume Manager GUI or the `metadetach` command to delete a transactional volume.	"How to Remove a Transactional Volume and Retain the Mount Device" on page 188
Share a log device	Use the Solaris Volume Manager GUI or the `metainit` command to share a transactional volume log device.	"How to Share a Log Device Among File Systems" on page 191
Recover a transactional volume with a file system panic	Use the `fsck` command to recover a transactional volume with a panic.	"How to Recover a Transactional Volume With a Panic" on page 192
Recover a transactional volume with hard errors	Use the `fsck` command to recover a transactional volume with hard errors.	"How to Recover a Transactional Volume With Hard Errors" on page 193

Creating Transactional Volumes

Note – Transactional volumes are scheduled to be removed from the Solaris operating environment in an upcoming Solaris release. UFS logging, available since the Solaris 8 release, provides the same capabilities but superior performance, as well as lower system administration requirements and overhead. These benefits provide a clear choice for optimal performance and capabilities.

▼ How to Create a Transactional Volume

1. **Check "Prerequisites for Creating Solaris Volume Manager Elements" on page 46 and "Background Information for Transactional Volumes" on page 169.**

2. **If possible, unmount the UFS file system for which you want to enable logging.**

   # `umount` */export*

   Note – If the file system cannot be unmounted, you can continue, but will have to reboot the system before the transactional volume can be active.

   ---

3. **Create the transactional volume by using one of the following methods:**

   - From the Enhanced Storage tool within the Solaris Management Console, open the Volumes node, then choose Action->Create Volume and follow the instructions in the wizard. For more information, see the online help.

   - Use the following form of the `metainit` command:

     `metainit` *trans-volume* `-t` *master-device* *log-device*

     - *trans-volume* is the name of the transactional volume to create.
     - *master-device* is the name of the device containing the file system you want to log.
     - *log-device* is the name of the device that will contain the log.

     The master device and log device can be either slices or logical volumes. See the `metainit`(1M) man page for more information.

     For example, to create a transactional volume (`d10`) logging the file system on slice `c0t0d0s6` to a log on `c0t0d0s7`, use the following syntax:

     ```
     # metainit d10 -t c0t0d0s6 c0t0d0s7
     ```

Note – You can use the same log device (c0t0d0s7 in this example) for several master devices. The sharing of log devices is fully supported.

---

4. **Edit the** /etc/vfstab **file so that the existing UFS file system information is replaced with that of the created transactional volume.**

   For example, if /export was on c0t0d0s6, and the new transactional volume is d10, edit /etc/vfstab as shown here, so the mount points to the transactional volume rather than to the raw disk slice:

   ```
   #/dev/dsk/c0t0d0s5    /dev/rdsk/c0t0d0s5    /export  ufs   2       yes    -
   /dev/md/dsk/d10    /dev/md/rdsk/d10    /export  ufs   2       yes    -
   ```

5. **If possible, remount the file system.**

Note – If you are creating a transactional volume for a file system that cannot be unmounted, such as /usr, then reboot the system now to remount the transactional volume and start logging.

Example—Creating a Transactional Volume for a Slice

```
# umount /home1
# metainit d63 -t c0t2d0s2 c2t2d0s1
d63: Trans is setup
     (Edit the /etc/vfstab file so that the file system references the transactional volume)
# mount /home1
```

The slice /dev/dsk/c0t2d0s2 contains a file system mounted on /home1. The slice that will contain the log device is /dev/dsk/c2t2d0s1. First, the file system is unmounted. The metainit command with the -t option creates the transactional volume, d63.

Next, the /etc/vfstab file must be edited to change the entry for the file system to reference the transactional volume. For example, the following line:

```
/dev/dsk/c0t2d0s2 /dev/rdsk/c0t2d0s2 /home1 ufs 2 yes -
```

should be changed to:

```
/dev/md/dsk/d63 /dev/md/rdsk/d63 /home1 ufs 2 yes -
```

Logging becomes effective for the file system when it is remounted.

On subsequent reboots, instead of checking the file system, the fsck command displays a log message for the transactional volume:

```
# reboot
. . .
```

```
/dev/md/rdsk/d63: is logging
```

Example—Creating a Transactional Volume for /usr

```
# metainit -f d20 -t c0t3d0s6 c1t2d0s1
d20: Trans is setup
    (Edit the /etc/vfstab file so that the file system references the transactional volume)
# reboot
```

Slice /dev/dsk/c0t3d0s6 contains the /usr file system. The slice that will contain the log device is /dev/dsk/c1t2d0s1. Because /usr cannot be unmounted, the metainit command is run with the -f option to force the creation of the transactional volume, d20. Next, the line in the /etc/vfstab file that mounts the file system must be changed to reference the transactional volume. For example, the following line:

```
/dev/dsk/c0t3d0s6 /dev/rdsk/c0t3d0s6 /usr ufs 1 no -
```

should be changed to:

```
/dev/md/dsk/d20 /dev/md/rdsk/d20 /usr ufs 1 no -
```

Logging becomes effective for the file system when the system is rebooted.

Example—Creating a Transactional Volume for a Logical Volume

```
# umount /home1
# metainit d64 -t d30 d12
d64: Trans is setup
    (Edit the /etc/vfstab file so that the file system references the transactional volume)
# mount /home1
```

RAID 1 volume d30 contains a file system that is mounted on /home1. The mirror that will contain the log device is d12. First, the file system is unmounted. The metainit command with the -t option creates the transactional volume, d64.

Next, the line in the /etc/vfstab file that mounts the file system must be changed to reference the transactional volume. For example, the following line:

```
/dev/md/dsk/d30 /dev/md/rdsk/d30 /home1 ufs 2 yes -
```

should be changed to:

```
/dev/md/dsk/d64 /dev/md/rdsk/d64 /home1 ufs 2 yes -
```

Logging becomes effective for the file system when the file system is remounted.

On subsequent file system remounts or system reboots, instead of checking the file system, the fsck command displays a log message for the transactional volume:

```
# reboot
...
/dev/md/rdsk/d64: is logging
```

Note – To avoid editing the `/etc/vfstab` file, you can use the `metarename`(1M) command to exchange the name of the original logical volume and the new transactional volume. For more information, see "Renaming Volumes" on page 221.

Converting Transactional Volumes to UFS Logging

Converting any existing transactional volumes on your system to use UFS logging could improve performance and maintainability. Additionally, because transactional volumes will not be supported at some time in the future, you will eventually need to move to UFS logging. The following section outlines the conversion process.

How to Convert a Transactional Volume to UFS Logging

Note – You must have at least one Mbyte of free space (using default system settings) to convert to UFS logging, because the log requires some space and resides on the logged volume. If you do not have sufficient free space, you will have to remove files or grow your file system before you can complete this conversion process.

▼ To Convert a Transactional Volume to Use UFS Logging

1. **Identify transactional volumes and their associated log devices by using the** `metastat` **command and looking for** `Trans` **and** `Logging device` **in the output.**

```
# metastat
d2: Trans
    State: Okay
    Size: 2869209 blocks
    Master Device: d0
    Logging Device: d20

d20: Logging device for d2
```

```
      State: Okay
      Size: 28470 blocks

d20: Concat/Stripe
      Size: 28728 blocks
      Stripe 0: (interlace: 32 blocks)
          Device                   Start Block  Dbase State          Reloc  Hot Spare
          d10                             0      No    Okay           No
          d11                             0      No    Okay           No
          d12
```

Note the names for these devices for later use.

2. **Check to see if the `Trans device` is currently mounted by using the `df` command and searching for the name of the transactional volume in the output. If the transactional volume is not mounted, go to Step 7.**

```
# df | grep d2
/mnt/transvolume     (/dev/md/dsk/d2   ): 2782756 blocks    339196 files
```

3. **Verify adequate free space on the transactional volume by using the `df -k` command.**

```
# df -k /mnt/transvolume
file system             kbytes      used    avail capacity  Mounted on
/dev/md/dsk/d2          1391387    91965 1243767     7%     /mnt/transvolume
```

4. **Stop all activity on the file system, either by halting applications or bringing the system to the single user mode.**

```
# init s
[roct@lexicon:lexicon-setup]$ init s
INIT: New run level: S
The system is coming down for administration.  Please wait.
Dec 11 08:14:43 lexicon syslogd: going down on signal 15
Killing user processes: done.

INIT: SINGLE USER MODE

Type control-d to proceed with normal startup,
(or give root password for system maintenance):
single-user privilege assigned to /dev/console.
Entering System Maintenance Mode

Dec 11 08:15:52 su: 'su root' succeeded for root on /dev/console
Sun Microsystems Inc.   SunOS 5.9       s81_51  May 2002
#
```

5. **Flush the log for the file system that is logged with `lockfs -f`.**

```
# /usr/sbin/lockfs -f /mnt/transvolume
```

6. **Unmount the file system.**

```
# umount /mnt/transvolume
```

7. **Clear the transactional volume that contains the file system.**

   This operation will not affect the data on the file system.

   ```
   # metaclear d2
   d2: Trans is cleared
   ```

   The Logging device, identified at the beginning of this procedure, is now unused
   and can be reused for other purposes. The master device, also identified at the
   beginning of this procedure, contains the file system and must be mounted for use.

8. **Edit the** /etc/vfstab **file to update the mount information for the file system.**

   You must change the raw and block mount points, and add logging to the options
   for that file system. With the transactional volume in use, the /etc/vfstab entry
   looks like this:

   ```
   /dev/md/dsk/d2  /dev/md/rdsk/d2 /mnt/transvolume   ufs  1   no  -
   ```

   After you update the file to change the mount point from the transactional volume d2
   to the underlying device d0, and add the logging option, that part of the
   /etc/vfstab file looks like this:

   ```
   #device        device       mount         FS    fsck    mount    mount
   #to mount      to fsck      point         type  pass    at boot  options
   #
   /dev/md/dsk/d0  /dev/md/rdsk/d0 /mnt/transvolume   ufs  1   no  logging
   ```

9. **Remount the file system.**

   ```
   # mount /mnt/transvolume
   ```

Note – The mount command might report an error, similar to"the state of
/dev/md/dsk/d0 is not okay and it was attempted to be mounted read/write. Please
run fsck and try again." If this happens, run fsck on the raw device (fsck
/dev/md/rdsk/d0 in this case), answer y to fixing the file system state in the
superblock, and try again.

---

10. **Verify that the file system is mounted with logging enabled by examining the**
    /etc/mnttab **file and confirming that the file system has logging listed as one of
    the options.**

    ```
    # grep mnt /etc/mnttab
    mnttab  /etc/mnttab      mntfs   dev=43c0000     1007575477
    /dev/md/dsk/d0  /mnt/transvolume     ufs  rw,intr,largefiles,
    logging,xattr,onerror=panic,suid,dev=1540000 1008085006
    ```

11. **If you changed to single-user mode during the process, you can now return to multiuser mode.**

Example—Converting From Transactional Volumes to UFS Logging

The following example shows the process of converting a transactional volume to UFS logging.

```
# metastat
    d50: Trans
    State: Okay
    Size: 204687 blocks
    Master Device: c1t14d0s0
    Logging Device: c1t12d0s0

        Master Device        Start Block  Dbase Reloc
        c1t14d0s0                     0   No    Yes

c1t12d0s0: Logging device for d50
    State: Okay
    Size: 30269 blocks

        Logging Device       Start Block  Dbase Reloc
        c1t12d0s0                  5641   No    Yes
```

Make note of the 'master' and 'log' devices as you will need this information in subsequent steps.

Determine if the transactional volume contains a mounted file system.

```
# df | grep d50
/home1              (/dev/md/dsk/d50   ):  161710 blocks    53701 files
```

Verify sufficient free space (more than 1 MByte)
```
# df -k /home1
filesystem             kbytes    used    avail capacity  Mounted on
/dev/md/dsk/d50         95510   14655    71304    18%    /home1
```

Go to single-user mode.

```
# /usr/sbin/lockfs -f /home1
# /usr/sbin/umount /home1
# /usr/sbin/metaclear d50
d50: Trans is cleared
```
Update /etc/vfstab file to mount underlying volume and add logging option.

```
# cat /etc/vfstab
#device             device              mount  FS   fsck   mount
mount
#to mount           to fsck             point  type pass   at boot
options
```

```
/dev/dsk/c1t14d0s0  /dev/rdsk/c1t14d0s0  /home1  ufs  2        yes
logging

# mount /home1
# /usr/bin/grep /home1 /etc/mnttab
/dev/dsk/c1t14d0s0       /home1  ufs
rw,intr,largefiles,logging,xattr,onerror=panic,suid,dev=740380
1008019906
```
Return to multi-user mode.

Maintaining Transactional Volumes

▼ How to Check the State of Transactional Volumes

● **To check the status of a transactional volume, use one of the following methods:**

- From the Enhanced Storage tool within the Solaris Management Console, open the Volumes node, then view the status of the volumes. Right-click a transactional volume and choose Properties for more detailed status information. For more information, see the online help.

- Use the `metastat` command.

  For more information, see the `metastat`(1M) man page.

Example—Checking the Status of Transactional Volumes

Here is sample transactional volume output from the `metastat` command:

```
# metastat
d20: Trans
    State: Okay
    Size: 102816 blocks
    Master Device: c0t3d0s4
    Logging Device: c0t2d0s3

        Master Device       Start Block  Dbase
        c0t3d0s4                     0   No

c0t2d0s3: Logging device for d0
    State:.Okay
    Size: 5350 blocks

        Logging Device      Start Block  Dbase
        c0t2d0s3                   250   No
```

The `metastat` command also shows master devices and log devices. For each device, the following information is displayed:

- "Device", which is the device name of the slice or volume
- "Start Block", which is the block on which the device begins
- "Dbase", which shows if the device contains a state database replica
- "State", which shows the state of the log device

The following table explains transactional volume states and possible actions to take.

TABLE 18–1 Transactional Volume States

State	Meaning	Action
Okay	The device is functioning properly. If mounted, the file system is logging and will not be checked at boot.	None.
Attaching	The log device will be attached to the transactional volume when the volume is closed or unmounted. When this occurs, the device transitions to the Okay state.	None.
Detached	The transactional volume does not have a log device. All benefits from UFS logging are disabled.	The `fsck` command automatically checks the device at boot time. See the `fsck`(1M) man page.
Detaching	The log device will be detached from the transactional volume when the volume is closed or unmounted. When this occurs, the device transitions to the Detached state.	None.
Hard Error	A device error or panic has occurred while the device was in use. An I/O error is returned for every read or write until the device is closed or unmounted. The first open causes the device to transition to the Error state.	Fix the transactional volume. See "How to Recover a Transactional Volume With a Panic" on page 192, or "How to Recover a Transactional Volume With Hard Errors" on page 193.

State	Meaning	Action
Error	The device can be read and written to. The file system can be mounted read-only. However, an I/O error is returned for every read or write that actually gets a device error. The device does not transition back to the Hard Error state, even when a later device error occurs.	Fix the transactional volume. See "How to Recover a Transactional Volume With a Panic" on page 192, or "How to Recover a Transactional Volume With Hard Errors" on page 193. Successfully completing the `fsck` or `newfs` commands transitions the device into the Okay state. When the device is in the Hard Error or Error state, the `fsck` command automatically checks and repairs the file system at boot time. The `newfs` command destroys whatever data might be on the device.

▼ How to Attach a Log Device to a Transactional Volume

1. **Check "Prerequisites for Creating Solaris Volume Manager Elements" on page 46 and "Background Information for Transactional Volumes" on page 169.**

2. **Unmount the UFS file system for which you want to enable logging.**

3. **Attach a log device to the transactional volume by using one of the following methods:**

   - From the Enhanced Storage tool within the Solaris Management Console, open the Volumes node, then choose the transactional volume from the listing. Right-click the volume, and choose Properties. For more information, see the online help.

   - Use the following form of the `metattach` command:

   `metattach` *master-volume logging-volume*

   master-volume is the name of the transactional volume that contains the file system to be logged.

   logging-volume is the name of the volume or slice that should contain the log.

   See the `metattach`(1M) man page for more information.

   ```
   # metattach d1 d23
   ```

4. **Remount the file system.**

Example—Attaching a Log Device to a Transactional Volume

This example shows a log device, the slice (`c1t1d0s1`), being attached to the transactional volume `d1`, which is mounted on `/fs2`.

```
# umount /fs2
# metattach d1 c1t1d0s1
d1: log device d0c1t1d0s1 is attached
# mount /fs2
```

▼ How to Detach a Log Device from a Transactional Volume

1. **Check "Prerequisites for Creating Solaris Volume Manager Elements" on page 46 and "Background Information for Transactional Volumes" on page 169.**

2. **Unmount the UFS file system for which you want to disable logging or change the log device.**

3. **Detach the log device from the transactional volume by using one of the following methods:**

   - From the Enhanced Storage tool within the Solaris Management Console, open the Volumes node, then choose the transactional volume from the listing. Right-click the volume, and choose Properties. For more information, see the online help.

   - Use the following form of the `metadetach` command:

     `metadetach` *master-volume*

     master-volume is the name of the transactional volume that contains the file system that is being logged.

     See the `metadetach`(1M) man page for more information.

4. **Remount the file system.**

Example—Detaching a Log Device from a Transactional Volume

This example show a log device, the slice (`c1t1d0s1`), being detached from the transactional volume `d1`, which is mounted on `/fs2`.

```
# umount /fs2
# metadetach d1
d1: log device c1t1d0s1 is detached
# mount /fs2
```

▼ How to Expand a Transactional Volume

Note – You can expand a master device within a transactional volume only when the master device is a volume (RAID 0, RAID 1, or RAID 5).

---

1. **Check "Prerequisites for Creating Solaris Volume Manager Elements" on page 46 and "Background Information for Transactional Volumes" on page 169.**

2. **If the master device is a volume (rather than a basic slice), attach additional slices to the master device by using one of the following methods:**

   - From the Enhanced Storage tool within the Solaris Management Console, open the Volumes node, then choose the transactional volume from the listing. Right-click the volume, and choose Properties, then the Components panel. For more information, see the online help.

   - Use the following form of the `metattach` command:

     `metattach` *master-volume component*

     master-volume is the name of the transactional volume that contains the file system to be logged.

     component is the name of the volume or slice that should be attached.

     See the `metattach`(1M) man page for more information.

   Note – If the master device is a mirror, you need to attach additional slices to each submirror.

   ---

3. **If the master device is a slice, you cannot expand it directly. Instead, you must do the following:**

   - Clear the existing transactional volume.
   - Put the master device's slice into a volume.
   - Recreate the transactional volume.

   Once you have completed this process, you can expand the master device as explained in the previous steps of this procedure.

Example—Expanding a RAID 1 Master Device Within a Transactional Volume

```
# metastat d10
d10: Trans
    State: Okay
```

```
      Size: 102816 blocks
      Master Device: d0
      Logging Device: d1
d0: Mirror
      Submirror 0: d11
        State: Okay
...
      Submirror 1: d12
        State: Okay
...
# metattach d11 c0t2d0s5
d11: component is attached
# metattach d12 c0t3d0s5
d12: component is attached
```

This example shows the expansion of a transactional device, d10, whose master device consists of a two-way RAID 1 volume, d0, which contains two submirrors, d11 and d12. The metattach command is run on each submirror. The system confirms that each slice was attached.

Where to Go From Here

For a UFS, run the growfs command on the transactional volume (not the master device). See "How to Grow a File System" on page 229.

An application, such as a database, that uses the raw volume must have its own way of growing the added space.

▼ How to Remove a Transactional Volume

1. **Check "Prerequisites for Creating Solaris Volume Manager Elements" on page 46 and "Background Information for Transactional Volumes" on page 169.**

2. **Unmount the UFS file system for which you want to remove the transactional volume and disable logging.**

   ```
   # umount /filesystem
   ```

3. **Detach the log device from the transactional volume by using one of the following methods:**

   - From the Enhanced Storage tool within the Solaris Management Console, open the Volumes node, then choose the transactional volume from the listing. Right-click the volume, and choose Properties. For more information, see the online help.

   - Use the following form of the metadetach command:

     ```
     metadetach master-volume
     ```

     master-volume is the name of the transactional volume that contains the file system that is being logged.

See the `metadetach`(1M) man page for more information.

4. **Remove (clear) the transactional volume by using one of the following methods:**

   - From the Enhanced Storage tool within the Solaris Management Console, open the Volumes node, then choose the transactional volume from the listing. Right-click the volume, and choose Delete. For more information, see the online help.

   - Use the following form of the `metaclear` command:

     `metaclear` *master-volume*

     See the `metaclear`(1M) man page for more information.

5. **If necessary, update `/etc/vfstab` to mount the underlying volume, rather than the transactional volume you just cleared.**

6. **Remount the file system.**

Example—Removing a Transactional Volume

This example shows the removal of a transactional volume `d1`, which was mounted on `/fs2`. The underlying slice, `c1t1d0s1`, is mounted directly after this procedure.

```
# umount /fs2
# metadetach d1
d1: log device d2 is detached
# metaclear d1
d1: Trans is cleared

    ( Edit /etc/vfstab to update mount point for /fs2 to mount on c1t1d0s1, not d1)
# mount /fs2
```

▼ How to Remove a Transactional Volume and Retain the Mount Device

This procedure works only for situations in which the transactional volume and the underlying device are both Solaris Volume Manager logical volumes.

1. **Check "Prerequisites for Creating Solaris Volume Manager Elements" on page 46 and "Background Information for Transactional Volumes" on page 169.**

2. **Unmount the UFS file system for which you want to remove the transactional volume and disable logging.**

3. **Detach the log device from the transactional volume by using one of the following methods:**

   - From the Enhanced Storage tool within the Solaris Management Console, open the Volumes node, then choose the transactional volume from the listing. Right-click the volume, and choose Properties. For more information, see the online help.

- Use the following form of the `metadetach` command:

  `metadetach` *master-volume*

  master-volume is the name of the transactional volume that contains the file system that is being logged.

  See the `metadetach`(1M) man page for more information.

4. **Exchange the name of the transactional volume with that of the master device.**

5. **Remove (clear) the transactional volume by using one of the following methods:**

   - From the Enhanced Storage tool within the Solaris Management Console, open the Volumes node, then choose the transactional volume from the listing. Right-click the volume, and choose Delete. For more information, see the online help.

   - Use the following form of the `metaclear` command:

     `metaclear` *master-volume*

     See the `metaclear`(1M) man page for more information.

6. **Run the `fsck` command on the master device.**

   When asked whether to fix the file system's state in the superblock, respond **y**.

7. **Remount the file system.**

Example—Removing a Transactional Volume While Retaining the Mount Device

This example begins with a transactional volume, d1, that contains a mounted file system, and ends up with a file system that is mounted on the transactional volume's underlying master device, which will be d1.

```
# metastat d1
d1: Trans
    State: Okay
    Size: 5600 blocks
    Master Device: d21
    Logging Device: d0

d21: Mirror
    Submirror 0: d20
      State: Okay
    Submirror 1: d2
      State: Okay
...

d0: Logging device for d1
    State: Okay
    Size: 5350 blocks
```

```
# umount /fs2
# metadetach d1
d1: log device d0 is detached
# metarename -f -x d1 d21
d1 and d21 have exchanged identities
# metastat d21
d21: Trans
    State: Detached
    Size: 5600 blocks
    Master Device: d1

d1: Mirror
    Submirror 0: d20
      State: Okay
    Submirror 1: d2
      State: Okay
# metaclear 21
# fsck /dev/md/dsk/d1
** /dev/md/dsk/d1
** Last Mounted on /fs2
** Phase 1 - Check Blocks and Sizes
** Phase 2 - Check Pathnames
** Phase 3 - Check Connectivity
** Phase 4 - Check Reference Counts
** Phase 5 - Check Cyl groups

FILE SYSTEM STATE IN SUPERBLOCK IS WRONG; FIX? y

3 files, 10 used, 2493 free (13 frags, 310 blocks, 0.5%
fragmentation)
# mount /fs2
```

The metastat command confirms that the transactional volume, d1, is in the "Okay"
state. The file system is unmounted before detaching the transactional volume's log
device. The transactional volume and its mirrored master device are exchanged by
using the -f (force) flag. Running the metastat command again confirms that the
exchange occurred. The transactional volume and the log device (if desired) are
cleared, in this case, d21 and d0, respectively. Next, the fsck command is run on the
mirror, d1, and the prompt is answered with a y. After the fsck command is done,
the file system is remounted. Note that because the mount device for /fs2 did not
change, the /etc/vfstab file does not require editing.

Sharing Log Devices

▼ How to Share a Log Device Among File Systems

This procedure assumes that you have already set up a transactional volume with a log for another file system.

1. **Check "Prerequisites for Creating Solaris Volume Manager Elements" on page 46 and "Background Information for Transactional Volumes" on page 169.**

2. **If possible, unmount the file system for which you want to enable logging.**

3. **If you already have an existing log device, detach it from the transactional volume by using one of the following methods:**

   - From the Enhanced Storage tool within the Solaris Management Console, open the Volumes node, then choose the transactional volume from the listing. Right-click the volume, and choose Properties. For more information, see the online help.

   - Use the following form of the `metadetach` command:

     `metadetach` *master-volume*

     See the `metadetach`(1M) man page for more information.

4. **Attach a log device to the transactional volume by using one of the following methods:**

   - From the Enhanced Storage tool within the Solaris Management Console, open the Volumes node, then choose the transactional volume from the listing. Right-click the volume, and choose Properties. For more information, see the online help.

   - Use the following form of the `metattach` command:

     `metattach` *master-volume* *logging-volume*

     See the `metattach`(1M) man page for more information.

5. **Edit the** `/etc/vfstab` **file to modify (or add) the entry for the file system to reference the transactional volume.**

6. **Remount the file system. If the file system cannot be unmounted, reboot the system to force your changes to take effect.**

Example—Sharing a Logging Device

```
# umount /xyzfs
# metainit d64 -t c0t2d0s4 d10
```

```
d64: Trans is setup
     (Edit the /etc/vfstab file so that the entry for /xyzfs references the transactional volume d64)
# mount /xyzfs
# metastat
. . .
d10: Logging device for d63 d64

. . .
```

This example shows the sharing of a log device (d10) defined as the log for a previous transactional volume, with a new transactional volume (d64). The file system to be set up as the master device is /xyzfs and is using slice /dev/dsk/c0t2d0s4. The metainit -t command specifies the configuration is a transactional volume. The /etc/vfstab file must be edited to change (or enter for the first time) the entry for the file system to reference the transactional volume. For example, the following line:

```
/dev/dsk/c0t2d0s4 /dev/rdsk/c0t2d0s4 /xyzfs ufs 2 yes -
```

should be changed to:

```
/dev/md/dsk/d64 /dev/md/rdsk/d64 /xyzfs ufs 2 yes -
```

The metastat command verifies that the log is being shared. Logging becomes effective for the file system when the system is rebooted.

Upon subsequent reboots, instead of checking the file system, the fsck command displays these messages for the two file systems:

```
/dev/md/rdsk/d63: is logging.
/dev/md/rdsk/d64: is logging.
```

Recovering Transactional Volumes When Errors Occur

▼ How to Recover a Transactional Volume With a Panic

● **For file systems that the fsck command cannot repair, run the fsck command on each transactional volume whose file systems share the affected log device.**

Example—Recovering a Transactional Volume

```
# fsck /dev/md/rdsk/trans
```

Only after all of the affected transactional volumes have been checked and successfully repaired will the fsck command reset the state of the failed transactional volume to "Okay."

▼ How to Recover a Transactional Volume With Hard Errors

Use this procedure to transition a transactional volume to the "Okay" state.

See "How to Check the State of Transactional Volumes " on page 182 to check the status of a transactional volume.

If either the master device or log device encounters errors while processing logged data, the device transitions from the "Okay" state to the "Hard Error" state. If the device is in the "Hard Error" or "Error" state, either a device error or panic occurred. Recovery from both scenarios is the same.

Note – If a log (log device) is shared, a failure in any of the slices in a transactional volume will result in all slices or volumes that are associated with the transactional volume switching to a failed state.

---

1. **Check "Prerequisites for Creating Solaris Volume Manager Elements" on page 46 and "Background Information for Transactional Volumes" on page 169.**

2. **Read "Background Information for Transactional Volumes" on page 169.**

3. **Run the** lockfs **command to determine which file systems are locked.**

   ```
   # lockfs
   ```

   Affected file systems are listed with a lock type of hard. Every file system that shares the same log device would be hard locked.

4. **Unmount the affected file system(s).**

   You can unmount locked file systems even if they were in use when the error occurred. If the affected processes try to access an opened file or directory on the hard locked or unmounted file system, an error is returned.

5. **(Optional) Back up any accessible data.**

   Before you attempt to fix the device error, you might want to recover as much data as possible. If your backup procedure requires a mounted file system (such as the tar command or the cpio command), you can mount the file system read-only. If your backup procedure does not require a mounted file system (such as the dump command or the volcopy command), you can access the transactional volume directly.

6. **Fix the device error.**

At this point, any attempt to open or mount the transactional volume for
read-and-write access starts rolling all accessible data on the log device to the
appropriate master devices. Any data that cannot be read or written is discarded.
However, if you open or mount the transactional volume for read-only access, the log
is simply rescanned and not rolled forward to the master devices, and the error is not
fixed. In other words, all data on the master device and log device remains unchanged
until the first read or write open or mount.

7. **Run the** `fsck` **command to repair the file system, or the** `newfs` **command if you
   need to restore data.**

   Run the `fsck` command on all of the transactional volumes that share the same log
   device. When all transactional volumes have been repaired by the `fsck` command,
   they then revert to the "Okay" state.

   The `newfs` command will also transition the file system back to the "Okay" state, but
   the command will destroy all of the data on the file system. The `newfs` command is
   generally used when you plan to restore file systems from backup.

   The `fsck` or `newfs` commands must be run on all of the transactional volumes that
   share the same log device before these devices revert back to the "Okay" state.

8. **Run the** `metastat` **command to verify that the state of the affected devices has
   reverted to "Okay."**

Example—Logging Device Error

```
# metastat d5
d5: Trans
    State: Hard Error
    Size: 10080 blocks
    Master Device: d4
    Logging Device: c0t0d0s6

d4: Mirror
    State: Okay
...
c0t0d0s6: Logging device for d5
    State: Hard Error
    Size: 5350 blocks

...
# fsck /dev/md/rdsk/d5
** /dev/md/rdsk/d5
** Last Mounted on /fs1
** Phase 1 - Check Blocks and Sizes
** Phase 2 - Check Pathnames
** Phase 3 - Check Connectivity
** Phase 4 - Check Reference Counts
** Phase 5 - Check Cyl groups
WARNING: md: log device: /dev/dsk/c0t0d0s6 changed state to
Okay
4 files, 11 used, 4452 free (20 frags, 554 blocks, 0.4%
fragmentation)
```

```
# metastat d5
d5: Trans
    State: Okay
    Size: 10080 blocks
    Master Device: d4
    Logging Device: c0t0d0s6

d4: Mirror
    State: Okay
...

c0t0d0s6: Logging device for d5
    State: Okay
...
```

This example shows a transactional volume, d5, which has a log device in the "Hard Error" state, being fixed. You must run the fsck command on the transactional volume itself, which transitions the state of the transactional volume to "Okay." The metastat command confirms that the state is "Okay."

## CHAPTER 19

Disk Sets (Overview)

This chapter provides conceptual information about disk sets. For information about performing related tasks, see Chapter 20.

This chapter includes the following information:

What Do Disk Sets Do?

A *shared disk set*, or simply *disk set*, is a set of disk drives that contain volumes and hot spares that can be shared exclusively but not at the same time by multiple hosts. Additionally, disk sets provide a separate namespace within which Solaris Volume Manager volumes can be managed.

A disk set supports data redundancy and data availability. If one host fails, the other host can take over the failed host's disk set. (This type of configuration is known as a *failover configuration*.) Although each host can control the set of disks, only one host can control it at a time.

Note – Disk sets are supported on both SPARC based and IA based platforms.

Note – Disk sets are intended primarily for use with Sun Cluster, Solstice HA (High Availability), or another supported third-party HA framework. Solaris Volume Manager by itself does not provide all the functionality necessary to implement a failover configuration.

How Does Solaris Volume Manager Manage Disk Sets?

In addition to the shared disk set, each host has a *local disk set*. The local disk set consists of all of the disks on a host that are not in a shared disk set. A local disk set belongs exclusively to a specific host. The local disk set contains the state database for that specific host's configuration.

Volumes and hot spare pools in a shared disk set must be built on drives from within that disk set. Once you have created a volume within the disk set, you can use the volume just as you would a physical slice. However, disk sets do not support mounting file systems from the `/etc/vfstab` file.

A file system that resides on a volume in a disk set cannot be mounted automatically at boot with the `/etc/vfstab` file. The necessary disk set RPC daemons (`rpc.metad` and `rpc.metamhd`) do not start early enough in the boot process to permit this. Additionally, the ownership of a disk set is lost during a reboot.

Similarly, volumes and hot spare pools in the local disk set can consist only of drives from within the local disk set.

When you add disks to a disk set, Solaris Volume Manager automatically creates the state database replicas on the disk set. When a drive is accepted into a disk set, Solaris Volume Manager might repartition the drive so that the state database replica for the disk set can be placed on the drive (see "Automatic Disk Partitioning" on page 199).

Unlike local disk set administration, you do not need to manually create or delete disk set state databases. Solaris Volume Manager places one state database replica (on slice 7) on each drive across all drives in the disk set, up to a maximum of 50 total replicas in the disk set.

Note – Although disk sets are supported in single-host configurations, they are often not appropriate for "local" (not dual-connected) use. Two common exceptions are the use of disk sets to provide a more managable namespace for logical volumes, and to more easily manage storage on a Storage Area Network (SAN) fabric (see "Scenario—Disk Sets" on page 204).

Automatic Disk Partitioning

When you add a new disk to a disk set, Solaris Volume Manager checks the disk format and, if necessary, repartitions the disk to ensure that the disk has a slice 7 with adequate space for a state database replica. The precise size of slice 7 depends on the disk geometry, but it will be no less than 4 Mbytes, and probably closer to 6 Mbytes (depending on where the cylinder boundaries lie). For example, the following output from the `prtvtoc` command shows a disk before it is added to a disk set.

```
[root@lexicon:apps]$ prtvtoc /dev/rdsk/c1t6d0s0
* /dev/rdsk/c1t6d0s0 partition map
*
* Dimensions:
*      512 bytes/sector
*      133 sectors/track
*       27 tracks/cylinder
*     3591 sectors/cylinder
*     4926 cylinders
*     4924 accessible cylinders
*
* Flags:
*    1: unmountable
*   10: read-only
*
*                           First      Sector      Last
* Partition  Tag  Flags     Sector      Count      Sector   Mount Directory
       0       2    00           0    4111695    4111694
       1       3    01     4111695    1235304    5346998
       2       5    01           0   17682084   17682083
       3       0    00     5346999    4197879    9544877
       4       0    00     9544878    4197879   13742756
       5       0    00    13742757    3939327   17682083
```

Note – Drives are repartitioned when they are added to a disk set only if slice 7 is not set up correctly. A small portion of each drive is reserved in slice 7 for use by Solaris Volume Manager. The remainder of the space on each drive is placed into slice 0. Any existing data on the disks is lost by repartitioning. After you add a drive to a disk set, it might be repartitioned as necessary, with the exception that slice 7 is not altered in any way.

If you have disk sets that you upgraded from Solstice DiskSuite software, the default state database replica size on those sets will be 1034 blocks, not the 8192 block size from Solaris Volume Manager. Also, slice 7 on the disks that were added under Solstice DiskSuite will be correspondingly smaller than slice 7 on disks that were added under Solaris Volume Manager.

After you add the disk to a disk set, the output of `prtvtoc` looks like the following:

```
[root@lexicon:apps]$ prtvtoc /dev/rdsk/c1t6d0s0
* /dev/rdsk/c1t6d0s0 partition map
*
* Dimensions:
*     512 bytes/sector
*     133 sectors/track
*      27 tracks/cylinder
*    3591 sectors/cylinder
*    4926 cylinders
*    4924 accessible cylinders
*
* Flags:
*    1: unmountable
*   10: read-only
*
*                          First     Sector    Last
* Partition  Tag  Flags    Sector    Count     Sector   Mount Directory
      0        0    00     10773   17671311   17682083
      7        0    01         0      10773      10772
[root@lexicon:apps]$
```

If disks you add to a disk set have acceptable slice 7s (that start at cylinder 0 and that have sufficient space for the state database replica), they will not be reformatted.

Disk Set Name Requirements

Disk set component names are similar to other Solaris Volume Manager component names, but the disk set name is part of the name.

- Volume path names include the disk set name after `/dev/md/` and before the actual volume name in the path.

- The following table shows some example disk set volume names.

`/dev/md/blue/dsk/d0`	Block volume d0 in disk set blue
`/dev/md/blue/dsk/d1`	Block volume d1 in disk set blue
`/dev/md/blue/rdsk/d126`	Raw volume d126 in disk set blue
`/dev/md/blue/rdsk/d127`	Raw volume d127 in disk set blue

Similarly, hot spare pools have the disk set name as part of the hot spare name.

Example—Two Shared Disk Sets

Figure 19–1 shows an example configuration that uses two disk sets.

In this configuration, Host A and Host B share disk sets A and B. They each have their own local disk set, which is not shared. If Host A fails, Host B can take over control of Host A's shared disk set (Disk set A). Likewise, if Host B fails, Host A can take control of Host B's shared disk set (Disk set B).

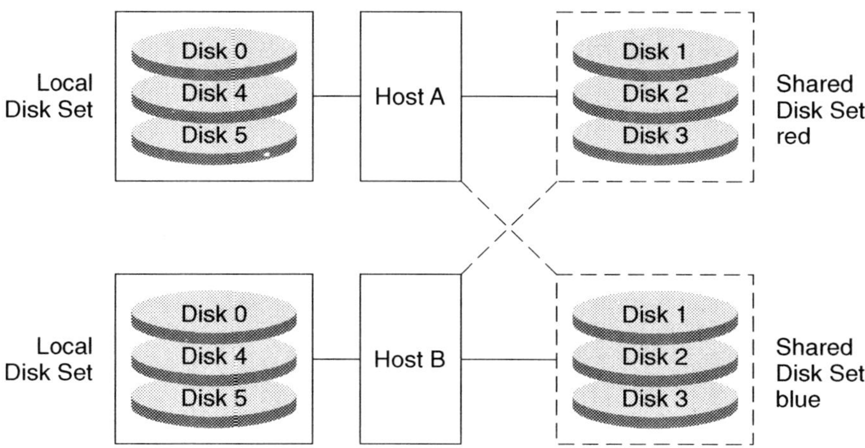

FIGURE 19–1 Disk Sets Example

Background Information for Disk Sets

When working with disk sets, consider the following "Background Information for Disk Sets" on page 202 and "Administering Disk Sets" on page 203.

Requirements for Disk Sets

- Solaris Volume Manager must be configured on each host that will be connected to the disk set.

- Each host must have its local state database set up before you can create disk sets.

- To create and work with a disk set in a clustering environment, root must be a member of Group 14, or the /.rhosts file must contain an entry for the other host name (on each host).

- To perform maintenance on a disk set, a host must be the owner of the disk set or have reserved the disk set. (A host takes implicit ownership of the disk set by putting the first drives into the set.)

- You cannot add a drive that is in use to a disk set. Before you add a drive, make sure it is not currently being used for a file system, database, or any other application.

- Do not add a drive with existing data that you want to preserve to a disk set. The process of adding the disk to the disk set repartitions the disk and destroys existing data.

- All disks that you plan to share between hosts in the disk set must be connected to each host and must have the exact same path, driver, and name on each host. Specifically, a shared disk drive must be seen on both hosts at the same device number (c#t#d#). If the numbers are not the same on both hosts, you will see the message "drive c#t#d# is not common with host *xxx*" when attempting to add drives to the disk set. The shared disks must use the same driver name (ssd). See "How to Add Drives to a Disk Set" on page 207 for more information on setting up shared disk drives in a disk set.

Guidelines for Disk Sets

- The default total number of disk sets on a system is 4. You can increase this value up to 32 by editing the /kernel/drv/md.conf file, as described in "How to Increase the Number of Default Disk Sets" on page 227. The number of shared disk sets is always one less than the md_nsets value, because the local set is included in md_nsets.

- Unlike local volume administration, it is not necessary to create or delete state database replicas manually on the disk set. Solaris Volume Manager tries to balance a reasonable number of replicas across all drives in a disk set.

- When drives are added to a disk set, Solaris Volume Manager re-balances the state database replicas across the remaining drives. Later, if necessary, you can change the replica layout with the `metadb` command.

Administering Disk Sets

Disk sets can be created and configured by using the Solaris Volume Manager command-line interface (the `metaset` command) or the Enhanced Storage tool within the Solaris Management Console.

After drives are added to a disk set, the disk set can be *reserved* (or *taken*) and *released* by hosts in the disk set. When a disk set is reserved by a host, the other host in the disk set cannot access the data on the drives in the disk set. To perform maintenance on a disk set, a host must be the owner of the disk set or have reserved the disk set. A host takes implicit ownership of the disk set by putting the first drives into the set.

Reserving a Disk Set

Before a host can use drives in a disk set, the host must reserve the disk set. There are two methods of reserving a disk set:

- **Safely** - When you safely reserve a disk set, Solaris Volume Manager attempts to take the disk set, and the other host attempts to release the disk set. The release (and therefore the reservation) might fail.

- **Forcibly** - When you forcibly reserve a disk set, Solaris Volume Manager reserves the disk set whether or not another host currently has the set reserved. This method is generally used when a host in the disk set is down or not communicating. All disks within the disk set are taken over. The state database is read in on the host performing the reservation and the shared volumes configured in the disk set become accessible. If the other host had the disk set reserved at this point, it would panic due to reservation loss.

  Normally, two hosts in a disk set cooperate with each other to ensure that drives in a disk set are reserved by only one host at a time. A normal situation is defined as both hosts being up and communicating with each other.

Note – If a drive has been determined unexpectedly not to be reserved (perhaps because another host using the disk set forcibly took the drive), the host will panic. This behavior helps to minimize data loss which would occur if two hosts were to simultaneously access the same drive.

For more information about taking or reserving a disk set, see"How to Take a Disk Set" on page 213.

Releasing a Disk Set

Releasing a disk set can be useful when you perform maintenance on the physical drives in the disk set. When a disk set is released, it cannot be accessed by the host. If both hosts in a disk set release the set, neither host in the disk set can access the drives in the disk set.

For more information about releasing a disk set, see "How to Release a Disk Set" on page 214.

Scenario—Disk Sets

The following example, drawing on the sample system shown in Chapter 4, describes how disk sets should be used to manage storage that resides on a SAN (Storage Area Network) fabric.

Assume that the sample system has an additional controller that connects to a fiber switch and SAN storage. Storage on the SAN fabric is not available to the system as early in the boot process as other devices, such as SCSI and IDE disks, and Solaris Volume Manager would report logical volumes on the fabric as unavailable at boot. However, by adding the storage to a disk set, and then using the disk set tools to manage the storage, this problem with boot time availability is avoided (and the fabric-attached storage can be easily managed within a separate, disk set controlled, namespace from the local storage).

## CHAPTER 20

Disk Sets (Tasks)

This chapter provides information about performing tasks that are associated with disk sets. For information about the concepts involved in these tasks, see Chapter 19.

Disk Sets (Task Map)

The following task map identifies the procedures needed to manage Solaris Volume Manager disk sets.

Task	Description	Instructions
Create a disk set	Use the Solaris Volume Manager GUI or the `metaset` command to create a disk set.	"How to Create a Disk Set" on page 206
Add drives to a disk set	Use the Solaris Volume Manager GUI or the `metaset` command to add drives to a disk set.	"How to Add Drives to a Disk Set" on page 207
Add a host to a disk set	Use the Solaris Volume Manager GUI or the `metaset` command to add a host to a disk set.	"How to Add a Host to a Disk Set" on page 209
Create Solaris Volume Manager volumes in a disk set	Use the Solaris Volume Manager GUI or the `metainit` command to create volumes in a disk set.	"How to Create Solaris Volume Manager Components in a Disk Set" on page 210

Task	Description	Instructions
Check the status of a disk set	Use the Solaris Volume Manager GUI or the `metaset` and `metastat` commands to check the status of a disk set.	"How to Check the Status of a Disk Set" on page 211
Remove disks from a disk set	Use the Solaris Volume Manager GUI or the `metaset` command to remove drives from a disk set.	"How to Remove Disks from a Disk Set" on page 212
Take a disk set	Use the Solaris Volume Manager GUI or the `metaset` command to take a disk set.	"How to Take a Disk Set" on page 213
Release a disk set	Use the Solaris Volume Manager GUI or the `metaset` command to release a disk set.	"How to Release a Disk Set" on page 214
Delete a host from a disk set	Use the Solaris Volume Manager GUI or the `metaset` command to delete hosts from a disk set.	"How to Delete a Host or Disk Set" on page 215
Delete a disk set	Use the Solaris Volume Manager GUI or the `metaset` command to delete the last host from a disk set, thus deleting the disk set.	"How to Delete a Host or Disk Set" on page 215

Creating Disk Sets

▼ How to Create a Disk Set

1. **Check "Background Information for Disk Sets" on page 202.**

2. **To create a disk set, use one of the following methods:**

   - From the Enhanced Storage tool within the Solaris Management Console, open the Disk Sets node. Choose Action->Create Disk Set, then follow the instructions in the wizard. For more information, see the online help.

   - To create a disk set from scratch from the command line, use the following form of the `metaset` command:

     `metaset` [-s *diskset-name*] [-a] [-h *hostname*]

-s *diskset-name*   Specifies the name of a disk set on which the `metaset` command will work.

-a   Adds hosts to the named disk set. Solaris Volume Manager supports a maximum of two hosts per disk set.

-h *hostname*   Specifies one or more hosts to be added to a disk set. Adding the first host creates the set. The second host can be added later, but it is not accepted if all the drives within the set cannot be found on the specified *hostname*. *hostname* is the same name found in the `/etc/nodename` file.

See `metaset`(1M) for more information.

3. **Check the status of the new disk set by using the** `metaset` **command.**

```
# metaset
```

Example—Creating a Disk Set

```
# metaset -s blue -a -h lexicon
# metaset
Set name = blue, Set number = 1

Host                Owner
  lexicon
```

In this example, you create a shared disk set called `blue`, from the host `lexicon`. The `metaset` command shows the status. At this point, the set has no owner. The host that adds disks to the set will become the owner by default.

Expanding Disk Sets

▼ How to Add Drives to a Disk Set

Only drives that meet the following conditions can be added to a disk set:

- The drive must not be in use in a volume or hot spare pool, or contain a state database replica.

- The drive must not be currently mounted, swapped on, or otherwise opened for use by an application.

1. **Check "Background Information for Disk Sets" on page 202.**

2. **To add drives to a disk set, use one of the following methods:**

   - From the Enhanced Storage tool within the Solaris Management Console, open the Disk Sets node. Select the disk set you want to modify, then right-click and choose Properties. Select the Disks tab, click Add Disk, then follow the instructions in the wizard. For more information, see the online help.

   - To add drives to a disk set from the command line, use the following form of the `metaset` command:

     metaset [-s *diskset-name*] [a] [*disk-name*]

-s *diskset-name*	Specifies the name of a disk set on which the `metaset` command will work.
-a	Adds drives to the named disk set.
disk-name	Specifies the drives to add to the disk set. Drive names are in the form c*x*t*x*d*x*; no "s*x*" slice identifiers are at the end of the name. They need to be the same as seen from all hosts in the disk set.

   See the `metaset` man page (`metaset`(1M)) for more information.

   The first host to add a drive to a disk set becomes the owner of the disk set.

Caution – Do not add a disk with data; the process of adding it to the disk set might repartition the disk, destroying any data. For more information, see "Example—Two Shared Disk Sets" on page 201

3. **Use the `metaset` command to verify the status of the disk set and drives.**

   ```
   # metaset
   ```

Example—Adding a Drive to a Disk Set

```
# metaset -s blue -a c1t6d0
# metaset
Set name = blue, Set number = 1

Host                Owner
   lexicon           Yes

Drive               Dbase
   c1t6d0            Yes
```

In this example, the host name is `lexicon`. The shared disk set is `blue`. At this point, only one disk has been added to the disk set `blue`.

Optionally, you could add multiple disks at once by listing each of them on the command line. For example, you could use the following:

```
# metaset -s blue -a c1t6d0 c2t6d0
```

▼ How to Add a Host to a Disk Set

Solaris Volume Manager supports a maximum of four hosts per disk set. This procedure explains how to add another host to an existing disk set that only has one host.

1. **Check "Background Information for Disk Sets" on page 202.**

2. **To add a host to a disk set, use one of the following methods:**

   - From the Enhanced Storage tool within the Solaris Management Console, open the Disk Sets node and choose the disk set you want to modify. Select the disk set you want to modify, then right-click and choose Properties. Select the Hosts tab, click Add Host, then follow the instructions in the wizard. For more information, see the online help.

   - To add hosts to a disk set from the command line, use the following form of the metaset command:

     metaset [-s *diskset-name*] [-a] [-h *hostname*]

-s *diskset-name*	Specifies the name of a disk set on which metaset will work.
-a	Adds drives to the named disk set.
-h *hostname*	Specifies one or more host names to be added to the disk set. Adding the first host creates the set. The host name is the same name found in the /etc/nodename file.

     See the metaset man page (metaset(1M)) for more information.

3. **Verify that the host has been added to the disk set by using the metaset command without any options.**

   ```
   # metaset
   ```

Example—Adding Another Host to a Disk Set

```
# metaset -s blue -a -h idiom
# metaset -s blue
Set name = blue, Set number = 1

Host                Owner
  lexicon                 Yes
  idiom
```

```
Drive               Dbase
   c1t6d0             Yes
   c2t6d0             Yes
```

This example shows the addition of host `idiom` to the disk set `blue`.

▼ How to Create Solaris Volume Manager Components in a Disk Set

After you create a disk set, you can create volumes and hot spare pools using the drives you added to the disk set. You can use either the Enhanced Storage tool within the Solaris Management Console or the command line utilities.

● **To create volumes or other Solaris Volume Manager devices within a disk set, use one of the following methods:**

■ From the Enhanced Storage tool within the Solaris Management Console, open the Volumes, State Database Replicas, or Hot Spare Pools node. Choose Action->Create, then follow the instructions in the wizard. For more information, see the online help.

■ Use the command line utilities with the same basic syntax you would without a disk set, but add `-s` *diskset-name* immediately after the command for every command.

Example—Creating Solaris Volume Manager Volumes in a Disk Set

```
# metainit -s blue d11 1 1 c1t6d0s0
blue/d11: Concat/Stripe is setup
# metainit -s blue d12 1 1 c2t6d0s0
blue/d12: Concat/Stripe is setup
# metainit -s blue d10 -m d11
blue/d10: Mirror is setup
# metattach -s blue d10 d12
blue/d10: submirror blue/d12 is attached

# metastat -s blue
blue/d10: Mirror
    Submirror 0: blue/d11
      State: Okay
    Submirror 1: blue/d12
      State: Resyncing
    Resync in progress: 0 % done
    Pass: 1
    Read option: roundrobin (default)
```

```
        Write option: parallel (default)
        Size: 17674902 blocks

blue/d11: Submirror of blue/d10
    State: Okay
    Size: 17674902 blocks
    Stripe 0:
        Device                    Start Block  Dbase State         Reloc  Hot Spare
        c1t6d0s0                            0  No    Okay


blue/d12: Submirror of blue/d10
    State: Resyncing
    Size: 17674902 blocks
    Stripe 0:
        Device                    Start Block  Dbase State         Reloc  Hot Spare
        c2t6d0s0                            0  No    Okay
```

This example shows the creation of a mirror, d10, in disk set blue, that consists of submirrors (RAID 0 devices) d11 and d12.

Maintaining Disk Sets

▼ How to Check the Status of a Disk Set

● **Use one of the following methods to check the status of a disk set.**

- From the Enhanced Storage tool within the Solaris Management Console, open the Disk Sets node. Right-click the Disk Set you want to monitor, then choose Properties from the menu. For more information, see the online help.

- Use the metaset command to view disk set status.

  See metaset(1M) for more information.

Note – Disk set ownership is only shown on the owning host.

Example—Checking the Status of a Specified Disk Set

```
red# metaset -s blue
```

```
Set name = blue, Set number = 1

Host                    Owner
   idiom                Yes

Drive                   Dbase
   c1t6d0               Yes
   c2t6d0               Yes
```

The `metaset` command with the `-s` option followed by the name of the `blue` disk set displays status information for that disk set. By issuing the `metaset` command from the owning host, `idiom`, it is determined that `idiom` is in fact the disk set owner. The `metaset` command also displays the drives in the disk set.

The `metaset` command by itself displays the status of all disk sets.

▼ How to Remove Disks from a Disk Set

To delete a disk set, you must first delete all drives from the disk set.

- From the Enhanced Storage tool within the Solaris Management Console, open the Disk Sets node. Right-click the Disk Set you want to release, then choose Properties from the menu. Click the Disks tab and follow the instructions in the online help.

- Use the following form of the `metaset` command:

  `metaset -s` *diskset-name* `-d` *drivename*

  `-s` *diskset-name*   Specifies the name of a disk set on which the `metaset` command will work.

  drive-name   Specifies the drives to delete from the disk set. Drive names are in the form *cxtxdx*; no "*sx*" slice identifiers are at the end of the name.

  See the `metaset`(1M) man page for more information.

- **Verify that the disk has been deleted from the disk set by using the** `metaset -s` *diskset-name* **command.**

  `# metaset -s blue`

Example—Deleting a Disk from a Disk Set

```
lexicon# metaset -s blue -d c1t6d0
lexicon# metaset -s blue

Set name = blue, Set number = 1

Host                    Owner
```

```
   lexicon
     idiom

Drive                 Dbase
   c2t6d0               Yes
```

This example deletes the disk from the disk set `blue`.

▼ How to Take a Disk Set

● **Use one of the following methods to take a disk set.**

- From the Enhanced Storage tool within the Solaris Management Console, open the Disk Sets node. Right-click the Disk Set you want to take, then choose Take Ownership from the menu. For more information, see the online help.

- Use the following form of the `metaset` command.

  `metaset -s` *diskset-name* `-t`

  -s *diskset-name*　　Specifies the name of a disk set on which the `metaset` command will work.

  -t　　Specifies to take the disk set.

  -f　　Specifies to take the disk set forcibly.

See the `metaset`(1M) man page for more information.

When one host in a disk set takes the disk set, the other host in the disk set cannot access data on drives in the disk set.

The default behavior of the `metaset` command takes the disk set for your host only if a release is possible on the other host.

Use the -f option to forcibly take the disk set. This option takes the disk set whether or not another host currently has the set. Use this method when a host in the disk set is down or not communicating. If the other host had the disk set taken at this point, it would panic when it attempts to perform an I/O operation to the disk set.

Note – Disk set ownership is only shown on the owning host.

Example—Taking a Disk Set

```
lexicon# metaset
...
Set name = blue, Set number = 1

Host                  Owner
```

```
    lexicon
    idiom
. . .
lexicon# metaset -s blue -t
lexicon# metaset

. . .
Set name = blue, Set number = 1

Host                Owner
  lexicon                 Yes
  idiom

. . .
```

In this example, host lexicon communicates with host idiom and ensures that host idiom has released the disk set before host lexicon attempts to take the set.

Note – In this example, if host idiom owned the set blue, the "Owner" column in the above output would still have been blank. The metaset command only shows whether the issuing host owns the disk set, and not the other host.

Example—Taking a Disk Set Forcibly

```
# metaset -s blue -t -f
```

In this example, the host that is taking the disk set does not communicate with the other host. Instead, the drives in the disk set are taken without warning. If the other host had the disk set, it would panic when it attempts an I/O operation to the disk set.

▼ How to Release a Disk Set

Releasing a disk set is useful when you perform maintenance on the physical drives in the disk set. When a disk set is released, it cannot be accessed by the host. If both hosts in a disk set release the set, neither host in the disk set can access volumes or hot spare pools defined in the set directly, although if both hosts release the set, the hosts can access the disks directly through their c*t*d* names.

1. **Check "Background Information for Disk Sets" on page 202.**

2. **Use one of the following methods to release a disk set.**

   - From the Enhanced Storage tool within the Solaris Management Console, open the Disk Sets node. Right-click the Disk Set you want to release, then choose Release Ownership from the menu. For more information, see the online help.

   - To release ownership of the disk set, use the following form of the metaset command.

```
metaset -s diskset-name-r
```

-s *diskset-name* Specifies the name of a disk set on which the `metaset` command will work.

-r Releases ownership of a disk set. The reservation of all the disks within the disk set is removed. The volumes within the disk set are no longer accessible.

See the `metaset`(1M) man page for more information.

Note – Disk set ownership is only shown on the owning host.

---

3. **Verify that the disk set has been released on this host by using the** `metaset` **command without any options.**

```
# metaset
```

Example—Releasing a Disk Set

```
lexicon# metaset -s blue -r
lexicon# metaset -s blue

Set name = blue, Set number = 1

Host                 Owner
    lexicon
      idiom

Drive                Dbase
    c1t6d0             Yes
    c2t6d0             Yes
```

This example shows the release of the disk set `blue`. Note that there is no owner of the disk set. Viewing status from host `lexicon` could be misleading. A host can only determine if it does or does not own a disk set. For example, if host `idiom` were to reserve the disk set, it would not appear so from host `lexicon`. Only host `idiom` would be able to determine the reservation in this case.

▼ How to Delete a Host or Disk Set

Deleting a disk set requires that the disk set contains no drives and that no other hosts are attached to the disk set. Deleting the last host will destroy the disk set.

1. **Use one of the following methods to delete a host from a disk set, or to delete a disk set.**

   - From the Enhanced Storage tool within the Solaris Management Console, open the Disk Sets node. Right-click the Disk Set you want to release, then choose Delete from the menu. Follow the instructions in the online help.

   - To delete the host and remove the disk set if the host removed is the last host on the disk set, use the following form of the `metaset` command.

     ```
     metaset -s diskset-name-d hostname
     ```

`-s` *diskset-name*	Specifies the name of a disk set on which the `metaset` command will work.
`-d`	Deletes a host from a disk set.
hostname	Specifies the name of the host to delete.

     ```
     # metaset -s blue -d idiom
     ```
     See the `metasetmetaset`(1M) man page for more information.

2. **Verify that the host has been deleted from the disk set by using the `metaset` command. Note that only the current (owning) host is shown. Other hosts have been deleted.**

   ```
   # metaset -s blue
   Set name = blue, Set number = 1

   Host              Owner
      lexicon          Yes

   Drive             Dbase
      c1t2d0           Yes
      c1t3d0           Yes
      c1t4d0           Yes
      c1t5d0           Yes
      c1t6d0           Yes
      c2t1d0           Yes
   ```

Example—Deleting the Last Host from a Disk Set

```
lexicon# metaset -s blue -d lexicon
lexicon# metaset -s blue

metaset: lexicon: setname "blue": no such set
```

This example shows the deletion of the last host from the disk set `blue`.

## CHAPTER 21

Maintaining Solaris Volume Manager (Tasks)

This chapter provides information about performing general storage administration maintenance tasks with Solaris Volume Manager.

This is a list of the information in this chapter:

- "Solaris Volume Manager Maintenance (Task Map)" on page 217
- "Viewing the Solaris Volume Manager Configuration" on page 218
- "Renaming Volumes" on page 221
- "Working with Configuration Files" on page 224
- "Changing Solaris Volume Manager Defaults" on page 226
- "Growing a File System" on page 228
- "Overview of Replacing and Enabling Components in RAID 1 and RAID 5 Volumes" on page 230

Solaris Volume Manager Maintenance (Task Map)

The following task map identifies the procedures needed to maintain Solaris Volume Manager.

Task	Description	Instructions
View the Solaris Volume Manager configuration	Use the Solaris Volume Manager GUI or the `metastat` command to view the system configuration.	"How to View the Solaris Volume Manager Volume Configuration" on page 218

Task	Description	Instructions
Rename a volume	Use the Solaris Volume Manager GUI or the `metarename` command to rename a volume.	"How to Rename a Volume" on page 223
Create configuration files	Use the `metastat -p` command and the `metadb` command to create configuration files.	"How to Create Configuration Files" on page 224
Initialize Solaris Volume Manager from configuration files	Use the `metainit` command to initialize Solaris Volume Manager from configuration files.	"How to Initialize Solaris Volume Manager from a Configuration File" on page 224
Increase the number of possible volumes	Edit the `/kernel/drv/md.conf` file to increase the number of possible volumes.	"How to Increase the Number of Default Volumes" on page 226
Increase the number of possible disk sets	Edit the `/kernel/drv/md.conf` file to increase the number of possible disk sets.	"How to Increase the Number of Default Disk Sets" on page 227
Grow a file system	Use the `growfs` command to grow a file system.	"How to Grow a File System" on page 229
Enable components	Use the Solaris Volume Manager GUI or the `metareplace` command to enable components.	"Enabling a Component" on page 230
Replace components	Use the Solaris Volume Manager GUI or the `metareplace` command to replace components.	"Replacing a Component With Another Available Component" on page 231

Viewing the Solaris Volume Manager Configuration

▼ How to View the Solaris Volume Manager Volume Configuration

● **To view the volume configuration, use one of the following methods:**

   ■ From the Enhanced Storage tool within the Solaris Management Console, open the Volumes node. For more information, see the online help.

   ■ Use the following format of the `metastat` command:

```
metastat -p -i component-name
```

- `-p` specifies to output a condensed summary, suitable for use in creating the `md.tab` file.

- `-i` specifies to verify that all devices can be accessed.

- *component-name* is the name of the volume to view. If no volume name is specified, a complete list of components will be displayed.

Tip – The `metastat` command does not sort output. Pipe the output of the `metastat -p` command to the `sort` or `grep` commands for a more managable listing of your configuration.

For more information, see `metastat`(1M).

Example—Viewing the Solaris Volume Manager Volume Configuration

The following example illustrates output from the `metastat` command.

```
# metastat
d50: RAID
    State: Okay
    Interlace: 32 blocks
    Size: 20985804 blocks
Original device:
    Size: 20987680 blocks
        Device                  Start Block  Dbase State      Reloc  Hot Spare
        c1t4d0s5                       330   No    Okay       Yes
        c1t5d0s5                       330   No    Okay       Yes
        c2t4d0s5                       330   No    Okay       Yes
        c2t5d0s5                       330   No    Okay       Yes
        c1t1d0s5                       330   No    Okay       Yes
        c2t1d0s5                       330   No    Okay       Yes

d1: Concat/Stripe
    Size: 4197879 blocks
    Stripe 0:
        Device                  Start Block  Dbase  Reloc
        c1t2d0s3                         0   No     Yes

d2: Concat/Stripe
    Size: 4197879 blocks
    Stripe 0:
        Device                  Start Block  Dbase  Reloc
        c2t2d0s3                         0   No     Yes


d80: Soft Partition
```

```
    Device: d70
    State: Okay
    Size: 2097152 blocks
        Extent                   Start Block              Block count
             0                             1                   2097152

d81: Soft Partition
    Device: d70
    State: Okay
    Size: 2097152 blocks
        Extent                   Start Block              Block count
             0                       2097154                   2097152

d70: Mirror
    Submirror 0: d71
      State: Okay
    Submirror 1: d72
      State: Okay
    Pass: 1
    Read option: roundrobin (default)
    Write option: parallel (default)
    Size: 12593637 blocks

d71: Submirror of d70
    State: Okay
    Size: 12593637 blocks
    Stripe 0:
        Device              Start Block  Dbase State      Reloc  Hot Spare
        c1t3d0s3                     0   No    Okay       Yes
    Stripe 1:
        Device              Start Block  Dbase State      Reloc  Hot Spare
        c1t3d0s4                     0   No    Okay       Yes
    Stripe 2:
        Device              Start Block  Dbase State      Reloc  Hot Spare
        c1t3d0s5                     0   No    Okay       Yes


d72: Submirror of d70
    State: Okay
    Size: 12593637 blocks
    Stripe 0:
        Device              Start Block  Dbase State      Reloc  Hot Spare
        c2t3d0s3                     0   No    Okay       Yes
    Stripe 1:
        Device              Start Block  Dbase State      Reloc  Hot Spare
        c2t3d0s4                     0   No    Okay       Yes
    Stripe 2:
        Device              Start Block  Dbase State      Reloc  Hot Spare
        c2t3d0s5                     0   No    Okay       Yes

hsp010: is empty

hsp014: 2 hot spares
        Device              Status       Length          Reloc
        c1t2d0s1            Available     617652 blocks   Yes
```

```
        c2t2d0s1                Available      617652 blocks  Yes

hsp050: 2 hot spares
        Device                  Status     Length          Reloc
        c1t2d0s5                Available      4197879 blocks Yes
        c2t2d0s5                Available      4197879 blocks Yes

hsp070: 2 hot spares
        Device                  Status     Length          Reloc
        c1t2d0s4                Available      4197879 blocks Yes
        c2t2d0s4                Available      4197879 blocks Yes

Device Relocation Information:
Device              Reloc       Device ID
c1t2d0              Yes         id1,sd@SSEAGATE_ST39204LCSUN9.0G3BV0N1S200002103AF29
c2t2d0              Yes         id1,sd@SSEAGATE_ST39204LCSUN9.0G3BV0P64Z00002105Q6J7
c1t1d0              Yes         id1,sd@SSEAGATE_ST39204LCSUN9.0G3BV0N1EM00002104NP2J
c2t1d0              Yes         id1,sd@SSEAGATE_ST39204LCSUN9.0G3BV0N93J000071040L3S
c0t0d0              Yes         id1,dad@s53554e575f4154415f5f53543339313430412525415933
```

Renaming Volumes

Background Information for Renaming Volumes

The `metarename` command with the `-x` option can exchange the names of volumes
that have a parent-child relationship. For more information, see "How to Rename a
Volume" on page 223 and the `metarename`(1M) man page.

Solaris Volume Manager enables you to rename most types of volumes at any time,
subject to some constraints.

Renaming volumes or switching volume names is an administrative convenience for
management of volume names. For example, you could arrange all file system mount
points in a desired numeric range. You might rename volumes to maintain a naming
scheme for your logical volumes or to allow a transactional volume to use the same
name as the underlying volume had been using.

Before you rename a volume, make sure that it is not currently in use. For a file
system, make sure it is not mounted or being used as `swap`. Other applications using
the raw device, such as a database, should have their own way of stopping access to
the data.

Specific considerations for renaming volumes include the following:

- You can rename any volume except the following:

  - Soft partitions
  - Volumes on which soft partitions are directly built
  - Volumes that are being used as log devices
  - Hot spare pools

- You can rename volumes within a disk set. However, you cannot rename volumes to move them from one disk set to another.

You can use either the Enhanced Storage tool within the Solaris Management Console or the command line (the `metarename`(1M) command) to rename volumes.

Exchanging Volume Names

When used with the `-x` option, the `metarename` command exchanges the names of an existing layered volume with one of its subdevices. This exchange can occur between a mirror and one of its submirrors, or a transactional volume and its master device.

Note – You must use the command line to exchange volume names. This functionality is currently unavailable in the Solaris Volume Manager GUI. However, you can rename a volume with either the command line or the GUI.

The `metarename -x` command can make it easier to mirror or unmirror an existing volume, and to create or remove a transactional volume of an existing volume.

- You cannot rename a volume that is currently in use. This includes volumes that are used as mounted file systems, as `swap`, or as active storage for applications or databases. Thus, before you use the `metarename` command, stop all access to the volume being renamed. For example, unmount a mounted file system.

- You cannot exchange volumes in a failed state, or volumes using a hot spare replacement.

- An exchange can only take place between volumes with a direct parent-child relationship. You could not, for example, directly exchange a stripe in a mirror that is a master device with the transactional volume.

- You must use the `-f` (force) flag when exchanging members of a transactional device.

- You cannot exchange (or rename) a logging device. The workaround is to either detach the logging device, rename it, then reattach it to the transactional device; or detach the logging device and attach another logging device of the desired name.

- Only volumes can be exchanged. You cannot exchange slices or hot spares.

▼ How to Rename a Volume

1. **Check the volume name requirements ("Volume Names" on page 42), and "Background Information for Renaming Volumes" on page 221.**

2. **Unmount the file system that uses the volume.**

3. **To rename the volume, use one of the following methods:**

   - From the Enhanced Storage tool within the Solaris Management Console, open the Volumes node and select the volume you want to rename. Right-click the icon and choose the Properties option, then follow the instructions on screen. For more information, see the online help.

   - Use the following format of the `metarename` command:

     `metarename` *old-volume-name* *new-volume-name*

     - *old-volume-name* is the name of the existing volume.
     - *new-volume-name* is the new name for the existing volume.

     See `metarename`(1M) for more information.

4. **Edit the `/etc/vfstab` file to refer to the new volume name, if necessary.**

5. **Remount the file system.**

Example—Renaming a Volume Used for a File System

```
# umount /home
# metarename d10 d100
d10: has been renamed to d100
     (Edit the /etc/vfstab file so that the file system references the new volume)
# mount /home
```

In this example, the volume `d10` is renamed to `d100`. Because `d10` contains a mounted file system, the file system must be unmounted before the rename can occur. If the volume is used for a file system with an entry in the `/etc/vfstab` file, the entry must be changed to reference the new volume name. For example, the following line:

```
/dev/md/dsk/d10 /dev/md/rdsk/d10 /docs ufs 2 yes -
```

should be changed to:

```
/dev/md/dsk/d100 /dev/md/rdsk/d100 /docs ufs 2 yes -
```

Then, the file system should be remounted.

Note – If you have an existing mirror or transactional volume, you can use the
`metarename -x` command to remove the mirror or transactional volume and keep
data on the underlying volume. For a transactional volume, as long as the master
device is a volume (RAID 0, RAID 1, or RAID 5 volume), you can keep data on that
volume.

Working with Configuration Files

Solaris Volume Manager configuration files contain basic Solaris Volume Manager
information, as well as most of the data necessary to reconstruct a configuration. The
following sections illustrate how to work with these files.

▼ How to Create Configuration Files

● **Once you have defined all appropriate parameters for the Solaris Volume Manager
environment, use the** `metastat -p` **command to create the** `/etc/lvm/md.tab` **file.**

```
# metastat -p > /etc/lvm/md.tab
```

This file contains all parameters for use by the `metainit`, and `metahs` commands, in
case you need to set up several similar environments or re-create the configuration
after a system failure.

For more information about the `md.tab` file, see "Overview of the `md.tab` File"
on page 279.

▼ How to Initialize Solaris Volume Manager from a Configuration File

Caution – Use this procedure only if you have experienced a complete loss of your
Solaris Volume Manager configuration, or if you have no configuration yet and you
want to create a configuration from a saved configuration file.

If your system loses the information maintained in the state database (for example,
because the system was rebooted after all state database replicas were deleted), and as
long as no volumes were created since the state database was lost, you can use the
`md.cf` or `md.tab` files to recover your Solaris Volume Manager configuration.

> **Note –** The md.cf file does not maintain information on active hot spares. Thus, if hot spares were in use when the Solaris Volume Manager configuration was lost, those volumes that were using active hot spares will likely be corrupted.

For more information about these files, see md.cf(4) and md.tab(4).

1. **Create state database replicas.**

   See "Creating State Database Replicas" on page 58 for more information.

2. **Create, or update the** /etc/lvm/md.tab **file.**

   - If you are attempting to recover the last known Solaris Volume Manager configuration, copy the md.cf file to the md.tab file.

   - If you are creating a new Solaris Volume Manager configuration based on a copy of the md.tab file that you preserved, put a copy of your preserved file at /etc/lvm/md.tab.

3. **Edit the "new"** md.tab **file and do the following:**

   - If you are creating a new configuration or recovering a configuration after a crash, configure the mirrors as one-way mirrors. If a mirror's submirrors are not the same size, be sure to use the smallest submirror for this one-way mirror. Otherwise data could be lost.

   - If you are recovering an existing configuration and Solaris Volume Manager was cleanly stopped, leave the mirror configuration as multi-way mirrors

   - Specify RAID 5 volumes with the -k option, to prevent reinitialization of the device. See the metainit(1M) man page for more information.

4. **Check the syntax of the** md.tab **file entries without committing changes by using the following form of the** metainit **command:**

   ```
   # metainit -n -a component-name
   ```

   - -n specifies not to actually create the devices. Use this to check to verify that the results will be as you expect

   - -a specifies to activate the devices.

   - *component-name* specifies the name of the component to initialize. IF no component is specified, all components will be created.

5. **If no problems were apparent from the previous step, re-create the volumes and hot spare pools from the** md.tab **file:**

   ```
   # metainit -a component-name
   ```

   - -a specifies to activate the devices.

   - *component-name* specifies the name of the component to initialize. If no component is specified, all components will be created.

6. **As needed, make the one-way mirrors into multi-way mirrors by using the**
   `metattach` **command.**

7. **Validate the data on the volumes.**

Changing Solaris Volume Manager Defaults

The Solaris Volume Manager configuration has the following default values:

- 128 volumes per disk set
- 4 disk sets
- State database replica maximum size of 8192 blocks

The values of total volumes and number of disk sets can be changed if necessary, and the tasks in this section tell you how.

▼ How to Increase the Number of Default Volumes

This task describes how to increase the number of volumes from the default value of 128. If you need to configure more than the default, you can increase this value up to 8192.

Caution – If you lower this number at any point, any volume existing between the old number and the new number might not be available, potentially resulting in data loss. If you see a message such as "md: d200: not configurable, check /kernel/drv/md.conf" you must edit the md.conf file and increase the value, as explained in this task.

1. **Check the prerequisites ("Prerequisites for Troubleshooting the System" on page 254).**

2. **Edit the** `/kernel/drv/md.conf` **file.**

3. **Change the value of the** nmd **field. Values up to 8192 are supported.**

4. **Save your changes.**

5. **Perform a reconfiguration reboot to build the volume names.**

   ```
   # boot -r
   ```

Example—`md.conf` File

Here is a sample `md.conf` file that is configured for 256 volumes.

```
#
#ident "@(#)md.conf   1.7     94/04/04 SMI"
#
# Copyright (c) 1992, 1993, 1994 by Sun Microsystems, Inc.
#
#
#pragma ident   "@(#)md.conf    2.1     00/07/07 SMI"
#
# Copyright (c) 1992-1999 by Sun Microsystems, Inc.
# All rights reserved.
#
name="md" parent="pseudo" nmd=256 md_nsets=4;
```

How to Increase the Number of Default Disk Sets

This task shows you how to increase the number of disk sets from the default value of
4.

Caution – Do not decrease the number of default disk sets if you have already
configured disk sets. Lowering this number could make existing disk sets unavailable
or unusable.

1. **Check the prerequisites ("Prerequisites for Troubleshooting the System"
   on page 254).**

2. **Edit the `/kernel/drv/md.conf` file.**

3. **Change the value of the `md_nsets` field. Values up to 32 are supported.**

4. **Save your changes.**

5. **Perform a reconfiguration reboot to build the volume names.**

   ```
   # boot -r
   ```

Example—`md.conf` File

Here is a sample `md.conf` file that is configured for five shared disk sets. The value of
`md_nsets` is six, which results in five shared disk sets and the one local disk set.

```
#
#
#pragma ident   "@(#)md.conf    2.1     00/07/07 SMI"
```

```
#
# Copyright (c) 1992-1999 by Sun Microsystems, Inc.
# All rights reserved.
#
name="md" parent="pseudo" nmd=128 md_nsets=6;
# Begin MDD database info (do not edit)
...
# End MDD database info (do not edit)
```

Growing a File System

After a volume that contains a file system is expanded (more space is added), if that volume contains a UFS, you also need to "grow" the file system to recognize the added space. You must manually grow the file system with the `growfs` command. The `growfs` command expands the file system, even while mounted. However, write access to the file system is not possible while the `growfs` command is running.

An application, such as a database, that uses the raw device must have its own method to grow added space. Solaris Volume Manager does not provide this capability.

The `growfs` command will "write-lock" a mounted file system as it expands the file system. The length of time the file system is write-locked can be shortened by expanding the file system in stages. For instance, to expand a 1 Gbyte file system to 2 Gbytes, the file system can be grown in 16 Mbyte stages using the `-s` option to specify the total size of the new file system at each stage.

During the expansion, the file system is not available for write access because of write-lock. Write accesses are transparently suspended and are restarted when the `growfs` command unlocks the file system. Read accesses are not affected, though access times are not kept while the lock is in effect.

Background Information for Expanding Slices and Volumes

Note – Solaris Volume Manager volumes can be expanded, but not shrunk.

- A volume, regardless if it is used for a file system, application, or database, can be expanded. So, you can expand RAID 0 (stripe and concatenation) volumes, RAID 1 (mirror) volumes, and RAID 5 volumes as well as soft partitions.

- You can concatenate a volume that contains an existing file system while the file system is in use. Then, as long as the file system is UFS, it can be expanded (with the growfs command) to fill the larger space without interrupting read access to the data.

- Once a file system is expanded, it cannot be shrunk, due to constraints in UFS.

- Applications and databases that use the raw device must have their own method to "grow" the added space so that they can recognize it. Solaris Volume Manager does not provide this capability.

- When a component is added to a RAID 5 volume, it becomes a concatenation to the device. The new component does not contain parity information. However, data on the new component is protected by the overall parity calculation that takes place for the volume.

- You can expand a log device by adding additional components. You do not need to run the growfs command, as Solaris Volume Manager automatically recognizes the additional space on reboot.

- Soft partitions can be expanded by adding space from the underlying volume or slice. All other volumes can be expanded by adding slices.

▼ How to Grow a File System

1. **Check "Prerequisites for Creating Solaris Volume Manager Elements" on page 46.**

2. **Use the growfs command to grow a UFS on a logical volume.**

   # **growfs -M** /mount-point **/dev/md/rdsk/**volumename

   See the following example and the growfs(1M) man page for more information.

Example—Growing a File System

```
# df -k
Filesystem                kbytes    used    avail capacity  Mounted on
...
/dev/md/dsk/d10            69047    65426        0    100%    /home2
...
# growfs -M /home2 /dev/md/rdsk/d10
/dev/md/rdsk/d10:       295200 sectors in 240 cylinders of 15 tracks, 82 sectors
        144.1MB in 15 cyl groups (16 c/g, 9.61MB/g, 4608 i/g)
super-block backups (for fsck -F ufs -o b=#) at:
 32, 19808, 39584, 59360, 79136, 98912, 118688, 138464, 158240, 178016, 197792,
 217568, 237344, 257120, 276896,
# df -k
Filesystem                kbytes    used    avail capacity  Mounted on
...
/dev/md/dsk/d10           138703    65426    59407     53%    /home2
...
```

In this example, a new slice was added to a volume, d10, which contains the mounted file system /home2. The growfs command specifies the mount point with the -M option to be /home2, which is expanded onto the raw volume /dev/md/rdsk/d10. The file system will span the entire volume when the growfs command is complete. You can use the df -hk command before and after to verify the total disk capacity.

Note – For mirror and transactional volumes, always run the growfs command on the top-level volume, not a submirror or master device, even though space is added to the submirror or master device.

Overview of Replacing and Enabling Components in RAID 1 and RAID 5 Volumes

Solaris Volume Manager has the capability to *replace* and *enable* components within RAID 1 (mirror) and RAID 5 volumes.

In Solaris Volume Manager terms, *replacing* a component is a way to substitute an available component on the system for a selected component in a submirror or RAID 5 volume. You can think of this process as logical replacement, as opposed to physically replacing the component. (See "Replacing a Component With Another Available Component" on page 231.)

Enabling a component means to "activate" or substitute a component with itself (that is, the component name is the same). See "Enabling a Component" on page 230.

Note – When recovering from disk errors, scan /var/adm/messages to see what kind of errors occurred. If the errors are transitory and the disks themselves do not have problems, try enabling the failed components. You can also use the format command to test a disk.

Enabling a Component

You can enable a component when any of the following conditions exist:

- Solaris Volume Manager could not access the physical drive. This problem might have occurred, for example, due to a power loss, or a loose drive cable. In this case, Solaris Volume Manager puts the components in the "Maintenance" state. You need to make sure that the drive is accessible (restore power, reattach cables, and so on), and then enable the components in the volumes.

- You suspect that a physical drive is having transitory problems that are not disk-related. You might be able to fix a component in the "Maintenance" state by simply enabling it. If this does not fix the problem, then you need to either physically replace the disk drive and enable the component, or replace the component with another available component on the system.

  When you physically replace a drive, be sure to partition it like the old drive to ensure adequate space on each used component.

Note – Always check for state database replicas and hot spares on the drive being replaced. Any state database replica shown to be in error should be deleted before replacing the disk. Then after enabling the component, they should be re-created (at the same size). You should treat hot spares in the same manner.

Replacing a Component With Another Available Component

You use the `metareplace` command when you replace or swap an existing component with a different component that is available and not in use on the system.

You can use this command when any of the following conditions exist:

- A disk drive has problems, and you do not have a replacement drive, but you do have available components elsewhere on the system.

  You might want to use this strategy if a replacement is absolutely necessary but you do not want to shut down the system.

- You are seeing soft errors.

  Physical disks might report soft errors even though Solaris Volume Manager shows the mirror/submirror or RAID 5 volume in the "Okay" state. Replacing the component in question with another available component enables you to perform preventative maintenance and potentially prevent hard errors from occurring.

- You want to do performance tuning.

  For example, by using the performance monitoring feature available from the Enhanced Storage tool within the Solaris Management Console, you see that a particular component in a RAID 5 volume is experiencing a high load average, even though it is in the "Okay" state. To balance the load on the volume, you can replace that component with a component from a disk that is less utilized. You can perform this type of replacement online without interrupting service to the volume.

Maintenance and Last Erred States

When a component in a mirror or RAID 5 volume experiences errors, Solaris Volume Manager puts the component in the "Maintenance" state. No further reads or writes are performed to a component in the "Maintenance" state. Subsequent errors on other components in the same volume are handled differently, depending on the type of volume. A RAID 1 volume might be able to tolerate many components in the "Maintenance" state and still be read from and written to. A RAID 5 volume, by definition, can only tolerate a single component in the "Maintenance" state.

When a component in a RAID 0 or RAID 5 volume experiences errors and there are no redundant components to read from (for example, in a RAID 5 volume, after one component goes into Maintenance state, there is no redundancy available, so the next component to fail would go into "Last Erred" state) When either a mirror or RAID 5 volume has a component in the "Last Erred" state, I/O is still attempted to the component marked "Last Erred." This happens because a "Last Erred" component contains the last good copy of data from Solaris Volume Manager's point of view. With a component in the "Last Erred" state, the volume behaves like a normal device (disk) and returns I/O errors to an application. Usually, at this point some data has been lost.

Always replace components in the "Maintenance" state first, followed by those in the "Last Erred" state. After a component is replaced and resynchronized, use the `metastat` command to verify its state, then validate the data to make sure it is good.

Mirrors –If components are in the "Maintenance" state, no data has been lost. You can safely replace or enable the components in any order. If a component is in the "Last Erred" state, you cannot replace it until you first replace all the other mirrored components in the "Maintenance" state. Replacing or enabling a component in the "Last Erred" state usually means that some data has been lost. Be sure to validate the data on the mirror after you repair it.

RAID 5 Volumes–A RAID 5 volume can tolerate a single component failure. You can safely replace a single component in the "Maintenance" state without losing data. If an error on another component occurs, it is put into the "Last Erred" state. At this point, the RAID 5 volume is a read-only device. You need to perform some type of error recovery so that the state of the RAID 5 volume is stable and the possibility of data loss is reduced. If a RAID 5 volume reaches a "Last Erred" state, there is a good chance it has lost data. Be sure to validate the data on the RAID 5 volume after you repair it.

Background Information For Replacing and Enabling Slices in Mirrors and RAID 5 Volumes

When you replace components in a mirror or a RAID 5 volume, follow these guidelines:

- Always replace components in the "Maintenance" state first, followed by those components in the "Last Erred" state.

- After a component is replaced and resynchronized, use the `metastat` command to verify the volume's state, then validate the data to make sure it is good. Replacing or enabling a component in the "Last Erred" state usually means that some data has been lost. Be sure to validate the data on the volume after you repair it. For a UFS, run the `fsck` command to validate the "metadata" (the structure of the file system) then check the actual user data. (Practically, users will have to examine their files.) A database or other application must have its own way of validating its internal data structure.

- Always check for state database replicas and hot spares when you replace components. Any state database replica shown to be in error should be deleted before you replace the physical disk. The state database replica should be added back before enabling the component. The same procedure applies to hot spares.

- RAID 5 volumes – During component replacement, data is recovered, either from a hot spare currently in use, or using the RAID level 5 parity, when no hot spare is in use.

- RAID 1 volumes– When you replace a component, Solaris Volume Manager automatically starts resynchronizing the new component with the rest of the mirror. When the resynchronization completes, the replaced component becomes readable and writable. If the failed component has been replaced with data from a hot spare, the hot spare is placed in the "Available" state and made available for other hot spare replacements.

- The new component must be large enough to replace the old component.

- As a precaution, back up all data before you replace "Last Erred" devices.

Note – A submirror or RAID 5 volume might be using a hot spare in place of a failed component. When that failed component is enabled or replaced by using the procedures in this section, the hot spare is marked "Available" in the hot spare pool, and is ready for use.

## CHAPTER 22

Best Practices for Solaris Volume Manager

This chapter provides general best practices information from real world storage scenarios using Solaris Volume Manager. In this section, you will see a typical configuration, followed by an analysis, followed by a recommended ("Best Practices") configuration to meet the same needs.

This chapter includes the following information:

Deploying Small Servers

Distributed computing environments, from ISPs to geographically distributed sales offices to telecommunication service providers, often need to deploy similar or identical servers at multiple locations. These servers might provide router or firewall services, email services, DNS caches, Usenet (Network News) servers, DHCP services, or other services best provided at a variety of locations. These small servers have several characteristics in common:

- High-reliability requirements
- High-availability requirements
- Routine hardware and performance requirements

As a starting point, consider a Netra with a single SCSI bus and two internal disks—an off-the-shelf configuration, and a good starting point for distributed servers. Solaris Volume Manager could easily be used to mirror some or all of the slices, thus providing redundant storage to help guard against disk failure. See the following figure for an example.

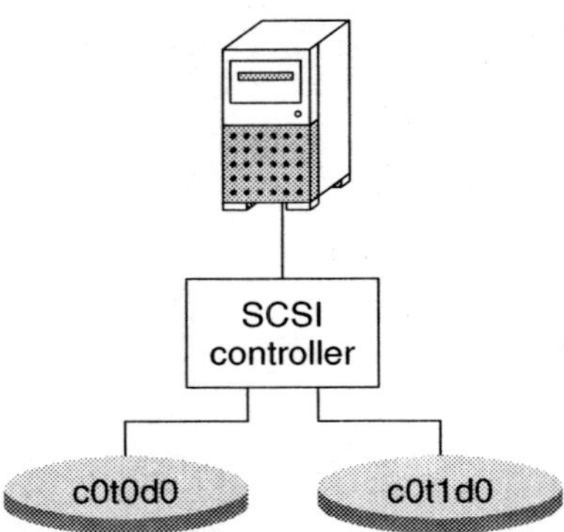

FIGURE 22–1 Small system configuration

A configuration like this example might include mirrors for the root (/), /usr, swap, /var, and /export file systems, plus state database replicas (one per disk). As such, a failure of either side of any of the mirrors would not necessarily result in system failure, and up to five discrete failures could possibly be tolerated. However, the system is not sufficiently protected against disk or slice failure. A variety of potential failures could result in a complete system failure, requiring operator intervention.

While this configuration does help provide some protection against catastrophic disk failure, it exposes key possible single points of failure:

- The single SCSI controller represents a potential point of failure. If the controller fails, the system will be down, pending replacement of the part.

- The two disks do not provide adequate distribution of state database replicas. The majority consensus algorithm requires that half of the state database replicas be available for the system to continue to run, and half plus one replica for a reboot. So, if one state database replica were on each disk and one disk or the slice containing the replica failed, the system could not reboot (thus making a mirrored root ineffective). If two or more state database replicas were on each disk, a single slice failure would likely not be problematic, but a disk failure would still prevent a reboot. If different number of replicas were on each disk, one would have more than half and one fewer than half. If the disk with fewer replicas failed, the system could reboot and continue. However, if the disk with more replicas failed, the system would immediately panic.

A "Best Practices" approach would be to modify the configuration by adding one more controller and one more hard drive. The resulting configuration could be far more resilient.

Using Solaris Volume Manager With Networked Storage Devices

Solaris Volume Manager works well with networked storage devices, particularly those devices that provide configurable RAID levels and flexible options. Usually, the combination of Solaris Volume Manager and other devices can result in performance and flexibility superior to either product alone.

Generally, do not establish Solaris Volume Manager RAID 5 volumes on any hardware storage devices that provide redundancy (for example, RAID 1 and RAID 5 volumes). Unless you have a very unusual situation, performance will suffer, and you will gain very little in terms of redundancy or higher availability

Configuring underlying hardware storage devices with RAID 5 volumes, on the other hand, is very effective, as it provides a good foundation for Solaris Volume Manager volumes. Hardware RAID 5 provides some additional redundancy for Solaris Volume Manager RAID 1 volumes, soft partitions, or other volumes.

Note – Do not configure similar software and hardware devices. For example, do not build software RAID 1 volumes on top of hardware RAID 1 devices. Configuring similar devices in hardware and software results in performance penalties without offsetting any gains in reliability.

Solaris Volume Manager RAID 1 volumes built on underlying hardware storage devices are not RAID 1+0, as Solaris Volume Manager cannot understand the underlying storage well enough to offer RAID 1+0 capabilities.

Configuring soft partitions on top of an Solaris Volume Manager RAID 1 volume, built in turn on a hardware RAID 5 device is a very flexible and resilient configuration.

## CHAPTER 23

Monitoring and Error Reporting (Tasks)

When Solaris Volume Manager encounters a problem, such as being unable to write to a volume due to physical errors at the slice level, it changes the status of the volume so system administrators can stay informed. However, unless you regularly check the status in the Solaris Volume Manager graphical user interface through the Solaris Management Console, or by running the `metastat` command, you might not see these status changes in a timely fashion.

This chapter provides information about various monitoring tools available for Solaris Volume Manager, including the Solaris Volume Manager SNMP agent, which is a subagent of the Solstice Enterprise Agents™ monitoring software. In addition to configuring the Solaris Volume Manager SNMP agent to report SNMP traps, you can create a shell script to actively monitor many Solaris Volume Manager functions. Such a shell script can run as a `cron` job and be valuable in identifying issues before they become problems.

This is a list of the information in this chapter:

Solaris Volume Manager Monitoring and Reporting (Task Map)

The following task map identifies the procedures needed to manage Solaris Volume Manager error reporting.

Task	Description	Instructions
Set the `mdmonitord` daemon to periodically check for errors	Set the error-checking interval used by the `mdmonitord` daemon by editing the `/etc/rc2.d/S95svm.sync` file.	"Setting the `mdmonitord` Command for Periodic Error Checking" on page 240
Configure the Solaris Volume Manager SNMP agent	Edit the configuration files in the `/etc/snmp/conf` directory so Solaris Volume Manager will throw traps appropriately, to the correct system.	"Configuring the Solaris Volume Manager SNMP Agent" on page 242
Monitor Solaris Volume Manager with scripts run by the `cron` command	Create or adapt a script to check for errors, then run the script from the `cron` command.	"Monitoring Solaris Volume Manager with a `cron` Job" on page 245

Setting the `mdmonitord` Command for Periodic Error Checking

Solaris Volume Manager includes the `/usr/sbin/mdmonitord` daemon, which is a program that checks Solaris Volume Manager volumes for errors. By default, this program checks all volumes for errors only when an error is detected (for example, through a write error) on a volume. However, you can set this program to actively check for errors at an interval you specify.

▼ How to Configure the `mdmonitord` Command for Periodic Error Checking

The `/etc/rc2.d/S95svm.sync` script starts the `mdmonitord` command at boot time. Edit the `/etc/rc2.d/S95svm.sync` script to add a time interval for periodic checking.

1. **Become superuser.**

2. **Edit the** `/etc/rc2.d/S95svm.sync` **script and change the line that starts the** `mdmonitord` **command by adding a** `-t` **flag and the number of seconds between checks.**

```
if [ -x $MDMONITORD ]; then
        $MDMONITORD -t 3600
        error=$?
        case $error in
        0)      ;;
        *)          echo "Could not start $MDMONITORD. Error $error."
                ;;
        esac
fi
```

3. **Stop and restart the** `mdmonitord` **command to activate your changes.**

```
# /etc/rc2.d/S95svm.sync stop
# /etc/rc2.d/S95svm.sync start
```

For more information, see `mdmonitord`(1M).

Solaris Volume Manager SNMP Agent Overview

The Solaris Volume Manager SNMP trap agent requires both the core packages `SUNWlvmr` and `SUNWlvma` and the Solstice Enterprise Agent packages. Those packages include the following:

- `SUNWmibii`
- `SUNWsacom`
- `SUNWsadmi`
- `SUNWsasnm`
- `SUNWsasnx`

These packages are part of the Solaris operating environment and are normally installed by default unless the package selection was modified at install time or a minimal set of packages was installed. After you confirm that all five packages are available (by using the `pkginfo` *pkgname* command, as in `pkginfo SUNWsasnx`), you need to configure the Solaris Volume Manager SNMP agent, as described in the following section.

Configuring the Solaris Volume Manager SNMP Agent

The Solaris Volume Manager SNMP agent is not enabled by default. Use the following procedure to enable SNMP traps.

▼ How to Configure the Solaris Volume Manager SNMP Agent

1. **Become superuser.**

2. **Move the** `/etc/snmp/conf/mdlogd.rsrc-` **configuration file to** `/etc/snmp/conf/mdlogd.rsrc`.

   ```
   # mv /etc/snmp/conf/mdlogd.rsrc- /etc/snmp/conf/mdlogd.rsrc
   ```

3. **Edit the** `/etc/snmp/conf/mdlogd.acl` **file to specify which hosts should receive SNMP traps. Look in the file for the following:**

   ```
   trap = {
       {
           trap-community = SNMP-trap
           hosts = corsair
           {
               enterprise = "Solaris Volume Manager"
               trap-num = 1, 2, 3
           }
   ```

   Change the line that contains `hosts = corsair` to specify the host name that you want to receive Solaris Volume Manager SNMP traps. For example, to send SNMP traps to `lexicon`, you would edit the line to `hosts = lexicon`. If you want to include multiple hosts, provide a comma-delimited list of host names, as in `hosts = lexicon, idiom`.

4. **Also edit the** `/etc/snmp/conf/snmpdx.acl` **file to specify which hosts should receive the SNMP traps.**

   Find the block that begins with `trap =` and add the same list of hosts that you added in the previous step. This section might be commented out with #'s. If so, you must remove the # at the beginning of the required lines in this section. Additional lines in the trap section are also commented out, but you can leave those lines alone or delete them for clarity. After uncommenting the required lines and updating the hosts line, this section could look like this:

   ```
   ###################
   # trap parameters #
   ###################
   ```

```
trap = {
   {
        trap-community = SNMP-trap
        hosts =lexicon
        {
          enterprise = "sun"
          trap-num = 0, 1, 2-5, 6-16
        }
#       {
#         enterprise = "3Com"
#         trap-num = 4
#       }
#       {
#         enterprise = "snmp"
#         trap-num = 0, 2, 5
#       }
#   }
#   {
#       trap-community = jerry-trap
#       hosts = jerry, nanak, hubble
#       {
#         enterprise = "sun"
#         trap-num = 1, 3
#       }
#       {
#         enterprise = "snmp"
#         trap-num = 1-3
#       }
   }
}
```

Note – Make sure that you have the same number of opening and closing brackets in the `/etc/snmp/conf/snmpdx.acl` file.

---

5. **Add a new Solaris Volume Manager section to the** `/etc/snmp/conf/snmpdx.acl` **file, inside the section you that uncommented in the previous step.**

```
        trap-community = SNMP-trap
        hosts = lexicon
        {
          enterprise = "sun"
          trap-num = 0, 1, 2-5, 6-16
        }
        {
            enterprise = "Solaris Volume Manager"
            trap-num = 1, 2, 3
        }
```

Note that the added four lines are placed immediately after the `enterprise = "sun"` block.

6. **Append the following line to the** `/etc/snmp/conf/enterprises.oid` **file:**

7. **Stop and restart the Solstice Enterprise Agents server.**

```
# /etc/init.d/init.snmpdx stop
# /etc/init.d/init.snmpdx start
```

Note – Whenever you upgrade your Solaris operating environment, you will probably need to edit the/etc/snmp/conf/enterprises.oid file and append the line in Step 6 again, then restart the Solaris Enterprise Agents server.

After you have completed this procedure, your system will issue SNMP traps to the host or hosts that you specified. You will need to use an appropriate SNMP monitor, such as Solstice Enterprise Agents software, to view the traps as they are issued.

Note – Set the mdmonitord command to probe your system regularly to help ensure that you receive traps if problems arise. See "Setting the mdmonitord Command for Periodic Error Checking" on page 240. Also, refer to "Monitoring Solaris Volume Manager with a cron Job" on page 245 for additional error-checking options.

Solaris Volume Manager SNMP Agent Limitations

The Solaris Volume Manager SNMP agent has certain limitations, and will not issue traps for all Solaris Volume Manager problems that system administrators will likely need to know about. Specifically, the agent issues traps *only* in the following instances:

- A RAID 1 or RAID 5 subcomponent goes into "needs maintenance" state
- A hot spare is swapped into service
- A hot spare starts to resynchronize
- A hot spare completes resynchronization
- A mirror is taken offline
- A disk set is taken by another host and the current host panics

Many problematic situations, such as an unavailable disk with RAID 0 volumes or soft partitions on it, do not result in SNMP traps, even when reads and writes to the device are attempted. SCSI or IDE errors are generally reported in these cases, but other SNMP agents must issue traps for those errors to be reported to a monitoring console.

Monitoring Solaris Volume Manager with a `cron` Job

▼ How to Automate Checking for Errors in Volumes

● **To automatically check your Solaris Volume Manager configuration for errors, create a script that the** `cron` **utility can periodically.**

The following example shows a script that you can adapt and modify for your needs.

Note – This script serves as a starting point for automating Solaris Volume Manager error checking. You will probably need to modify this script for your own configuration.

```
#
#ident "@(#)metacheck.sh   1.3     96/06/21 SMI"
#!/bin/ksh
#!/bin/ksh -x
#!/bin/ksh -v
# ident='%Z%%M%    %I%      %E% SMI'
#
# Copyright (c) 1999 by Sun Microsystems, Inc.
#
# metacheck
#
# Check on the status of the metadevice configuration.  If there is a problem
# return a non zero exit code.  Depending on options, send email notification.
#
# -h
#    help
# -s setname
#    Specify the set to check.  By default, the 'local' set will be checked.
# -m recipient [recipient...]
#    Send email notification to the specified recipients.  This
#    must be the last argument. The notification shows up as a short
#    email message with a subject of
#        "Solaris Volume Manager Problem: metacheck.who.nodename.setname"
#    which summarizes the problem(s) and tells how to obtain detailed
#    information. The "setname" is from the -s option, "who" is from
#    the -w option, and "nodename" is reported by uname(1).
#    Email notification is further affected by the following options:
#        -f    to suppress additional messages after a problem
#              has been found.
#        -d    to control the supression.
#        -w    to identify who generated the email.
#        -t    to force email even when there is no problem.
```

```
# -w who
#     indicate who is running the command. By default, this is the
#     user-name as reported by id(1M). This is used when sending
#     email notification (-m).
# -f
#     Enable filtering.  Filtering applies to email notification (-m).
#     Filtering requires root permission.  When sending email notification
#     the file /etc/lvm/metacheck.setname.pending is used to
#     controll the filter.  The following matrix specifies the behavior
#     of the filter:
#
#     problem_found      file_exists
#       yes                no          Create file, send notification
#       yes                yes          Resend notification if the current date
#                        (as specified by -d datefmt) is
#                        different than the file date.
#       no              yes          Delete file, send notification
#                      that the problem is resolved.
#       no              no           Send notification if -t specified.
#
# -d datefmt
#     Specify the format of the date for filtering (-f).  This option
#     controls the how often re-notification via email occurs. If the
#     current date according to the specified format (strftime(3C)) is
#     identical to the date contained in the
#     /etc/lvm/metacheck.setname.pending file then the message is
#     suppressed. The default date format is "%D", which will send one
#     re-notification per day.
# -t
#     Test mode.  Enable email generation even when there is no problem.
#     Used for end-to-end verification of the mechanism and email addresses.
#
#
# These options are designed to allow integration of metacheck
# into crontab.  For example, a root crontab entry of:
#
# 0,15,30,45 * * * * /usr/sbin/metacheck -f -w SVMcron \
#   -d '\%D \%h' -m notice@example.com 2148357243.8333033@pager.example.com
#
# would check for problems every 15 minutes, and generate an email to
# notice@example.com (and send to an email pager service) every hour when
# there is a problem.  Note the \ prior to the '%' characters for a
# crontab entry.  Bounced email would come back to root@nodename.
# The subject line for email generated by the above line would be
# Solaris Volume Manager Problem: metacheck.SVMcron.nodename.local
#

# display a debug line to controlling terminal (works in pipes)
decho()
{
    if [ "$debug" = "yes" ] ; then
    echo "DEBUG: $*"     < /dev/null > /dev/tty 2>&1
    fi
}
```

```
# if string $1 is in $2-* then return $1, else return ""
strstr()
{
    typeset    look="$1"
    typeset    ret=""

    shift
#   decho "strstr LOOK .$look. FIRST .$1."
    while [ $# -ne 0 ] ; do
    if [ "$look" = "$1" ] ; then
        ret="$look"
    fi
    shift
    done
    echo "$ret"
}

# if string $1 is in $2-* then delete it. return result
strdstr()
{
    typeset    look="$1"
    typeset    ret=""

    shift
#   decho "strdstr LOOK .$look. FIRST .$1."
    while [ $# -ne 0 ] ; do
    if [ "$look" != "$1" ] ; then
        ret="$ret $1"
    fi
    shift
    done
    echo "$ret"
}

merge_continued_lines()
{
    awk -e '\
    BEGIN { line = "";} \
    $NF == "\\" { \
        $NF = ""; \
        line = line $0; \
        next; \
    } \
    $NF != "\\" { \
        if ( line != "" ) { \
        print line $0; \
        line = ""; \
        } else { \
        print $0; \
        } \
    }'
}

# trim out stuff not associated with metadevices
find_meta_devices()
```

```
{
	typeset	devices=""

#	decho "find_meta_devices .$*."
	while [ $# -ne 0 ] ; do
	case $1 in
	d+([0-9]) )	# metadevice name
	    devices="$devices $1"
	    ;;
	esac
	shift
	done
	echo "$devices"
}


# return the list of top level metadevices
toplevel()
{
	typeset	comp_meta_devices=""
	typeset	top_meta_devices=""
	typeset	devices=""
	typeset	device=""
	typeset	comp=""

	metastat$setarg -p | merge_continued_lines | while read line ; do
	echo "$line"
	devices=`find_meta_devices $line`
	set -- $devices
	if [ $# -ne 0 ] ; then
	    device=$1
	    shift
	    # check to see if device already refered to as component
	    comp=`strstr $device $comp_meta_devices`
	    if [ -z $comp ] ; then
	    top_meta_devices="$top_meta_devices $device"
	    fi
	    # add components to component list, remove from top list
	    while [ $# -ne 0 ] ; do
	    comp=$1
	    comp_meta_devices="$comp_meta_devices $comp"
	    top_meta_devices=`strdstr $comp $top_meta_devices`
	    shift
	    done
	fi
	done > /dev/null 2>&1
	echo $top_meta_devices
}


#
# - MAIN
#
METAPATH=/usr/sbin
PATH=//usr/bin:$METAPATH
USAGE="usage: metacheck [-s setname] [-h] [[-t] [-f [-d datefmt]] \
    [-w who] -m recipient [recipient...]]"
```

```
datefmt="%D"
debug="no"
filter="no"
mflag="no"
set="local"
setarg=""
testarg="no"
who=`id | sed -e 's/^uid=[0-9][0-9]*(//' -e 's/).*//'`

while getopts d:Dfms:tw: flag
do
    case $flag in
    d)     datefmt=$OPTARG;
    ;;
    D)     debug="yes"
    ;;
    f)     filter="yes"
    ;;
    m)     mflag="yes"
    ;;
    s)     set=$OPTARG;
    if [ "$set" != "local" ] ; then
        setarg=" -s $set";
    fi
    ;;
    t)     testarg="yes";
    ;;
    w)     who=$OPTARG;
    ;;
    \?)    echo $USAGE
    exit 1
    ;;
    esac
done

# if mflag specified then everything else part of recipient
shift `expr $OPTIND - 1`
if [ $mflag = "no" ] ; then
    if [ $# -ne 0 ] ; then
    echo $USAGE
    exit 1
    fi
else
    if [ $# -eq 0 ] ; then
    echo $USAGE
    exit 1
    fi
fi
recipients="$*"

curdate_filter=`date +$datefmt`
curdate=`date`
node=`uname -n`
```

```
# establish files
msg_f=/tmp/metacheck.msg.$$
msgs_f=/tmp/metacheck.msgs.$$
metastat_f=/tmp/metacheck.metastat.$$
metadb_f=/tmp/metacheck.metadb.$$
metahs_f=/tmp/metacheck.metahs.$$
pending_f=/etc/lvm/metacheck.$set.pending
files="$metastat_f $metadb_f $metahs_f $msg_f $msgs_f"

rm -f $files                                    > /dev/null 2>&1
trap "rm -f $files > /dev/null 2>&1; exit 1" 1 2 3 15

# Check to see if metadb is capable of running
have_metadb="yes"
metadb$setarg                                   > $metadb_f 2>&1
if [ $? -ne 0 ] ; then
    have_metadb="no"
fi
grep "there are no existing databases"      < $metadb_f     > /dev/null 2>&1
if [ $? -eq 0 ] ; then
    have_metadb="no"
fi
grep "/dev/md/admin"                       < $metadb_f     > /dev/null 2>&1
if [ $? -eq 0 ] ; then
    have_metadb="no"
fi

# check for problems accessing metadbs
retval=0
if [ "$have_metadb" = "no" ] ; then
    retval=1
    echo "metacheck: metadb problem, can't run '$METAPATH/metadb$setarg'" \
                                >> $msgs_f
else
    # snapshot the state
    metadb$setarg 2>&1 | sed -e '1d' | merge_continued_lines     > $metadb_f
    metastat$setarg 2>&1 | merge_continued_lines          > $metastat_f
    metahs$setarg -i 2>&1 | merge_continued_lines          > $metahs_f

    #
    # Check replicas for problems, capital letters in the flags
    # indicate an error, fields are seperated by tabs.
    #
    problem=`awk < $metadb_f -F\t '{if ($1 ~ /[A-Z]/) print $1;}'`
    if [ -n "$problem" ] ; then
    retval=`expr $retval + 64`
    echo "\
metacheck: metadb problem, for more detail run:\n\t$METAPATH/metadb$setarg -i" \
                                >> $msgs_f
    fi

    #
    # Check the metadevice state
    #
    problem=`awk < $metastat_f -e \
```

```
            '/State:/ {if ($2 != "Okay" && $2 != "Resyncing") print $0;}''
        if [ -n "$problem" ] ; then
        retval=`expr $retval + 128`
        echo "\
metacheck: metadevice problem, for more detail run:" \
                                >> $msgs_f


        # refine the message to toplevel metadevices that have a problem
        top=`toplevel`
        set -- $top
        while [ $# -ne 0 ] ; do
            device=$1
            problem=`metastat $device | awk -e \
            '/State:/ {if ($2 != "Okay" && $2 != "Resyncing") print $0;}''
            if [ -n "$problem" ] ; then
            echo "\t$METAPATH/metastat$setarg $device"    >> $msgs_f
            # find out what is mounted on the device
            mp=`mount|awk -e '/\/dev\/md\/dsk\/'$device'[ \t]/{print $1;}'`
            if [ -n "$mp" ] ; then
                echo "\t\t$mp mounted on $device"        >> $msgs_f
            fi
            fi
            shift
        done
        fi


        #
        # Check the hotspares to see if any have been used.
        #
        problem=""
        grep "no hotspare pools found"    < $metahs_f        > /dev/null 2>&1
        `if [ $? -ne 0 ] ; then
        problem=`awk < $metahs_f -e \
            '/blocks/ { if ( $2 != "Available" ) print $0;}''
        fi
        if [ -n "$problem" ] ; then
        retval=`expr $retval + 256`
        echo "\
metacheck: hot spare in use, for more detail run:\n\t$METAPATH/metahs$setarg -i" \
                                >> $msgs_f
        fi
fi


# If any errors occurred, then mail the report
if [ $retval -ne 0 ] ; then
    if [ -n "$recipients" ] ; then
    re=""
    if [ -f $pending_f ] && [ "$filter" = "yes" ] ; then
        re="Re: "
        # we have a pending notification, check date to see if we resend
        penddate_filter=`cat $pending_f | head -1`
        if [ "$curdate_filter" != "$penddate_filter" ] ; then
        rm -f $pending_f                  > /dev/null 2>&1
        else
          if [ "$debug" = "yes" ] ; then
```

```sh
                echo "metacheck: email problem notification still pending"
                cat $pending_f
            fi
            fi
        fi
        if [ ! -f $pending_f ] ; then
            if [ "$filter" = "yes" ] ; then
            echo "$curdate_filter\n\tDate:$curdate\n\tTo:$recipients" \
                                > $pending_f
            fi
            echo "\
Solaris Volume Manager: $node: metacheck$setarg: Report: $curdate"          >> $msg_f
            echo "\
-------------------------------------------------------------" >> $msg_f
            cat $msg_f $msgs_f | mailx -s \
            "${re}Solaris Volume Manager Problem: metacheck.$who.$set.$node" $recipients
        fi
        else
        cat $msgs_f
        fi
else
    # no problems detected,
    if [ -n "$recipients" ] ; then
    # default is to not send any mail, or print anything.
    echo "\
Solaris Volume Manager: $node: metacheck$setarg: Report: $curdate"          >> $msg_f
    echo "\
-------------------------------------------------------------" >> $msg_f
    if [ -f $pending_f ] && [ "$filter" = "yes" ] ; then
        # pending filter exista, remove it and send OK
        rm -f $pending_f                        > /dev/null 2>&1
        echo "Problem resolved"                 >> $msg_f
        cat $msg_f | mailx -s \
        "Re: Solaris Volume Manager Problem: metacheck.$who.$node.$set" $recipients
    elif [ "$testarg" = "yes" ] ; then
        # for testing, send mail every time even thought there is no problem
        echo "Messaging test, no problems detected"         >> $msg_f
        cat $msg_f | mailx -s \
        "Solaris Volume Manager Problem: metacheck.$who.$node.$set" $recipients
    fi
    else
    echo "metacheck: Okay"
    fi
fi

rm -f $files                                    > /dev/null 2>&1
exit $retval
```

For information on invoking scripts by using the cron utility, see the cron(1M) man page.

## CHAPTER 24

Troubleshooting Solaris Volume Manager

This chapter describes how to troubleshoot problems related to Solaris Volume Manager. This chapter provides both general troubleshooting guidelines and specific procedures for resolving some particular known problems.

This chapter includes the following information:

- "Troubleshooting Solaris Volume Manager (Task Map)" on page 253
- "Overview of Troubleshooting the System" on page 254
- "General Troubleshooting Approach" on page 255
- "Replacing Disks" on page 255
- "Boot Problems" on page 258

This chapter describes some Solaris Volume Manager problems and their appropriate solution. It is not intended to be all-inclusive but rather to present common scenarios and recovery procedures.

Troubleshooting Solaris Volume Manager (Task Map)

The following task map identifies some procedures needed to troubleshoot Solaris Volume Manager.

Task	Description	Instructions
Replace a failed disk	Replace a disk, then update state database replicas and logical volumes on the new disk.	"How to Replace a Failed Disk" on page 255

Task	Description	Instructions
Recover from improper /etc/vfstab entries	Use the `fsck` command on the mirror, then edit the /etc/vfstab file so the system will boot correctly.	"How to Recover From Improper /etc/vfstab Entries" on page 258
Recover from a boot device failure	Boot from a different submirror.	"How to Recover From a Boot Device Failure" on page 261
Recover from insufficient state database replicas	Delete unavailable replicas by using the `metadb` command.	"How to Recover From Insufficient State Database Replicas" on page 265
Recover configuration data for a lost soft partition	Use the `metarecover` command to recover configuration data for soft partitions.	"How to Recover Configuration Data for a Soft Partition" on page 268
Recover a Solaris Volume Manager configuration from salvaged disks	Attach disks to a new system and have Solaris Volume Manager rebuild the configuration from the existing state database replicas.	"How to Recover a Configuration" on page 271

Overview of Troubleshooting the System

Prerequisites for Troubleshooting the System

To troubleshoot storage management problems related to Solaris Volume Manager, you need to do the following:

- Have root privilege
- Have a current backup of all data

General Guidelines for Troubleshooting Solaris Volume Manager

You should have the following information on hand when you troubleshoot Solaris Volume Manager problems:

- Output from the `metadb` command.
- Output from the `metastat` command.
- Output from the `metastat -p` command.

- Backup copy of the `/etc/vfstab` file.
- Backup copy of the `/etc/lvm/mddb.cf` file.
- Disk partition information, from the `prtvtoc` command (SPARC™ systems) or the `fdisk` command (IA–based systems)
- Solaris version
- Solaris patches installed
- Solaris Volume Manager patches installed

Tip – Any time you update your Solaris Volume Manager configuration, or make other storage or operating environment-related changes to your system, generate fresh copies of this configuration information. You could also generate this information automatically with a `cron` job.

General Troubleshooting Approach

Although there is no one procedure that will enable you to evaluate all problems with Solaris Volume Manager, the following process provides one general approach that might help.

1. Gather information about current configuration.
2. Look at the current status indicators, including the output from the `metastat` and `metadb` commands. There should be information here that indicates which component is faulty.
3. Check the hardware for obvious points of failure. (Is everything connected properly? Was there a recent electrical outage? Have you recently added or changed equipment?)

Replacing Disks

This section describes how to replace disks in a Solaris Volume Manager environment.

▼ How to Replace a Failed Disk

1. **Identify the failed disk to be replaced by examining the** `/var/adm/messages` **file and the** `metastat` **command output.**

2. **Locate any state database replicas that might have been placed on the failed disk.**

Use the `metadb` command to find the replicas.

The `metadb` command might report errors for the state database replicas located on the failed disk. In this example, `c0t1d0` is the problem device.

```
# metadb
    flags             first blk          block count
    a m     u            16                 1034           /dev/dsk/c0t0d0s4
    a       u          1050                 1034           /dev/dsk/c0t0d0s4
    a       u          2084                 1034           /dev/dsk/c0t0d0s4
    W    pc luo          16                 1034           /dev/dsk/c0t1d0s4
    W    pc luo        1050                 1034           /dev/dsk/c0t1d0s4
    W    pc luo        2084                 1034           /dev/dsk/c0t1d0s4
```

The output shows three state database replicas on slice 4 of the local disks, `c0t0d0` and `c0t1d0`. The `W` in the flags field of the `c0t1d0s4` slice indicates that the device has write errors. Three replicas on the `c0t0d0s4` slice are still good.

3. **Record the slice name where the state database replicas reside and the number of state database replicas, then delete the state database replicas.**

The number of state database replicas is obtained by counting the number of appearances of a slice in the `metadb` command output in Step 2. In this example, the three state database replicas that exist on `c0t1d0s4` are deleted.

```
# metadb -d c0t1d0s4
```

Caution – If, after deleting the bad state database replicas, you are left with three or fewer, add more state database replicas before continuing. This will help ensure that configuration information remains intact.

4. **Locate any submirrors that use slices on the failed disk and detach them.**

The `metastat` command can show the affected mirrors. In this example, one submirror, `d10`, is using `c0t1d0s4`. The mirror is `d20`.

```
# metadetach d20 d10
d20: submirror d10 is detached
```

5. **Delete any hot spares on the failed disk.**

```
# metahs -d hsp000 c0t1d0s6
hsp000: Hotspare is deleted
```

6. **Halt the system and boot to single-user mode.**

```
# halt
. . .
ok boot -s
. . .
```

7. **Physically replace the failed disk.**

8. **Repartition the new disk.**

   Use the `format` command or the `fmthard` command to partition the disk with the same slice information as the failed disk. If you have the `prtvtoc` output from the failed disk, you can format the replacement disk with `fmthard -s` */tmp/failed-disk-prtvtoc-output*

9. **If you deleted state database replicas in Step 3, add the same number back to the appropriate slice.**

   In this example, `/dev/dsk/c0t1d0s4` is used.

   ```
   # metadb -a c 3 c0t1d0s4
   ```

10. **Depending on how the disk was used, you have a variety of things to do. Use the following table to decide what to do next.**

    TABLE 24–1 Disk Replacement Decision Table

Type of Device...	Task
Slice	Use normal data recovery procedures.
Unmirrored RAID 0 volume or Soft Partition	If the volume is used for a file system, run the `newfs` command, mount the file system then restore data from backup. If the RAID 0 volume is used for an application that uses the raw device, that application must have its own recovery procedures.
RAID 1 volume (Submirror)	Run the `metattach` command to reattach a detached submirror, which causes the resynchronization to start.
RAID 5 volume	Run the `metareplace` command to re-enable the slice, which causes the resynchronization to start.
Transactional volume	Depends on underlying volume type. If the transactional volume is on a RAID 5 volume, for example, follow those instructions in this table.

11. **Replace hot spares that were deleted, and add them to the appropriate hot spare pool or pools.**

    ```
    # metahs -a hsp000 c0t0d0s6
    hsp000: Hotspare is added
    ```

12. **Validate the data.**

    Check the user/application data on all volumes. You might have to run an application-level consistency checker or use some other method to check the data.

Boot Problems

Because Solaris Volume Manager enables you to mirror the root (/), `swap`, and `/usr` directories, special problems can arise when you boot the system, either through hardware failures or operator error. The tasks in this section provide solutions to such potential problems.

The following table describes these problems and points you to the appropriate solution.

TABLE 24–2 Common Solaris Volume Manager Boot Problems

Reason for the Boot Problem	Instructions
The `/etc/vfstab` file contains incorrect information.	"How to Recover From Improper `/etc/vfstab` Entries" on page 258
There are not enough state database replicas.	"How to Recover From Insufficient State Database Replicas" on page 265
A boot device (disk) has failed.	"How to Recover From a Boot Device Failure" on page 261
The boot mirror has failed.	

Background Information for Boot Problems

- If Solaris Volume Manager takes a volume offline due to errors, unmount all file systems on the disk where the failure occurred. Because each disk slice is independent, multiple file systems can be mounted on a single disk. If the software has encountered a failure, other slices on the same disk will likely experience failures soon. File systems mounted directly on disk slices do not have the protection of Solaris Volume Manager error handling, and leaving such file systems mounted can leave you vulnerable to crashing the system and losing data.

- Minimize the amount of time you run with submirrors disabled or offline. During resynchronization and online backup intervals, the full protection of mirroring is gone.

▼ How to Recover From Improper `/etc/vfstab` Entries

If you have made an incorrect entry in the `/etc/vfstab` file, for example, when mirroring root (/), the system will appear at first to be booting properly then fail. To remedy this situation, you need to edit the `/etc/vfstab` file while in single-user mode.

The high-level steps to recover from improper `/etc/vfstab` file entries are as follows:

1. Booting the system to single-user mode
2. Running the `fsck` command on the mirror volume
3. Remounting file system read-write
4. Optional: running the `metaroot` command for a root (/) mirror
5. Verifying that the `/etc/vfstab` file correctly references the volume for the file system entry
6. Rebooting

Example—Recovering the root (/) Mirror

In the following example, root (/) is mirrored with a two-way mirror, d0. The root (/) entry in the `/etc/vfstab` file has somehow reverted back to the original slice of the file system, but the information in the `/etc/system` file still shows booting to be from the mirror d0. The most likely reason is that the `metaroot` command was not used to maintain the `/etc/system` and `/etc/vfstab` files, or an old copy of the`/etc/vfstab` file was copied back.

The incorrect `/etc/vfstab` file would look something like the following:

```
#device                device          mount           FS      fsck    mount     mount
#to mount              to fsck          point           type    pass    at boot   options
#
/dev/dsk/c0t3d0s0 /dev/rdsk/c0t3d0s0   /               ufs     1       no        -
/dev/dsk/c0t3d0s1 -                    -               swap    -       no        -
/dev/dsk/c0t3d0s6 /dev/rdsk/c0t3d0s6   /usr            ufs     2       no        -
#
/proc             -                    /proc   proc    -       no        -
floppy            -                    /dev/floppy floppy      -       no        -
swap              -                    /tmp    tmpfs   -       yes       -
```

Because of the errors, you automatically go into single-user mode when the system is booted:

```
ok boot
...
configuring network interfaces: hme0.
Hostname: lexicon
mount: /dev/dsk/c0t3d0s0 is not this fstype.
setmnt: Cannot open /etc/mnttab for writing

INIT: Cannot create /var/adm/utmp or /var/adm/utmpx

INIT: failed write of utmpx entry:"   "

INIT: failed write of utmpx entry:"   "
```

```
INIT: SINGLE USER MODE

Type Ctrl-d to proceed with normal startup,
(or give root password for system maintenance): <root-password>
```

At this point, root (/) and /usr are mounted read-only. Follow these steps:

1. **Run the `fsck` command on the root (/) mirror.**

Note – Be careful to use the correct volume for root.

```
# fsck /dev/md/rdsk/d0
** /dev/md/rdsk/d0
** Currently Mounted on /
** Phase 1 - Check Blocks and Sizes
** Phase 2 - Check Pathnames
** Phase 3 - Check Connectivity
** Phase 4 - Check Reference Counts
** Phase 5 - Check Cyl groups
2274 files, 11815 used, 10302 free (158 frags, 1268 blocks,
0.7% fragmentation)
```

2. **Remount root (/) read/write so you can edit the `/etc/vfstab` file.**

```
# mount -o rw,remount /dev/md/dsk/d0 /
mount: warning: cannot lock temp file </etc/.mnt.lock>
```

3. **Run the `metaroot` command.**

```
# metaroot d0
```

This command edits the `/etc/system` and `/etc/vfstab` files to specify that the
root (/) file system is now on volume d0.

4. **Verify that the `/etc/vfstab` file contains the correct volume entries.**

The root (/) entry in the `/etc/vfstab` file should appear as follows so that the entry
for the file system correctly references the RAID 1 volume:

```
#device                device              mount      FS     fsck   mount    mount
#to mount              to fsck             point      type   pass   at boot  options
#
/dev/md/dsk/d0         /dev/md/rdsk/d0     /          ufs    1      no       -
/dev/dsk/c0t3d0s1      -                   -          swap   -      no       -
/dev/dsk/c0t3d0s6      /dev/rdsk/c0t3d0s6  /usr       ufs    2      no       -
#
/proc                 -                   /proc      proc   -      no       -
floppy                -                   /dev/floppy   floppy    -      no      -
swap                  -                   /tmp       tmpfs  -      yes      -
```

5. **Reboot the system.**

The system returns to normal operation.

▼ How to Recover From a Boot Device Failure

If you have a root (/) mirror and your boot device fails, you'll need to set up an alternate boot device.

The high-level steps in this task are as follows:

1. Booting from the alternate root (/) submirror
2. Determining the errored state database replicas and volumes
3. Repairing the failed disk
4. Restoring state database and volumes to their original state

In the following example, the boot device contains two of the six state database replicas and the root (/), swap, and /usr submirrors fails.

Initially, when the boot device fails, you'll see a message similar to the following. This message might differ among various architectures.

```
Rebooting with command:
Boot device: /iommu/sbus/dma@f,81000/esp@f,80000/sd@3,0
The selected SCSI device is not responding
Can't open boot device
...
```

When you see this message, note the device. Then, follow these steps:

1. **Boot from another root (/) submirror.**

   Since only two of the six state database replicas in this example are in error, you can still boot. If this were not the case, you would need to delete the inaccessible state database replicas in single-user mode. This procedure is described in "How to Recover From Insufficient State Database Replicas" on page 265.

   When you created the mirror for the root (/) file system, you should have recorded the alternate boot device as part of that procedure. In this example, disk2 is that alternate boot device.

   ```
   ok boot disk2
   SunOS Release 5.9 Version s81_51 64-bit
   Copyright 1983-2001 Sun Microsystems, Inc.  All rights reserved.
   Hostname: demo
   ...
   demo console login: root
   Password: <root-password>
   Dec 16 12:22:09 lexicon login: ROOT LOGIN /dev/console
   Last login: Wed Dec 12 10:55:16 on console
   Sun Microsystems Inc.   SunOS 5.9        s81_51  May 2002
   ...
   ```

2. **Determine that two state database replicas have failed by using the** metadb **command.**

   ```
   # metadb
         flags          first blk      block count
      M     p           unknown        unknown        /dev/dsk/c0t3d0s3
   ```

```
    M     p            unknown        unknown        /dev/dsk/c0t3d0s3
    a m   p  luo       16             1034           /dev/dsk/c0t2d0s3
    a     p  luo       1050           1034           /dev/dsk/c0t2d0s3
    a     p  luo       16             1034           /dev/dsk/c0t1d0s3
    a     p  luo       1050           1034           /dev/dsk/c0t1d0s3
```

The system can no longer detect state database replicas on slice
/dev/dsk/c0t3d0s3, which is part of the failed disk.

3. **Determine that half of the root (/), swap, and /usr mirrors have failed by using the**
   metastat **command.**

```
# metastat
d0: Mirror
    Submirror 0: d10
      State: Needs maintenance
    Submirror 1: d20
      State: Okay
...

d10: Submirror of d0
    State: Needs maintenance
    Invoke: "metareplace d0 /dev/dsk/c0t3d0s0 <new device>"
    Size: 47628 blocks
    Stripe 0:
    Device              Start Block  Dbase State        Hot Spare
    /dev/dsk/c0t3d0s0             0   No    Maintenance

d20: Submirror of d0
    State: Okay
    Size: 47628 blocks
    Stripe 0:
    Device              Start Block  Dbase State        Hot Spare
    /dev/dsk/c0t2d0s0             0   No    Okay

d1: Mirror
    Submirror 0: d11
      State: Needs maintenance
    Submirror 1: d21
      State: Okay
...

d11: Submirror of d1
    State: Needs maintenance
    Invoke: "metareplace d1 /dev/dsk/c0t3d0s1 <new device>"
    Size: 69660 blocks
    Stripe 0:
    Device              Start Block  Dbase State        Hot Spare
    /dev/dsk/c0t3d0s1             0   No    Maintenance

d21: Submirror of d1
    State: Okay
    Size: 69660 blocks
    Stripe 0:
    Device              Start Block  Dbase State        Hot Spare
```

```
     /dev/dsk/c0t2d0s1            0     No     Okay

  d2: Mirror
      Submirror 0: d12
        State: Needs maintenance
      Submirror 1: d22
        State: Okay
  ...

  d2: Mirror
      Submirror 0: d12
        State: Needs maintenance
      Submirror 1: d22
        State: Okay
  ...

  d12: Submirror of d2
      State: Needs maintenance
      Invoke: "metareplace d2 /dev/dsk/c0t3d0s6 <new device>"
      Size: 286740 blocks
      Stripe 0:
      Device                Start Block   Dbase State         Hot Spare
      /dev/dsk/c0t3d0s6             0     No    Maintenance

  d22: Submirror of d2
      State: Okay
      Size: 286740 blocks
      Stripe 0:
      Device                Start Block   Dbase State         Hot Spare
      /dev/dsk/c0t2d0s6             0     No    Okay
```

In this example, the `metastat` command shows that following submirrors need maintenance:

- Submirror d10, device c0t3d0s0
- Submirror d11, device c0t3d0s1
- Submirror d12, device c0t3d0s6

4. **Halt the system, replace the disk, and use the** `format` **command or the** `fmthard` **command, to partition the disk as it was before the failure.**

Tip – If the new disk is identical to the existing disk (the intact side of the mirror in this example), use `prtvtoc /dev/rdsk/c0t2d0s2 | fmthard - -s /dev/rdsk/c0t3d0s2` to quickly format the new disk (c0t3d0 in this example)

```
# halt
...
Halted
...
ok boot
...
# format /dev/rdsk/c0t3d0s0
```

5. **Reboot.**

   Note that you must reboot from the other half of the root (/) mirror. You should have
   recorded the alternate boot device when you created the mirror.

   ```
   # halt
   ...
   ok boot disk2
   ```

6. **To delete the failed state database replicas and then add them back, use the** metadb
   command.

   ```
   # metadb
           flags               first blk       block count
       M       p               unknown         unknown         /dev/dsk/c0t3d0s3
       M       p               unknown         unknown         /dev/dsk/c0t3d0s3
       a m   p   luo           16              1034            /dev/dsk/c0t2d0s3
       a     p   luo           1050            1034            /dev/dsk/c0t2d0s3
       a     p   luo           16              1034            /dev/dsk/c0t1d0s3
       a     p   luo           1050            1034            /dev/dsk/c0t1d0s3
   # metadb -d c0t3d0s3
   # metadb -c 2 -a c0t3d0s3
   # metadb
           flags               first blk       block count
       a m   p   luo           16              1034            /dev/dsk/c0t2d0s3
       a     p   luo           1050            1034            /dev/dsk/c0t2d0s3
       a     p   luo           16              1034            /dev/dsk/c0t1d0s3
       a     p   luo           1050            1034            /dev/dsk/c0t1d0s3
       a         u             16              1034            /dev/dsk/c0t3d0s3
       a         u             1050            1034            /dev/dsk/c0t3d0s3
   ```

7. **Re-enable the submirrors by using the** metareplace **command.**

   ```
   # metareplace -e d0 c0t3d0s0
   Device /dev/dsk/c0t3d0s0 is enabled

   # metareplace -e d1 c0t3d0s1
   Device /dev/dsk/c0t3d0s1 is enabled

   # metareplace -e d2 c0t3d0s6
   Device /dev/dsk/c0t3d0s6 is enabled
   ```

   After some time, the resynchronization will complete. You can now return to booting
   from the original device.

Recovering From State Database Replica Failures

▼ How to Recover From Insufficient State Database Replicas

If the state database replica quorum is not met, for example, due to a drive failure, the system cannot be rebooted into multiuser mode. This situation could follow a panic (when Solaris Volume Manager discovers that fewer than half the state database replicas are available) or could occur if the system is rebooted with exactly half or fewer functional state database replicas. In Solaris Volume Manager terms, the state database has gone "stale." This task explains how to recover from this problem.

1. **Boot the system to determine which state database replicas are down.**

2. **Determine which state database replicas are unavailable**

   Use the following format of the `metadb` command:

   ```
   metadb -i
   ```

3. **If one or more disks are known to be unavailable, delete the state database replicas on those disks. Otherwise, delete enough errored state database replicas (W, M, D, F, or R status flags reported by `metadb`) to ensure that a majority of the existing state database replicas are not errored.**

   Delete the state database replica on the bad disk using the `metadb -d` command.

   Tip – State database replicas with a capitalized status flag are in error, while those with lowercase status flags are functioning normally.

   ---

4. **Verify that the replicas have been deleted by using the `metadb` command.**

5. **Reboot.**

6. **If necessary, you can replace the disk, format it appropriately, then add any state database replicas needed to the disk. Following the instructions in "Creating State Database Replicas" on page 58.**

   Once you have a replacement disk, halt the system, replace the failed disk, and once again, reboot the system. Use the `format` command or the `fmthard` command to partition the disk as it was configured before the failure.

Example—Recovering From Stale State Database Replicas

In the following example, a disk containing seven replicas has gone bad. This leaves
the system with only three good replicas, and the system panics, then cannot reboot
into multi-user mode.

```
panic[cpu0]/thread=70a41e00: md: state database problem

403238a8 md:mddb_commitrec_wrapper+6c (2, 1, 70a66ca0, 40323964, 70a66ca0, 3c)
  %l0-7: 0000000a 00000000 00000001 70bbcce0 70bbcd04 70995400 00000002 00000000
40323908 md:alloc_entry+c4 (70b00844, 1, 9, 0, 403239e4, ff00)
  %l0-7: 70b796a4 00000001 00000000 705064cc 70a66ca0 00000002 00000024 00000000
40323968 md:md_setdevname+2d4 (7003b988, 6, 0, 63, 70a71618, 10)
  %l0-7: 70a71620 00000000 705064cc 70b00844 00000010 00000000 00000000 00000000
403239f8 md:setnm_ioctl+134 (7003b968, 100003, 64, 0, 0, ffbffc00)
  %l0-7: 7003b988 00000000 70a71618 00000000 00000000 000225f0 00000000 00000000
40323a58 md:md_base_ioctl+9b4 (157ffff, 5605, ffbffa3c, 100003, 40323ba8, ff1b5470)
  %l0-7: ff3f2208 ff3f2138 ff3f26a0 00000000 00000000 00000064 ff1396e9 00000000
40323ad0 md:md_admin_ioctl+24 (157ffff, 5605, ffbffa3c, 100003, 40323ba8, 0)
  %l0-7: 00005605 ffbffa3c 00100003 0157ffff 0aa64245 00000000 7efefeff 81010100
40323b48 md:mdioctl+e4 (157ffff, 5605, ffbffa3c, 100003, 7016db60, 40323c7c)
  %l0-7: 0157ffff 00005605 ffbffa3c 00100003 0003ffff 70995598 70995570 0147c800
40323bb0 genunix:ioctl+1dc (3, 5605, ffbffa3c, fffffff8, ffffffe0, ffbffa65)
  %l0-7: 0114c57c 70937428 ff3f26a0 00000000 00000001 ff3b10d4 0aa64245 00000000


panic:
stopped at       edd000d8:       ta       %icc,%g0 + 125
Type  'go' to resume

ok boot -s
Resetting ...

Sun Ultra 5/10 UPA/PCI (UltraSPARC-IIi 270MHz), No Keyboard
OpenBoot 3.11, 128 MB memory installed, Serial #9841776.
Ethernet address 8:0:20:96:2c:70, Host ID: 80962c70.



Rebooting with command: boot -s
Boot device: /pci@1f,0/pci@1,1/ide@3/disk@0,0:a  File and args: -s
SunOS Release 5.9 Version s81_39 64-bit

Copyright 1983-2001 Sun Microsystems, Inc.  All rights reserved.
configuring IPv4 interfaces: hme0.
Hostname: dodo

metainit: dodo: stale databases

Insufficient metadevice database replicas located.

Use metadb to delete databases which are broken.
Ignore any "Read-only file system" error messages.
Reboot the system when finished to reload the metadevice database.
After reboot, repair any broken database replicas which were deleted.
```

```
Type control-d to proceed with normal startup,
(or give root password for system maintenance): root password
single-user privilege assigned to /dev/console.
Entering System Maintenance Mode

Jun  7 08:57:25 su: 'su root' succeeded for root on /dev/console
Sun Microsystems Inc.    SunOS 5.9        s81_39  May 2002
# metadb -i
        flags            first blk        block count
    a m  p  lu           16               8192                /dev/dsk/c0t0d0s7
    a    p  l            8208             8192                /dev/dsk/c0t0d0s7
    a    p  l            16400            8192                /dev/dsk/c0t0d0s7
      M  p               16               unknown             /dev/dsk/c1t1d0s0
      M  p               8208             unknown             /dev/dsk/c1t1d0s0
      M  p               16400            unknown             /dev/dsk/c1t1d0s0
      M  p               24592            unknown             /dev/dsk/c1t1d0s0
      M  p               32784            unknown             /dev/dsk/c1t1d0s0
      M  p               40976            unknown             /dev/dsk/c1t1d0s0
      M  p               49168            unknown             /dev/dsk/c1t1d0s0
# metadb -d c1t1d0s0
# metadb
        flags            first blk        block count
    a m  p  lu           16               8192                /dev/dsk/c0t0d0s7
    a    p  l            8208             8192                /dev/dsk/c0t0d0s7
    a    p  l            16400            8192                /dev/dsk/c0t0d0s7
#
```

The system paniced because it could no longer detect state database replicas on slice /dev/dsk/c1t1d0s0, which is part of the failed disk or attached to a failed controller. The first metadb -i command identifies the replicas on this slice as having a problem with the master blocks.

When you delete the stale state database replicas, the root (/) file system is read-only. You can ignore the mddb.cf error messages displayed.

At this point, the system is again functional, although it probably has fewer state database replicas than it should, and any volumes that used part of the failed storage are also either failed, errored, or hot-spared; those issues should be addressed promptly.

Repairing Transactional Volumes

Because a transactional volume is a "layered" volume, consisting of a master device and logging device, and because the logging device can be shared among file systems, repairing a failed transactional volume requires special recovery tasks.

Any device errors or panics must be managed by using the command line utilities.

Panics

If a file system detects any internal inconsistencies while it is in use, it will panic the system. If the file system is configured for logging, it notifies the transactional volume that it needs to be checked at reboot. The transactional volume transitions itself to the "Hard Error" state. All other transactional volumes that share the same log device also go into the "Hard Error" state.

At reboot, fsck checks and repairs the file system and transitions the file system back to the "Okay" state. fsck completes this process for all transactional volumes listed in the /etc/vfstab file for the affected log device.

Transactional Volume Errors

If a device error occurs on either the master device or the log device while the transactional volume is processing logged data, the device transitions from the "Okay" state to the "Hard Error" state. If the device is either in the "Hard Error" or "Error" state, either a device error has occurred, or a panic has occurred.

Any devices sharing the failed log device also go the "Error" state.

Recovering From Soft Partition Problems

The following sections show how to recover configuration information for soft partitions. You should only use these techniques if all of your state database replicas have been lost and you do not have a current or accurate copy of metastat -p output, the md.cf file, or an up-to-date md.tab file.

How to Recover Configuration Data for a Soft Partition

At the beginning of each soft partition extent, a sector is used to mark the beginning of the soft partition extent. These hidden sectors are called extent headers and do not appear to the user of the soft partition. If all Solaris Volume Manager configuration is lost, the disk can be scanned in an attempt to generate the configuration data.

This procedure is a last option to recover lost soft partition configuration information. The metarecover command should only be used when you have lost both your metadb and your md.cf files, and your md.tab is lost or out of date.

> **Note –** This procedure only works to recover soft partition information, and does not assist in recovering from other lost configurations or for recovering configuration information for other Solaris Volume Manager volumes.

> **Note –** If your configuration included other Solaris Volume Manager volumes that were built on top of soft partitions, you should recover the soft partitions before attempting to recover the other volumes.

Configuration information about your soft partitions is stored on your devices and in your state database. Since either of these sources could be corrupt, you must tell the `metarecover` command which source is reliable.

First, use the `metarecover` command to determine whether the two sources agree. If they do agree, the `metarecover` command cannot be used to make any changes. If the `metarecover` command reports an inconsistency, however, you must examine its output carefully to determine whether the disk or the state database is corrupt, then you should use the `metarecover` command to rebuild the configuration based on the appropriate source.

1. **Read the "Background Information About Soft Partitions" on page 122.**

2. **Review the soft partition recovery information by using the** `metarecover` **command.**

   metarecover *component*-**p** {-d }

   In this case, component is the c*t*d*s* name of the raw component. The -d option indicates to scan the physical slice for extent headers of soft partitions.

   For more information, see the `metarecover`(1M) man page.

Example—Recovering Soft Partitions from On-Disk Extent Headers

```
# metarecover c1t1d0s1 -p -d
The following soft partitions were found and will be added to
your metadevice configuration.
  Name              Size        No. of Extents
     d10             10240              1
     d11             10240              1
     d12             10240              1
# metarecover c1t1d0s1 -p -d
The following soft partitions were found and will be added to
your metadevice configuration.
  Name              Size        No. of Extents
```

```
      d10             10240           1
      d11             10240           1
      d12             10240           1
WARNING: You are about to add one or more soft partition
metadevices to your metadevice configuration.  If there
appears to be an error in the soft partition(s) displayed
above, do NOT proceed with this recovery operation.
Are you sure you want to do this (yes/no)?yes
c1t1d0s1: Soft Partitions recovered from device.
bash-2.05# metastat
d10: Soft Partition
    Device: c1t1d0s1
    State: Okay
    Size: 10240 blocks
        Device                  Start Block  Dbase Reloc
        c1t1d0s1                          0  No    Yes

        Extent                  Start Block              Block count
             0                            1                    10240


d11: Soft Partition
    Device: c1t1d0s1
    State: Okay
    Size: 10240 blocks
        Device                  Start Block  Dbase Reloc
        c1t1d0s1                          0  No    Yes

        Extent                  Start Block              Block count
             0                        10242                    10240


d12: Soft Partition
    Device: c1t1d0s1
    State: Okay
    Size: 10240 blocks
        Device                  Start Block  Dbase Reloc
        c1t1d0s1                          0  No    Yes

        Extent                  Start Block              Block count
             0                        20483                    10240
```

This example recovers three soft partitions from disk, after the state database replicas
were accidentally deleted.

Recovering Configuration From a Different System

You can recover a Solaris Volume Manager configuration, even onto a different system from the original. For example, assume you have a system with an external Multipack of six disks in it, and a Solaris Volume Manager configuration, including at least one state database replica, on some of those disks. If you experience a system failure, you can attach the Multipack to a different system and recover the complete configuration from the local disk set.

Note – Only recover a Solaris Volume Manager configuration onto a system with no preexisting Solaris Volume Manager configuration. Otherwise, you risk replacing a logical volume on your system with a logical volume that you are recovering, and possibly corrupting your system.

Note – This process only works to recover volumes from the local disk set.

How to Recover a Configuration

▼ How to Recover a Configuration

1. **Attach the disk or disks that contain the Solaris Volume Manager configuration to a system with no preexisting Solaris Volume Manager configuration.**

2. **Do a reconfiguration reboot to ensure that the system recognizes the newly added disks.**

   ```
   # reboot -- -r
   ```

3. **Determine the major/minor number for a slice containing a state database replica on the newly added disks.**

   Use `ls -lL`, and note the two numbers between the group name and the date. Those are the major/minor numbers for this slice.

   ```
   # ls -Ll /dev/dsk/c1t9d0s7
   brw-r-----   1 root      sys          32, 71 Dec  5 10:05 /dev/dsk/c1t9d0s7
   ```

4. **If necessary, determine the major name corresponding with the major number by looking up the major number in** `/etc/name_to_major`.

```
# grep " 32" /etc/name_to_major
sd 32
```

5. **Update the** `/kernel/drv/md.conf` **file with two commands: one command to tell
   Solaris Volume Manager where to find a valid state database replica on the new
   disks, and one command to tell it to trust the new replica and ignore any conflicting
   device ID information on the system.**

   In the line in this example that begins with `mddb_bootlist1`, replace the *sd* in the
   example with the major name you found in the previous step. Replace *71* in the
   example with the minor number you identified in Step 3.

```
#pragma ident    "@(#)md.conf    2.1    00/07/07 SMI"
#
# Copyright (c) 1992-1999 by Sun Microsystems, Inc.
# All rights reserved.
#
name="md" parent="pseudo" nmd=128 md_nsets=4;
#
#pragma ident    "@(#)md.conf    2.1    00/07/07 SMI"
#
# Copyright (c) 1992-1999 by Sun Microsystems, Inc.
# All rights reserved.
#
name="md" parent="pseudo" nmd=128 md_nsets=4;
# Begin MDD database info (do not edit)
mddb_bootlist1="sd:71:16:id0";
md_devid_destroy=1;# End MDD database info (do not edit)
```

6. **Reboot to force Solaris Volume Manager to reload your configuration.**

   You will see messages similar to the following displayed to the console.

```
volume management starting.
Dec  5 10:11:53 lexicon metadevadm: Disk movement detected
Dec  5 10:11:53 lexicon metadevadm: Updating device names in
Solaris Volume Manager
The system is ready.
```

7. **Verify your configuration by using the** `metadb` **and** `metastat` **commands.**

```
# metadb
        flags              first blk        block count
    a m  p  luo            16               8192            /dev/dsk/c1t9d0s7
    a        luo           16               8192            /dev/dsk/c1t10d0s7
    a        luo           16               8192            /dev/dsk/c1t11d0s7
    a        luo           16               8192            /dev/dsk/c1t12d0s7
    a        luo           16               8192            /dev/dsk/c1t13d0s7
# metastat
d12: RAID
    State: Okay
    Interlace: 32 blocks
    Size: 125685 blocks
Original device:
    Size: 128576 blocks
        Device              Start Block  Dbase State      Reloc  Hot Spare
```

```
        c1t11d0s3                    330    No    Okay         Yes
        c1t12d0s3                    330    No    Okay         Yes
        c1t13d0s3                    330    No    Okay         Yes

d20: Soft Partition
    Device: d10
    State: Okay
    Size: 8192 blocks
        Extent              Start Block              Block count
             0                   3592                     8192

d21: Soft Partition
    Device: d10
    State: Okay
    Size: 8192 blocks
        Extent              Start Block              Block count
             0                  11785                     8192

d22: Soft Partition
    Device: d10
    State: Okay
    Size: 8192 blocks
        Extent              Start Block              Block count
             0                  19978                     8192

d10: Mirror
    Submirror 0: d0
      State: Okay
    Submirror 1: d1
      State: Okay
    Pass: 1
    Read option: roundrobin (default)
    Write option: parallel (default)
    Size: 82593 blocks

d0: Submirror of d10
    State: Okay
    Size: 118503 blocks
    Stripe 0: (interlace: 32 blocks)
        Device            Start Block  Dbase State         Reloc  Hot Spare
        c1t9d0s0                    0    No  Okay           Yes
        c1t10d0s0                3591    No  Okay           Yes


d1: Submirror of d10
    State: Okay
    Size: 82593 blocks
    Stripe 0: (interlace: 32 blocks)
        Device            Start Block  Dbase State         Reloc  Hot Spare
        c1t9d0s1                    0    No  Okay           Yes
        c1t10d0s1                   0    No  Okay           Yes


Device Relocation Information:
Device          Reloc      Device ID
```

```
c1t9d0          Yes         id1,sd@SSEAGATE_ST39103LCSUN9.0GLS3487980000U00907AZ
c1t10d0         Yes         id1,sd@SSEAGATE_ST39103LCSUN9.0GLS3397070000W0090A8Q
c1t11d0         Yes         id1,sd@SSEAGATE_ST39103LCSUN9.0GLS3449660000U00904NZ
c1t12d0         Yes         id1,sd@SSEAGATE_ST39103LCSUN9.0GLS32655400007010H04J
c1t13d0         Yes         id1,sd@SSEAGATE_ST39103LCSUN9.0GLS3461190000701001T0
#
# metadb
        flags               first blk           block count
    a m  p  luo             16                  8192            /dev/dsk/c1t9d0s7
    a       luo             16                  8192            /dev/dsk/c1t10d0s7
    a       luo             16                  8192            /dev/dsk/c1t11d0s7
    a       luo             16                  8192            /dev/dsk/c1t12d0s7
    a       luo             16                  8192            /dev/dsk/c1t13d0s7
# metastat
d12: RAID
    State: Okay
    Interlace: 32 blocks
    Size: 125685 blocks
Original device:
    Size: 128576 blocks
        Device              Start Block  Dbase State         Reloc  Hot Spare
        c1t11d0s3                  330   No    Okay          Yes
        c1t12d0s3                  330   No    Okay          Yes
        c1t13d0s3                  330   No    Okay          Yes

d20: Soft Partition
    Device: d10
    State: Okay
    Size: 8192 blocks
        Extent              Start Block             Block count
            0                   3592                    8192

d21: Soft Partition
    Device: d10
    State: Okay
    Size: 8192 blocks
        Extent              Start Block             Block count
            0                  11785                    8192

d22: Soft Partition
    Device: d10
    State: Okay
    Size: 8192 blocks
        Extent              Start Block             Block count
            0                  19978                    8192

d10: Mirror
    Submirror 0: d0
      State: Okay
    Submirror 1: d1
      State: Okay
    Pass: 1
    Read option: roundrobin (default)
    Write option: parallel (default)
    Size: 82593 blocks
```

```
d0: Submirror of d10
    State: Okay
    Size: 118503 blocks
    Stripe 0: (interlace: 32 blocks)
        Device                 Start Block  Dbase State       Reloc  Hot Spare
        c1t9d0s0                         0  No    Okay        Yes
        c1t10d0s0                     3591  No    Okay        Yes


d1: Submirror of d10
    State: Okay
    Size: 82593 blocks
    Stripe 0: (interlace: 32 blocks)
        Device                 Start Block  Dbase State       Reloc  Hot Spare
        c1t9d0s1                         0  No    Okay        Yes
        c1t10d0s1                        0  No    Okay        Yes


Device Relocation Information:
Device          Reloc     Device ID
c1t9d0          Yes       id1,sd@SSEAGATE_ST39103LCSUN9.0GLS3487980000U00907AZ1
c1t10d0         Yes       id1,sd@SSEAGATE_ST39103LCSUN9.0GLS3397070000W0090A8Q
c1t11d0         Yes       id1,sd@SSEAGATE_ST39103LCSUN9.0GLS3449660000U00904NZ
c1t12d0         Yes       id1,sd@SSEAGATE_ST39103LCSUN9.0GLS32655400007010H04J
c1t13d0         Yes       id1,sd@SSEAGATE_ST39103LCSUN9.0GLS3461190000701001T0
# metastat -p
d12 -r c1t11d0s3 c1t12d0s3 c1t13d0s3 -k -i 32b
d20 -p d10 -o 3592 -b 8192
d21 -p d10 -o 11785 -b 8192
d22 -p d10 -o 19978 -b 8192
d10 -m d0 d1 1
d0 1 2 c1t9d0s0 c1t10d0s0 -i 32b
d1 1 2 c1t9d0s1 c1t10d0s1 -i 32b
#
```

Important Solaris Volume Manager Files

This appendix contains information about Solaris Volume Manager files for reference purposes. It contains the following:

- "System Files and Startup Files" on page 277
- "Manually Configured Files" on page 279

System Files and Startup Files

This section explains the files that are necessary for Solaris Volume Manager to operate correctly. With the exception of a few specialized configuration changes, you will not need to access or modify these files.

- `/etc/lvm/mddb.cf`

Caution – Do not edit this file. If you change this file, you could corrupt your Solaris Volume Manager configuration.

The `/etc/lvm/mddb.cf` file records the locations of state database replicas. When state database replica locations change, Solaris Volume Manager makes an entry in the `mddb.cf` file that records the locations of all state databases. See `mddb.cf`(4) for more information.

- `/etc/lvm/md.cf`

The `/etc/lvm/md.cf` file contains automatically generated configuration information for the default (unspecified or local) disk set. When you change the Solaris Volume Manager configuration, Solaris Volume Manager automatically updates the `md.cf` file (except for information about hot spares in use). See `md.cf`(4) for more information.

Caution – Do not edit this file. If you change this file, you could corrupt your Solaris Volume Manager configuration or be unable to recover your Solaris Volume Manager configuration.

If your system loses the information maintained in the state database, and as long as no volumes were changed or created in the meantime, you can use the `md.cf` file to recover your configuration. See "How to Initialize Solaris Volume Manager from a Configuration File" on page 224.

- `/kernel/drv/md.conf`

  The `md.conf` configuration file is read by Solaris Volume Manager at startup. You can edit two fields in this file: nmd, which sets the number of volumes (metadevices) that the configuration can support, and `md_nsets`, which is the number of disk sets. The default value for nmd is 128, which can be increased to 8192. The default value for `md_nsets` is 4, which can be increased to 32. The total number of named disk sets is always one less than the `md_nsets` value, because the default (unnamed or local) disk set is included in `md_nsets`.

  Note – Keep the values of nmd and `md_nsets` as low as possible. Memory structures exist for all possible devices as determined by nmd and `md_nsets`, even if you have not created those devices. For optimal performance, keep nmd and `md_nsets` only slightly higher than the number of volumes you will use.

- `/etc/rcS.d/S35svm.init`

  This file configures and starts Solaris Volume Manager at boot and allows administrators to start and stop the daemons.

- `/etc/rc2.d/S95svm.sync`

  This file checks the Solaris Volume Manager configuration at boot, starts resynchronization of mirrors if necessary, and starts the active monitoring daemon. (For more information, see `mdmonitord`(1M)).

Manually Configured Files

Overview of the `md.tab` File

The `/etc/lvm/md.tab` file contains Solaris Volume Manager configuration information that can be used to reconstruct your Solaris Volume Manager configuration. Solaris Volume Manager can use this file as input to the command line utilities `metainit`, `metadb`, and `metahs` to reconstruct a configuration. Volumes, disk sets, and hot spare pools might have entries in this file. See "How to Create Configuration Files" on page 224 for instructions on creating this file (using `metastat -p > /etc/lvm/md.tab`).

Note – The configuration information in the `/etc/lvm/md.tab` file might differ from the current volumes, hot spares, and state database replicas in use. It is used manually, by the system administrator, to capture the intended configuration. After you change your Solaris Volume Manager configuration, re-create this file and preserve a backup copy.

Once you have created and updated the file, the `metainit`, `metahs`, and `metadb` commands then activate the volumes, hot spare pools, and state database replicas defined in the file.

In the `/etc/lvm/md.tab` file, one complete configuration entry for a single volume appears on each line using the syntax of the `metainit`, `metadb`, and `metahs` commands.

You then run the `metainit` command with either the `-a` option, to activate all volumes in the `/etc/lvm/md.tab` file, or with the volume name that corresponds to a specific entry in the file.

Note – Solaris Volume Manager does not write to or store configuration information in the `/etc/lvm/md.tab` file. You must edit the file by hand and run the `metainit`, `metahs`, or `metadb` commands to create Solaris Volume Manager components.

For more information, see `md.tab`(4) man page.

Solaris Volume Manager Quick Reference

This appendix provides quick access information about the features and functions available with Solaris Volume Manager.

Command Line Reference

Listed here are all the commands that you use to administer Solaris Volume Manager. For more detailed information, see the man pages.

TABLE B–1 Solaris Volume Manager Commands

Solaris Volume Manager Command	Description	Man page
growfs	Expands a UFS file system in a nondestructive fashion.	growfs(1M)
metaclear	Deletes active volumes and hot spare pools.	metaclear(1M)
metadb	Creates and deletes state database replicas.	metadb(1M)
metadetach	Detaches a volume from a RAID 1 (mirror) volume, or a logging device from a transactional volume.	metadetach(1M)
metadevadm	Checks device ID configuration.	metadevadm(1M)
metahs	Manages hot spares and hot spare pools.	metahs(1M)
metainit	Configures volumes.	metainit(1M)
metaoffline	Places submirrors offline.	metaoffline(1M)

TABLE B–1 Solaris Volume Manager Commands   *(Continued)*

Solaris Volume Manager Command	Description	Man page
metaonline	Places submirrors online.	metaonline(1M)
metaparam	Modifies volume parameters.	metaparam(1M)
metarecover	Recovers configuration information for soft partitions.	metarecover(1M)
metarename	Renames and exchanges volume names.	metarename(1M)
metareplace	Replaces components in submirrors and RAID 5 volumes.	metareplace(1M)
metaroot	Sets up system files for mirroring root (/).	metaroot(1M)
metaset	Administers disk sets.	metaset(1M)
metastat	Displays the status of volumes or hot spare pools.	metastat(1M)
metasync	Resynchronizes volumes during reboot.	metasync(1M)
metattach	Attaches a component to a RAID 0 or RAID 1 volume, or a log device to a transactional volume.	metattach(1M)

Solaris Volume Manager CIM/WBEM API

Managing Solaris Volume Manager

The Solaris Volume Manager CIM/WBEM Application Programming Interface (API) provides a public, standards-based programmatic interface to observe and configure the Solaris Volume Manager. This API is based on the Distributed Management Task Force (DMTF) Common Information Model (CIM). For more information about DMTF, see `http://www.dmtf.org`.

CIM defines the data model, referred to as the "schema" which describes the following:

- attributes of and the operations against SVM devices
- relationships among the various SVM devices
- relationships among the SVM devices and other aspects of the operating system, such as file systems

This model is made available through the Solaris Web Based Enterprise Management (WBEM) SDK. The WBEM SDK is a set of Java™ technology-based API's that allow access to system management capabilities that are represented by CIM.

For more information about the CIM/WBEM SDK, see the *Solaris WBEM SDK Developer's Guide*.

Index

DiskSuite Tool, *See* graphical interface

E

enabling a hot spare,   162
enabling a slice in a RAID 5 volume,   143
enabling a slice in a submirror,   107
Enhanced Storage, *See* graphical interface
errors
    checking for using a script,   245
/etc/lvm/md.cf file,   277
/etc/lvm/mddb.cf file,   277
/etc/rc2.d/S95lvm.sync file,   278
/etc/rcS.d/S35lvm.init file,   278
/etc/vfstab file,   116, 177, 192
    recovering from improper entries,   258

F

failover configuration,   44, 197
file system
    expanding by creating a concatenation,   77
    expansion overview,   41
    growing,   228
    guidelines,   45
    panics,   268
    unmirroring,   118
fmthard command,   263, 265
format command,   263, 265
fsck command,   193

G

general performance guidelines,   30
graphical interface
    overview,   36
growfs command,   41, 229, 281
GUI
    sample,   37

H

hot spare,   148
    adding to a hot spare pool,   156

hot spare *(continued)*
    conceptual overview,   148
    enabling,   163
    replacing in a hot spare pool,   161
hot spare pool,   44
    administering,   150
    associating,   157
    basic operation,   44
    changing association,   158
    conceptual overview,   147, 149
    creating,   155
    definition,   39, 44
    example with mirror,   149
    states,   160

I

I/O,   31
interfaces, *See* Solaris Volume Manager
    interfaces
interlace
    specifying,   74

K

/kernel/drv/md.conf file,   226, 278

L

local disk set,   198
lockfs command,   119, 193
log device
    definition,   167
    problems when sharing,   193
    recovering from errors,   194
    shared,   167, 170
    sharing,   192
    space required,   170
logging device
    hard error state,   268

M

majority consensus algorithm,   52

RAID 5 volume *(continued)*
  initializing slices,   131
  maintenance vs. last erred,   232
  overview of replacing and enabling
     slices,   230
  parity information,   131, 134
  replacing a failed slice,   145
  resynchronizing slices,   131
random I/O,   31
raw volume,   75, 96, 138
read policies overview,   86
releasing a disk set,   212, 214
renaming volumes,   221
replica,   43
reserving a disk set,   213
resynchronization
  full,   87
  optimized,   88
  partial,   88
root (/)
  mirroring,   100
  unmirroring,   116

S

SCSI disk
  replacing,   255, 257
sequential I/O,   32
shared disk set,   44
simple volume
  See RAID 0 volume
  definition,   40
slices
  adding to a RAID 5 volume,   142
  expanding,   78
soft partition
  checking status,   127
  creating,   126
  deleting,   129
  expanding,   128
  growing,   128
  recovering configuration for,   268
  removing,   129
soft partitioning
  definition,   122
  guidelines,   122
  locations,   122

Solaris Volume Manager
  See Solaris Volume Manager
  configuration guidelines,   45
  recovering the configuration,   224
Solaris Volume Manager elements
  overview,   38
Solaris Volume Manager interfaces
  command line,   36
  sample GUI,   37
  Solaris Management Console,   36
state database
  conceptual overview,   43, 52
  corrupt,   52
  definition,   39, 43
  recovering from stale replicas,   265
state database replicas,   43
  adding larger replicas,   61
  basic operation,   52
  creating additional,   58
  creating multiple on a single slice,   53
  definition,   43
  errors,   56
  location,   44, 54
  minimum number,   54
  recovering from stale replicas,   265
  two-disk configuration,   55
  usage,   51
status,   212
stripe
  creating,   74
  definition,   64
  example with three slices,   65
  expanding,   79
  information for creating,   70
  information for recreating,   70
  removing,   80
striped volume, *See* stripe
striping
  definition,   64
submirror,   82
  attaching,   82
  detaching,   82
  enabling a failed slice,   107
  operation while offline,   82
  placing offline and online,   105
  replacing a failed slice,   113
  replacing entire,   114

swap
  mirroring, 101
  unmirroring, 118
system files, 277

T

three-way mirror, 89
transactional volume
  and /etc/vfstab file, 176
  creating for a file system that cannot be
    unmounted, 177
  creating using metarename, 185, 188
  creating using mirrors, 177
  definition, 40
  determining file systems to log, 170
  example with mirrors, 167
  example with shared log device, 168
  expanding, 187
  guidelines, 169
  recovering from errors, 195, 267
  removing using metarename, 189
  states, 183
  usage, 167
troubleshooting
  general guidelines, 254

U

UFS logging
  definition, 165
/usr
  logging, 177
  mirroring, 100
  unmirroring, 116

V

/var/adm/messages file, 230, 255
volume
  checking status, 183
  conceptual overview, 39
  default number, 226
  definition, 39
  expanding disk space, 41

volume *(continued)*
  increasing the default number, 226
  name switching, 222
  naming conventions, 42, 200
  renaming, 223
  types, 40
  uses, 40
  using file system commands on, 40
  virtual disk, 35
volume name switching, 43, 222

W

write policies overview, 86

X

x86
  See IA